W9-AKT-633

The New GE

How Jack Welch Revived
an American Institution

The New GE

How Jack Welch Revived
an American Institution

Robert Slater

Business One Irwin
Homewood, Illinois 60430

Sponsoring editor:	Jeffrey A. Krames
Project editor:	Jane Lightell
Production manager:	Diane Palmer
Designer:	Julie Smith
Compositor:	BookMasters, Inc.
Typeface:	11/13 Electra
Printer:	R. R. Donnelley & Sons Company

Library of Congress Cataloging-in-Publication Data

Slater, Robert (Robert I.)
    The new GE : how Jack Welch revived an American institution / by
Robert Slater.
        p.   cm.
    Includes bibliographical references and index.
    ISBN 1-55623-670-0
    1. General Electric Company.   2. Electric industries—United
States.   3. Welch, Jack (John Francis), 1935.   I. Welch, Jack
(John Francis), 1935.   II. Title.
    HD9697.A3U568   1993
    338.7'62138'0973—dc20   92–11676

In memory of my father, Joseph G. Slater

Acknowledgments

To write a book that would present readers with the first in-depth look at Jack Welch and his decade-long effort as chairman and CEO of GE, I needed access to Welch. I also needed access to a wide variety of GE employees, from senior executives to factory floor workers. Informing General Electric that I planned to write *The New GE*, I asked for that access. It took a day or so before I was told that GE would help me as much as possible with my project and that Welch would be available for at least one interview.

The Jack Welch era at General Electric has not been treated systematically in book form. A few books devote a chapter to the company's recent years. Business periodicals have focused on Welch and GE, sometimes with cover-story articles. Considering that the Welch years at GE constitute one of the most intriguing business stories of our age, there seemed ample room for a book on the subject. Hence *The New GE*.

To tell Jack Welch's story I conducted interviews with a wide variety of people, including Welch himself, his senior executives, rank-and-file employees at GE, former GE employees, Wall Street analysts, and business school professors.

A word about my contact with Jack Welch. I was told by GE's public relations people that Welch gave few interviews and had gone through long periods in which he had not seen any writers. I persisted, indicating that it would not be easy to do a portrait of a man whom I could not meet. In the end I talked with Welch on four occasions. On July 8, 1991, I held the first of my two long interviews with Welch at

◇

GE's corporate headquarters in Fairfield, Connecticut. On October 14, 1991, Welch took me along on his helicopter from Fairfield to Crotonville, New York, where he gave some talks to GE employees. (I was told that I was the first "outsider" who had been permitted to attend such sessions.) Eight days later I held my second interview with Welch at Fairfield. My fourth encounter with Welch took the form of a long phone conversation to clarify some points toward the end of my research.

I wish to give special thanks to Joyce Hergenhan, vice president for public relations at General Electric. She fielded my questions, put me in touch with a host of people at GE, and explained the company to me on dozens of occasions. I also wish to thank GE spokespersons Jim Allen (Appliance Park, Louisville), Leonard K. Doviak (Power Generation, Schenectady), Peter Van Avery (GE Research and Development, Schenectady), Helen Brightrall Platt (Kidder, Peabody, New York), and George Jamison and Bruce Bunch (Corporate Public Relations, Fairfield).

My gratitude goes to Maxine J. Hilderley, associate executive director, Hall of History Foundation, Schenectady, New York, for supplying me with photos from the early years of GE.

The following people were interviewed: Angie Abell, Fran Ahl, Jim Allen, James P. Baughman, John D. Bergen, Lawrence A. Bossidy, Stephen P. Bradley, Rodger H. Bricknell, Johnnie D. Brown, Bruce Bunch, Richard L. Burke, Mary Byrum, Bill Bywater, Michael A. Carpenter, Jim Carter, Bob Colman, Joseph P. Connolly, James C. Corman, Dave Cote, Roger Creal, Wally Croote, Dennis D. Dammerman, J. P. Donlon, Leonard K. Doviak, Frank P. Doyle, John Dyer, Peter V. Edwards, Herman L. Finkbeiner, Paolo Fresco, Pat Friar, Michael G. Gartner, Harry Geller, David C. Genever-Watling, Kathryn Rudie Harrigan, Joyce Hergenhan, Nicholas P. Heymann, Edward E. Hood, Jr., George Jamison, Reginald Jones, Bill Kline, Ken Kolling, John Kotter, Robert W. Lear, Bob Lewis, Carl C. Liebert, Jim Lochenberg, Nancy Dodd McCann, Louis McNeill, Gertrude S. Michelson, Bob Murray, Dan Nault, Denis J. Nayden, Charles E. Okosky, Louise O'Reilly, James A. Parke, Helen Brightrall Platt, Craig Pollard, James D. Pollock, John Rice, Larry Riddell, Walter L. Robb, Peter B. Roemer, Gary L. Rogers, Harvey W. Schadler, Leonard Schlesinger, Gaylord Seemann, Norman K. Sondheimer, Edward G. Synfelt, Tom Tiller, Brad Tobin, Peter Van

Avery, Paul Van Orden, Fred Walker, Gary C. Wendt, John Wilson, Robert C. Wright, Walter B. Wriston, Boris Yavitz, and numerous others who asked not to be identified.

Once again, I have had the pleasure of working with Jeff Krames, the editor of *The New GE* and a true partner of mine in this endeavor from beginning to end. His support and his friendship have meant a great deal to me. His contributions to the final shape of this book have been enormous, and I thank him for all of his efforts.

I also wish to thank Leslie Dickstein for technical assistance rendered during various parts of the research.

I thank too Miriam and Shimi, Adam, Rachel, and Dotty for their patience and understanding during all the time it took to get *The New GE* into print. And for making my travels much easier, I thank Roslyn and Judd Winick, Jack and Bea Slater, Michael and Bobbi Winick.

Lastly, I owe the greatest gratitude to my wife, Elinor. As with my previous books, she has helped me to find the time and the energy for this current effort. The fruits of our many conversations about Jack Welch and General Electric have frequently found their way into the text. Her editing of early drafts helped in many, many ways to improve the text.

Robert Slater

Contents

◇

Prologue

Often the two men breakfasted in New York City and talked of potential deals. This time Jack Welch, the chairman and chief executive officer of General Electric, had a whopper of a deal in mind.

One day in early November of 1985 he called his investment banker friend Felix Rohatyn and asked to see him.

A shrewd man, with antennas out to every possible corner of the business world, Rohatyn, a partner at Lazard Frères, was one of Wall Street's most important merger wizards.

When the call from Welch came, Rohatyn's antennas were working full-time.

Rohatyn was fully aware that since taking over in April of 1981, the GE chairman had acquired 300 businesses as part of his plan to restructure one of America's great business icons. It was no secret that Welch's dream was to create America's foremost business enterprise by nurturing GE's good ventures and shedding the bad ones.

Rohatyn knew too that Welch had been eager to acquire CBS the previous spring and that he had remained on the prowl after his hopes were dashed.

He had good reason. Suddenly the media giants of America were in play, a brand-new phenomenon. Until the mid-80s it was unthinkable that an outsider like Welch would even dream of buying a media company like RCA and its flagship business, NBC. Yet in the spring of 1985 Capital Cities Communications had grabbed off ABC and Ted Turner had gone after CBS. NBC automatically became part of the turmoil that was sweeping the world of the media giants.

It was no coincidence, the investment banker suspected, that Welch's phone call came as another big media fish named RCA appeared increasingly ripe for a merger. By trimming down in recent years, casting off nonessential businesses, and concentrating more on electronics, satellite communications, and its entertainment businesses, RCA had improved its balance sheet immeasurably. From 1981 to 1984 its earnings had increased eightfold, to $341 million.

What did Jack Welch want? For GE to be bigger than IBM, bigger than Exxon? Unlikely. Size was not crucial to him. Being good at the game of business would achieve his main goal. He wanted General Electric to be the most competitive enterprise in America.

Arriving at that goal was a struggle.

For 4 1/2 years the GE chairman had altered his company as no other leader of the 113-year-old enterprise had ever done.

He had not only bought and sold hundreds of businesses, he had changed the very nature and shape of the corporation. Thousands of employees had been laid off. Whole layers of management had been dissolved. A once diffuse and confusing array of hundreds of business units and product lines had been recast in order to construct a tighter, more coherent organization.

All of these transactions had been essential. But not enough. Not nearly enough.

Eluding Jack Welch was a critical business decision, a step forward that he considered crucial to realizing his plans for General Electric.

He called it "a quantum leap."

A leap that would advance GE toward his goals more quickly, more conclusively than anything he had done before.

Before picking up the phone to Felix Rohatyn, Jack Welch sensed that he knew what that quantum leap was. He needed to act quickly. He felt excited about the phone call.

Like a long-distance runner about to cross the finish line. The crowd would soon applaud.

He was going to make the earth tremble. And he liked the idea.

"Can you arrange for me to meet Brad?" Welch asked.

Brad was the 68-year-old Thornton Bradshaw, chairman of RCA, whom Rohatyn's Lazard Frères served as an adviser.

Rohatyn was delighted. He loved playing matchmaker when the stakes were so high.

The date was set for the evening of November 6. Drinks at Felix Rohatyn's Park Avenue apartment in Manhattan. The first thing that Jack Welch noticed about Thornton Bradshaw was that the RCA chairman was wearing a tuxedo. He had to attend a Navy League dinner later that evening. The dinner seemed far more important than the get-together with the chairman of General Electric. Throughout the 45-minute session Bradshaw looked at his watch constantly.

Bradshaw knew the purpose of the meeting. He told none of his RCA colleagues that Welch was sniffing around RCA. Many other companies had made similar overtures. Bradshaw felt no compulsion to bring in Robert Frederick, RCA's CEO, or members of the RCA board when the hounds had come sniffing. Much too early for that.

The three men sat there over drinks and, like the good actors that they were, performed their roles beautifully. No one dared to broach The Subject. They all knew why they were in Rohatyn's apartment, and it was not just to talk about the calamitous state of the consumer electronics industry. Or the fact that the Japanese and the Koreans were genuine pains for producing things so cheaply.

Yet the conversation centered on these topics. The subject of a merger between General Electric and the Radio Corporation of America never arose.

It hovered, however, in the air, too premature, too delicate to be broached just now. It was as if they were playing poker and no one wanted to show his hand too early.

Avoiding The Subject, Bradshaw and Rohatyn left Jack Welch in a state ranging between bewilderment and buoyancy. He could not be certain that Rohatyn had even raised the idea of a merger with Brad in advance of their get-together. That aside, the RCA chairman seemed like an appealing fellow and Welch concluded that he and Bradshaw thought alike, and that was sufficient for him to power up his strategic planners and move the plan forward.

Jack Welch's plan would bring together under one corporate roof two of the most familiar names in American business. It was all terribly ironic, for General Electric had helped to found RCA in 1919 and seven years later had been part owner of the newly formed NBC radio network. That alliance ended in 1933, when a federal court forced General Electric to divest RCA. In subsequent years both companies became household words because of their incredibly popular product lines. Consumers knew GE for its light bulbs and refrigerators. Consumers knew RCA for its Elvis Presley records and television sets. Now, in the mid-80s, these two giants moved toward a merger: GE, with 300,000 employees and sales of $27.95 billion, was the ninth-largest industrial company in America; RCA, with 106,000 employees and sales of $10.11 billion, was the second-largest service firm. Together they would form the seventh-largest industrial company in the United States. GE was by far the more valuable company: Its income in 1984 had been $2.28 billion; RCA's only $341 million.

November 7. Jack Welch issued instructions to his strategic planners. They were to concentrate on RCA. Was it a sensible strategic fit? Should GE and RCA merge? The secret project was dubbed "Island."

Two weeks later the planning team had a 60-page report on Island circulating within General Electric. Its main advice to Jack Welch: Go for it! RCA's defense electronics business made a natural fit with GE's defense activities. NBC too was most attractive. On its way to becoming the top-rated network. A cash cow that was immune to the threat of foreign competition. True, viewers had begun moving away from the three major networks and drifting toward the cable upstarts, but so what? It was a money machine today. Definitely worth grabbing.

Thanksgiving. November 28. Four days of vacation. The strategic planners had written their report. The numbers looked promising. Jack Welch wanted time to think. To decide once and for all if this was the quantum leap he had been after. He and his family spent the holiday in West Palm Beach. He waited until Monday, December 2, to make the momentous phone call.

Again he dialed Felix Rohatyn's number. Again he asked to see Thornton Bradshaw.

Thursday, December 5. Welch and Bradshaw met one-on-one in the RCA chairman's duplex at the Dorset on West 54th Street. For Bradshaw the day had already been fateful. Over lunch Grant Tinker, president of the NBC network, the man responsible for NBC's incredible turnaround in the early 80s, had dropped a bombshell.

He had been commuting back and forth from California to New York every week and, having brought NBC to within sight of becoming the number one network, wanted to quit. He would wait until next July, his fifth anniversary at NBC. Bradshaw did not tell Tinker of his plan to see Welch later that day.

Welch wasted no words after greeting Brad.

"I'd like to buy your company."

The GE chairman gave all sorts of reasons why it made sense. Most important, a merger would make the two companies more competitive around the world. Welch offered to pay $61 a share, $13 more than the current price of RCA's stock.

Think about it, Welch said, and let him know.

Bradshaw was stunned.

He knew Welch was interested in RCA. But so were others. The shock was in hearing a genuine offer being made.

Too low, Bradshaw responded matter-of-factly. But yes, he would take it back to his board.

As soon as Welch left, Bradshaw began telephoning. He hunted for Bob Frederick. He hunted for Grant Tinker. Both men were on the West Coast.

They were recalled to New York at once. Meanwhile, Bradshaw scheduled a board meeting for Sunday, December 8.

The board liked Welch's offer. Liked it very much. It decided not to seek other bidders. And to pursue talks with General Electric.

Monday, December 9. Bob Frederick placed a phone call to Jack Welch. His message: RCA wanted to negotiate. But on two conditions.

Condition 1: General Electric had to sign a standstill agreement promising not to launch a hostile takeover if the talks failed.

Condition 2: GE had to indicate what parts of RCA it planned to sell.

Welch agreed to Condition 1 on the spot. He would launch no hostile takeover. Welch said he would respond to Condition 2 in person in a few hours.

Monday afternoon. Welch choppered from Fairfield, Connecticut, to New York City to meet with Bradshaw and Frederick in Brad's apartment. Welch promised not to sell any part of RCA without giving the business a careful look first.

Accepting that, Bradshaw and Frederick authorized Felix Rohatyn to get the ball rolling.

Then the hard part began. The negotiations. They occurred at different locations. At GE's law firm of Fried, Frank, Harris, Shriver & Jacobson in the Wall Street area; at GE's corporate headquarters in Fairfield; at GE's Waldorf Towers apartment, where Welch and Bradshaw met several times.

Documents went back and forth. Secrecy was vital while the lawyers and the investment bankers and the brass of both companies worked round the clock.

Price was an issue. General Electric offered $61 a share. RCA held out for more.

GE was worried that a second bidder would surface with a higher offer. It wanted protection. GE proposed that a "crown jewel" arrangement be invoked if RCA got a better offer. In that event RCA would guarantee the sale of two of its five television stations—the ones in New York and Los Angeles—to General Electric, depriving another suitor of gaining much value from a deal with RCA.

The RCA negotiators demurred. How could RCA split up the television network that way, selling part of it to one company, part of it to another? Instead the two companies agreed on a "stock lockup." General Electric had the option of purchasing 28 million shares of RCA stock at $53 a share.

Tuesday, December 10. The secret emerged. Something was happening at RCA. The attorneys worked throughout the evening on final drafts.

Wednesday, December 11. Wall Street reacted. RCA's stock jumped $10.375. It closed at $63.50. An incredible 5.1 million shares were traded. That evening both boards huddled and agreed to the merger. A press release was readied. General Electric agreed to pay $66.50 a share, $6.28 billion in cash, for RCA.

Jack Welch had his quantum leap.

That leap, and Jack Welch's other razzle-dazzle accomplishments, forged the most extraordinary success story in American business in the 80s and early 90s. Two decades earlier a storm cloud appeared over the heady, marvelous growth years of the 1960s and 1970s, a storm cloud that began in Japan, swept over Western Europe, and hovered over America.

Foreign competitors, with their high-quality, inexpensive goods, were beginning to spread their wings on a global basis. They presented the gravest of threats to American business. And yet few American business leaders wanted to believe that the threat was real.

Only Jack Welch took serious notice of the storm signals gathering on the horizon.

When he became the chairman and chief executive officer of General Electric in April 1981, he could have pretended that all was well, that the 110-year-old business icon over which he presided would continue to sell its light bulbs and refrigerators and turbines no matter what was occurring to America's business environment.

He could have pretended that GE, with its 350 business units, was so diversified and large that little could disturb its steady financial ascent.

But Welch understood that change was afoot, and he chose to act on his instincts.

He chose to reshape a corporation that outwardly exhibited no sign of needing repair. GE employees and business analysts alike greeted him with disdain, disbelief, fear. He was tampering with tradition. He was fixing something that was not broken. He was playing with fire.

Stirrings of fierce patriotism raced through people both inside and outside GE who failed to understand how Jack Welch could tamper with a sacred American institution. General Electric was not just the outcome of Tom Edison's marvelous invention, the light bulb. It was, by virtue of the products it provided for the military, a bulwark of America's national defense. It was, thanks to its kitchen appliances, a household word. It was a company with a proud history whose leaders had been men like Ralph Cordiner and Fred Borch and Reg Jones—and whose spokesman had been no less a figure than Ronald Reagan.

How could Jack Welch tamper with all of that?

He might as well have defaced the Statue of Liberty—or Mount Rushmore.

Other business leaders in the early 80s chose to ignore the storm signals. They did so at their peril. Had they acted with the same courage and skill and tenacity that Welch did and as early as he did, they might have avoided the crises that affected their companies in the early 90s. The leaders of IBM and General Motors are but two prominent examples.

Welch understood, better than anyone else among his peers on the American business scene, that time was running out for companies like General Electric. That keeping one's head buried in the sand would dissipate the strong and steady profits of the 70s.

Others extolled General Electric as the model for American business. When GE developed a new management style, that style was emulated by the rest of American business. When it decentralized in the 50s, decentralization became the wave of the future. When it built up huge bureaucracies in the 60s and 70s, that too became the model for business.

Jack Welch alone saw the real GE. Where others saw virtue in a decentralized organization, he saw chaos. Where others saw orderliness in the company's bureaucracy, he saw sluggishness. Where others believed that layers upon layers of management created the best possible command-and-control system, he saw a leadership wasting its precious time and spinning its wheels, losing sight of its basic purpose.

Which was running successful businesses—and making money.

To make money for General Electric Welch decided that he would need to set a revolution in motion.

A revolution that would recast the very nature of this institution. Businesses that were making strong profits and had little potential for high growth would have to go. People who were costing the company too much money would have to leave. The entire management structure would have to be redefined and streamlined.

Welch was indeed playing with fire. And he knew it.

But he felt he had no choice.

He did not want to wait until General Electric was in trouble. He did not want to have to act with a gun pointed at his head. This was a company that at the start of the 80s was generating $25 billion in sales—and $1.5 billion in profits.

To keep those figures from declining, Welch knew that he had to push the company to become more competitive. His goal was to make General Electric the most competitive business enterprise on earth.

By the early 90s Jack Welch had accomplished that goal. Though its employee rolls were 25 percent smaller, the company, now organized into 13 businesses, had blossomed into one of the strongest companies in America. Its sales had mushroomed to over $60 billion a year. Its earnings were nearly $4.5 billion a year. Its market value stood at nearly $60 billion.

No other American company had increased its market value as much as GE during the 80s. No other major American corporation had gone through a radical restructuring, yet continued to churn out earnings increases. At the beginning of the 90s General Electric was being touted with growing frequency as the number one company in America.

How did Jack Welch revive this American institution? How did he create this new GE? He did it the hard way.

By being an activist, a football coach, a preacher, a business philosopher.

By being willing to inflict pain. Knowing that firing people was the one thing that would make people hate him. But knowing that he had no choice.

By facing down his critics, who called him "Neutron Jack." Who called him "the toughest boss in America."

By wooing the community that was the key to his success—his own employees. Unwilling to promise them a job for life, he created an atmosphere in which, if they had the talent and the will, they could flourish.

By waking up every morning as if it were January 1. Ready to rewrite his agenda.

Welch's incredible success has magnified his virtues and made people forget about the pain that his revolution caused thousands of General Electric employees. Or the turmoil that he set in motion when he fashioned the company. To bring off his revolution Welch forced many of those employees to pay the ultimate price—giving up their jobs!

A myth grew up around Jack Welch in the 80s: that the secret of his success was his charisma, his leadership skills, his ability to—manage. And yet Welch knew that the real secret had been his ability to delegate power and authority down the line.

He has given American business a new outlook on how to manage. Or, more aptly, how not to manage. In arguing that managing less is managing better, Welch has set a new style for the management of the large American corporation. It is a standard that many others have begun to follow.

He began the decade of the 80s by getting rid of senior management, making it possible for him to talk directly to the leaders of his businesses. But even that he found was not enough. He closed the decade with a plan that enabled him to turn managerial responsibilities over to the factory workers themselves.

He thus opened one decade as the pioneer of restructuring.

He was opening the next decade as the pioneer in the reshaping of the American workplace.

The 80s belonged to Jack Welch and General Electric. The revival of this great American institution became one of America's greatest business stories.

By shaking the place up, by saying no to tradition, Jack Welch brought General Electric to heights it had never known before. By carrying out a revolution and showing that it could work, he offered the most valuable lesson for American business leaders.

This, then, is the story of how Jack Welch brought revolution to General Electric. How he created a new GE. How he revived an American institution.

CHAPTER ONE

◇

"Shining in the Palace of the Mikado"

It bothered Thomas Alva Edison that the company he helped to found was not named after him. He had a point. For Edison had been the catalyst that brought General Electric to life. He was also the inventor of the phonograph, motion pictures, and the electric light bulb. He was the supreme inventor of his age, and many of the conveniences of modern life were due to his genius. Because of Edison's invention of the light bulb, a company was founded that eventually became General Electric. It was a company that based itself entirely on the electrical manufacturing business, GE's core business for years—indeed until World War II. Then it diversified. Although electrical manufacturing remained an essential part of GE's identity, its expansion into many other fields suggested to some in the company that its past did not matter. GE had become, one might say, more "General" than "Electric." What the debunkers of the company's earliest decades overlooked was this one overriding truth: General Electric's stellar reputation in recent years had much to do with the richness of its history. So, before we look at the changes that occurred in the company in modern times, it makes sense to step back into the past.

October 15, 1878, is the date when General Electric was founded. Then it was called the Edison Electric Light Company. Edison Light came into being when a handful of investors put together the then tidy sum of $50,000 to support Thomas Alva Edison's incandescent lamp experiments at Menlo Park, New Jersey. Edison was America's most prolific inventor, with over 100 patents. Born in Milan, Ohio,

◇

1

on February 11, 1847, Edison was only seven years old when he set up his first chemical laboratory in the cellar of his parents' roomy home in Port Huron, Michigan. At age 21 he arrived in New York, virtually penniless. He fixed a broken-down machine in the Gold and Stock Telegraph Company, however, and out of that came a $300-a-month job as the firm's superintendent.

He began inventing. He won his first patent the next year for an electric vote-recording machine, although he was unable to market the device. At 29, Edison was in Menlo Park, New Jersey, where he began work on what he called "the electric light problem."

Electric light. Was it possible? Could light be produced other than by a flame? Other than by oil lamps and candles? By the 1830s electricity had been produced. Then, in 1872, dynamos and the first commercially successful generator were developed. Steady and reliable electric current was possible. In 1805 a scientist named Humphry Davy had forced an electric discharge across the space between two conductors. When the current was maintained, the discharge was continuous, creating an electric arc. Once electricity became cheaper, by the 1870s, arc lamps were introduced. Though the lamps gave off harsh, flickering light and constituted a fire hazard, they were used to light the streets of Paris and other cities. For all its promise, the arc lamp had the drawback of giving off a light too brilliant to be utilized inside small areas.

Edison was among the researchers who were looking for ways to subdivide arc light into units small enough for home and office use. Though by 1877 he had already invented the phonograph, what he embarked on now was the incandescent lamp, his most important invention. None of the others could compare with its impact on people's lives. It was incandescence that Edison and others were trying to produce, essentially using electricity to create a glow in a filament of some material as a way of subdividing the arc light's glare. The key was finding a filament material that could withstand much heat.

Edison obtained the needed financial backing by striking a business deal with the New York attorney Grosvenor P. Lowrey, his close friend and counsel to the Western Union Telegraph Company. Lowrey put up $300,000, and he and Edison created the Edison Electric Light Company in October 1878. In return for half the shares of the company, Edison promised that he would develop incandescent lighting. While others experimented with heavy elements, Edison sensed that a hair-thin filament was essential. The breakthrough was a scorched cotton thread that he was ready to test on Sunday, October 19, 1879. The current was turned on. All eyes turned to the bulb. It was glowing. But would it continue to burn brightly? Hour after hour passed. When the bulb had burned for 40 hours—it was now Tuesday afternoon—Edison proclaimed with great satisfaction: "If it will burn that number of hours now, I know that I can make it burn a hundred!"[1] The inefficient, impractical arc light had been surpassed. Thanks to Tom Edison, incandescent light was a reality.

It took a full two months before the press touted Edison's achievement. Cynics branded Edison's invention a fake. Gas stocks, however, plummeted, and stock in the Edison Light Company raced upward (reaching $3,500 a share in time). Obviously some believers were out there. Edison's greatest moment came on New Year's Eve, when he showed off his invention to an audience of 3,000, who watched as the streets and buildings of Menlo Park were illuminated by electric light.

In 1880 Edison obtained a patent for the new invention (Number 223,898) and formed a company to furnish lamps to the parent Edison Electric Light Company. By the fall of 1882 he was ready to unveil an electrical system over a large portion of a city. His plan was to make the Pearl Street Station in New York City the first commercial central generating system in America: It was intended to provide light from 14,000 incandescent lamps for 900 buildings. Success was not a foregone conclusion. Jittery about the outcome, Edison banned the press. He had good reason. A few weeks earlier, when the system was tested, a young man burst into the dynamo room shouting, "Your electricity has got into the pavement up in Fulton Street and all the horses are dancing."[2]

Entering the dynamo room at Pearl Street about 9 A.M. on a Monday morning, Edison wore a frock coat and a tall derby. Only 20 others stood around when he gave the signal for the connection to be established. Suddenly 600 kilowatts of electricity surged through 14 miles of underground cable. On this day just 59 customers received Edison's lighting, but they were a Who's Who among prominent New Yorkers, including the bankers Drexel, Morgan and Company; two newspapers, the *Herald* and the *Times*; and Sweet's restaurant. The *New York Times* wrote: "The giant dynamos were started up at three in the afternoon, and according to Mr. Edison, they will go on forever unless stopped by an earthquake."

Electrification was unstoppable. The electric chair was introduced in 1890. In 1895 electric elevators were employed in a skyscraper for the first time, in Chicago. Large American cities began using the electric trolley. Factories turned to electric motors. Homes were also using electricity.

In 1889 Edison Electric Light Company was consolidated with several of Tom Edison's other companies to form the Edison General Electric Company. A year later Edison Electric's sales had risen to $10 million. Like many other inventors, however, Edison was more successful as a scientist than as a businessman. Not that he did not try to commercialize on his new technologies. He was shrewd enough to secure strong patent protection for his inventions of the phonograph and the electric light bulb. Early investors in his lighting technology marveled that he had indeed come up with an invention superior to arc lighting.

Edison, however, believed in direct-current applications for his invention. Direct electric current flowed in one direction only. Edison's generating station in New York used it. Others favored alternating current, an electric current that reversed its direction at regular intervals. Edison was convinced that alternating current was dangerous, noting that it was used in electric chairs. The turning point came in 1893, when George Westinghouse won a contract to develop the Niagara Falls power plants on an alternating-current basis. In later years Charles Steinmetz, General Electric's mathematical and electrical engineering wizard, put the theory of alternating currents on a firm mathematical basis. At present alternating current is used almost universally in power distribution systems.

Edison discovered that certain investors were not pleased with his insistence on direct current. Accordingly, one group, which included Charles A. Coffin, a Massachusetts businessman, purchased Edison's patents and combined them with Thomson-Houston's alternating-current patents. Coffin had founded a shoe manufacturing company in Lynn, Massachusetts. After that business succeeded, he was asked to join American Electric Company, a struggling young firm that had relocated in Lynn. American Electric's greatest asset was the inventor Elihu Thomson. Coffin's business acumen was needed to supplement Thomson's technical genius. Coffin ran the new company, called Thomson-Houston, and it soon became a worthy competitor of Thomas Edison's companies.

A businessman through and through, Coffin asked J. R. McKee, one of his former shoe customers, to manage a Thomson-Houston commercial department.

"But I don't even know what electricity is," observed McKee.

"That's just our trouble," Coffin replied, laughing. "We've too many men who know what electricity is, or think they do. What we want now is somebody to care for the commerical side. Perhaps the less you know about what electricity is, the better."[3]

Edison General Electric and Thomson-Houston merged on April 15, 1892, and the new enterprise was called the General Electric Company. Edison General Electric contributed such important assets as basic incandescent lamp patents, the Edison system of distributing electrical energy, and a growing electric traction business. For its part, Thomson-Houston provided a profitable arc lighting business and important developments in alternating-current systems. The two firms, employing 10,000 people, had grossed $20 million in sales altogether. Tom Edison remained a consultant to General Electric, and he held a seat on its board for 10 years. He adopted a low profile, however, selling all of his shares in 1894 and attending only one board meeting in a decade. One of his chief disappointments was the omission of his own name from that of the new company.

Charles Coffin was elected GE's first president. He was the first in a line of General Electric executives who possessed special managerial abilities: He never issued orders. He gave suggestions. He encouraged his underlings, called "associates," to speak out. He was a great salesman, a wonderful storyteller, and he laced his staff meetings with anecdotes that eased tensions. For the next 30 years he served as GE's leader.

In its first seven months—ending December 31, 1892—the General Electric Company earned almost $3 million. All seemed fine. An 1893 GE publication boasted somewhat hyperbolically: "Our incandescent and arc lamps extend in an unbroken line around the earth; they shine in the Palace of the Mikado as well as in the Opera House in Paris."[4]

Some months later, however, America was hit by a sharp recession that lasted five years. Companies failed. The young electric industry was at grave risk. Only Coffin's sound business skills kept GE alive. Short of cash, Coffin saved the day by negotiating an arrangement with J. P. Morgan in which GE got the money it needed from New York banks as payment for GE-held utility stocks.

Sensing that the mood in Congress was increasingly antitrust, Coffin wisely decided that GE should abandon the utility business. If Congress could regulate the railroad and telegraph industries, it could also regulate the electrical utility business. Selling off GE's holdings in the various "Edison" public utility companies in New York, Boston, and Detroit, Coffin astutely positioned GE as the high-profit, nonregulated supplier to the electrical utilities. Thus he avoided owning a part of the electric industry that could in time fall prey to government regulation.

With great foresight the founders of General Electric understood at the beginning of the 20th century that the company had to devote a certain share of its resources to research and development. They created an industrial laboratory that attracted the finest minds in the electrical field. The nucleus of GE's fledgling laboratory consisted of men like Willis R. Whitney, the first chief of the laboratory, and William D. Coolidge and Irving Langmuir, marvels who took Thomas Edison's lighting invention to more sophisticated levels.

The GE laboratory began in December 1900, when Whitney, then a 32-year-old assistant professor of chemistry at MIT, set up experimental equipment in a barn behind the Schenectady home of Charles Proteus Steinmetz, a hunchbacked German immigrant who was later nicknamed "the wizard of electricity."

From the outset Willis Whitney worried about whether the GE laboratory would benefit the company. In 1901 he wrote: "I know that I was put here for a purpose. The company is not primarily a philanthropic asylum for indigent chemists and I must not let it become one even secondarily."[5]

Determined to prove the value of science to the electric industry, Whitney invented the GEM (General Electric Metallized) lamp in 1904. This lamp, which utilized a metallized carbon filament, was 25 percent more efficient than regular carbon lamps. GEM lamps were sold from 1905 until 1918.

Scientists searched relentlessly for improved filament materials. Eventually they focused on tungsten because of its high melting point. Whitney sought a leading researcher to head the GE laboratory's tungsten efforts. He came upon MIT's William D. Coolidge, who joined the GE operation in 1905. For two years Coolidge experimented, trying to make tungsten a commercially feasible filament. He hammered and squeezed and rolled the tungsten, and finally, in 1908, he produced the first commercially usable ductile tungsten. A public announcement of the breakthrough took another two years. With Coolidge's new technology a filament existed that could absorb the shocks and vibrations of railroad cars, streetcars, and automobiles. Now it was possible to have a lamp with twice the output of the GEM design. "Electric Light is Now Cheaper," an ad proclaimed. "Ask your Electric Light Company about this new lamp tomorrow morning. Find out why it is so economical. Learn how you can have Electricity Light at one half of the old cost. When you have these new facts you will plan to use Electricity immediately."[6]

The Coolidge ductile tungsten process has stood the test of time: It is still used to manufacture nearly all of the filaments for incandescent lamps. In the 1990s GE laboratory scientists were trying to make it even more productive.

Coolidge was active on other research fronts as well. In 1913 he produced the first X-ray tube that was highly predictable and consistent in operation. It combined the scientific notion of a "pure electronic discharge" with the use of a tungsten X-ray target. The device produced far more penetrating X rays than earlier models. It set the stage for the use of X rays in therapy and industrial inspection as well as medical diagnostics.

Thanks to ductile tungsten and other innovations, the reputation of the GE laboratory was growing. Irving Langmuir, a Brooklyn-born chemist, joined the laboratory in the summer of 1909. His research in 1912 and 1913 produced another major advance in lighting: a light bulb filled with inert gas. This bulb tripled the hours of light and reduced the problem of bulb blackening. ("Use 3 lights at the old cost of One," went the GE ad.) Other lamp and lighting improvements emerged from General Electric's laboratory over the years: the first American photoflash lamp in 1930; the high-pressure gaseous discharge lamp line in 1934; the fluorescent lamp in 1938. Fluorescent lamps lasted twice as long as incandescents. Langmuir also came up with improvements in the vacuum tube that helped to make radio and modern electronics possible. His contributions to surface chemistry won him the 1932 Nobel Prize in chemistry. Langmuir has been credited more than anyone else with proving the value of industrial research to industry as well as science.

But the key force during the first decades of the GE laboratory was Charles Proteus Steinmetz. He had left his native Germany, fled to Switzerland, and then in 1889 immigrated to America. His body was misshapen, his figure diminutive. He looked like a pygmy. Steinmetz had acquired a reputation in scientific circles for talks he had given on electromagnetic theory, but uninterested in pursuing a career in electrical work, he found a job in Yonkers as an electrical draftsman for the Rudolf Eickemeyer factory. General Electric had its eye on the factory. Edwin Rice, a member of GE's board of directors, visited the factory and noticed something special in Steinmetz. He had a "small, frail body, surmounted by a large head with long hair hanging to the shoulders, clothed in an old cardigan jacket, cigar in mouth, sitting cross-legged on a laboratory worktable." When Steinmetz spoke, Rice felt the "strange power of his piercing, but kindly, eyes."[7]

Among Steinmetz's many dazzling findings was his discovery of the law governing losses in the magnetic circuit of an electric motor— the law of hysteresis. A major obstacle to electrical engineering had been applying mathematics to the phenomena of alterations, cycles, and phases. This had been done by slow and complicated means. Steinmetz's discovery came as interest in expanding the uses of electric light was growing. Relying on direct current, however, would have been expensive, requiring either a large investment in copper wire or the building of many generation stations. By coming up with the mathematics for the law of hysteresis and of alternating current, Steinmetz enabled the less expensive and more flexible alternating current to be used, speeding the electrification of America.

Tom Edison immodestly but accurately proclaimed electricity to be "the greatest factor in human progress" in people's daily lives. Nowhere was that statement truer than in the kitchen. As late as 1910 no American kitchen had an electric refrigerator, an electric range, an electric coffee maker, or an electric dishwasher. The dominant feature of the American kitchen in the preelectric days was the black cast-iron stove, fueled by wood, coal, or kerosene. A familiar sight at the time was the delivery of ice from a horse-drawn cart.

It took General Electric some time to take on the challenge of the American kitchen. In its early years GE produced the heavy apparatus for the new electric industry. Its only consumer products were electric lamps and fans. The first electrical product to be used in homes was the 'Hot Point' iron, the idea of an Ontario, California, housewife named Mary Richardson. Mary's husband, an employee at the local power company, had experimented with electric flatirons. In 1905 Mary advised him that if he wanted to win over women customers, his best bet was an iron with a hot point that would press around button-holes and reach into ruffles and pleats. Earl Richardson came up with an iron whose heating elements converged at the tip—a hot point! He offered some acquaintances a chance to sample the new device, and the response was positive. He set up the Pacific Electric Heating Company and within a short time became the leading manufacturer of electric flatirons in America.

At around the same time a Fargo, North Dakota, entrepreneur named George Alexander Hughes was trying to devise an electric range. Hughes had founded his own electric power firm. He was con-vinced that only if the cook could see the source of the heat would the notion of electric cooking be accepted. His first range was primitive: The heating elements were open wire set in bricks. They burned out after only a few hours. By 1910, having set up the Hughes Electric Heating Company in a Chicago loft, he was ready to ship his first six electric ranges, to Billings, Montana. A brass band welcomed the ranges at the railroad station! Now stoves no longer had to be painted black to hide their soot: Hughes's ranges were white, adding brightness to the kitchen.

Though General Electric had produced a fan in 1894, an iron in 1905, and a toaster in 1908, it moved into kitchen products slowly. After Hughes and Richardson had built up their businesses, General Electric decided that the time was ripe. It experimented with electric cooking devices and electric refrigerators but eventually chose to merge with the Hotpoint Electric Company and the Hughes Electric Heating Company. The new firm, the Edison Electric Appliance Company, offered a series of Hotpoint electric appliances and house-wares, including radiant heaters, ranges, electric percolators, foot warmers, sewing machines, and three kinds of hand irons.

In 1913 Charles Coffin became chairman of GE and Edwin Rice became president. During the Rice years GE produced an increasing amount of electrical apparatus that was needed for the industrializa-tion of the country. Powering production machinery now were more efficient motors, generators, and steam turbines—devices that also made it possible to light streets and electrify ships of the U.S. Navy and streetcars.

In 1922 Owen D. Young became GE's chairman and Gerard Swope became its president. By that time GE's annual sales, $12 million in 1892, had grown to $243 million. Three fourths of General Electric's business was then in capital goods equipment used by utilities, industrial plants, and transportation systems. Most of the rest was in incandescent lamps, electric fans, and a few small appliances. Refrigerators and electric stoves were still only for the wealthy.

Electrifying the home, Young and Swope believed, was the key to GE's success. Demand for household electric goods would rise dramatically when they were cheap and reliable. That in turn would increase demand for electricity, leading to greater sales in generating and distribution equipment.

Electrification expanded a good deal after World War I. Electric lines reached only one out of every four American homes in 1919; five years later they reached nearly two out of every three homes. During the 1920s General Electric made great headway in marketing that most important kitchen appliance—the refrigerator. Until the early 20s only a few thousand American homes had refrigerators: At $1,000 they cost twice as much as an automobile and nearly a year's average annual income! Nearly half of American homes went without even an icebox in the early 20s. The GE Monitor Top refrigerator, introduced in 1927, began to change all that. The Monitor Top was the first practical electric home refrigerator. Unlike previous models it had no external motors and pulleys. Its round top-mounted compressor unit sprouted like a mushroom from the storage cabinet—hence the name Monitor Top. It came in two sizes, 5 and 7 cubic feet. The smaller model sold for $250, the larger for $350.

Where none had existed 10 years earlier, by 1928 1.25 million refrigerators and 7.5 million radios were in American households. At the same time the number of electrically wired homes increased from 7 million to 19 million. That produced a rise in power consumed from 25 million to nearly 100 million kilowatt-hours a year.

Accordingly, GE broadened its consumer product line to include an electric mixer and a vacuum cleaner in the late 20s and, by the 30s, clocks, clothes washers, dishwashers, air conditioners, radios, and food waste disposers. During the depression years GE adopted this advertising slogan; "More Goods for More People at Less Cost."

Charles Wilson succeeded Swope as president of GE in 1940, serving through 1952. During World War II Washington borrowed Wilson, asking him to head the War Mobilization Board. Swope returned from retirement to fill Wilson's shoes at GE. With the onset of war GE stopped making consumer goods in favor of military products. It entered many wartime technologies, including aircraft engines, radar, nuclear energy, and aerospace. With this diversification GE went through changes in its culture. From Charles Coffin's tenure through the 30s GE had always avoided being captive to suppliers. It had a "make" rather than a "buy" mentality. "Do-it-yourself" was its watchword. With the outbreak of war GE felt obligated to pursue new technologies that forced it to become less self-sufficient.

Like many other American companies, GE received a big boost from postwar demand. The Marshall Plan, which underwrote Europe's reconstruction, further boosted the demand for GE products. Armed with a new advertising theme, "You Can Put Your Confidence in General Electric," the company rode the tide of the postwar consumer boom. In 1947 it came out with an automatic clothes washer and two-door refrigerator freezer units. Television sets followed. During Wilson's presidency GE grew enormously: By 1950 it had 183,000 employees, 117 plants, and sales of $1.96 billion.

The 50s brought a housing explosion. Americans flooded the stores to buy appliances for their new homes. Taking over as GE's president in 1950 and as its chairman and chief executive officer in 1958, Ralph Cordiner sensed that consumer goods would be the biggest growth area in the postwar environment. General Electric was among the first corporations to exploit the new medium of television as a vehicle of advertising: In April 1953 an actor named Ronald Reagan, a newly appointed spokesman for GE, hosted "GE Theater," which debuted over 120 CBS-affiliated stations. (The future president also appeared six times each year in the program's dramas.) "Progress Is Our Most Important Product," GE boasted in its advertising slogans then. By the 50s GE was producing toaster ovens, portable hair dryers, table-top broilers, and pocket radios. It introduced microwave ovens in 1956.

With GE's production facilities strained, Cordiner bought 942 acres of farmland near Louisville, Kentucky, in order to build Appliance Park, the largest and most efficient appliance plant in the world. Six large manufacturing buildings and a warehouse provided 4 million square feet of space. In 1956 *Reader's Digest* described the park as "that factory of the future you've heard about." The park was huge, with 20 miles of paved roads and 93 acres of buildings, one of which was large enough to enclose 15 football fields. It had its own police force, fire department, taxi service, and railroad, and its own newspaper for the 12,000 employees. The cynics, doubting that the need for appliances would warrant a facility that large, dubbed the place "Cordiner's folly." In time it proved no blunder.

During the 50s General Electric had a strong technological presence. It built nuclear reactors; it also provided the U.S. Air Force with the Mark 2 reentry vehicle, from which the first payload ever recovered from outer space, a data capsule, was ejected. GE was to the 1950s what IBM would be to the 60s and 70s. Apart from dominating the electrical equipment field, GE entered the field of electronics early via audio products and semiconductors. It had much cash and recognition. Not surprisingly, General Electric staked out a leading position in fields that would become important industries in later years—computers, semiconductors, and robotics. However, it eventually failed to establish itself in any of them.

It was under Cordiner that General Electric decentralized. He understood that GE had changed and grown since World War II, that GE was no longer essentially an electrical manufacturer but a diverse and far-flung company. It was important, he felt, to bring order to the company, and that, he thought, meant transferring power from corporate headquarters to the business leaders. Accordingly, he made each of 120 department general managers responsible for a segment of GE business. The theory was that the sum total of many wise individual decisions would be more fruitful than decisions handed down from headquarters. By dividing businesses into small slices, GE offered its business managers and their staffs a chance to get closer to the customer and thus to respond to market changes much faster. However, one effect of pushing responsibility down to the product managers was to allow improbable start-ups time to develop. GE's Plastics and Aircraft Engines might have been scrapped at an earlier stage had it not been for decentralization.

Cordiner implemented decentralization with an eye to symmetry and order. Buildings were the same height. Pay was uniform. Organizational structure, span of control, and policies and practices were the same no matter what the size of the business unit or the maturity of the product line.

Decentralization, for all its advantages, carried one critical flaw: It spawned bureaucracy. At the outset it had seemed wise to invest as much control as possible in the business units, to get them to make decisions on their own. In practice, however, the business managers turned to senior management much more frequently than had been planned. More and more management layers were needed to impose order on the "decentralized" system. The bureaucracy developed a life of its own, and sometimes it took nine approvals for some business units to act.

Breeding an atmosphere of fear, however unintentionally, Cordiner, all 5 feet 2 inches of him, was not well liked. He insisted that each general manager bear responsibility for a "profit center." The manager had to achieve "hurdle rates": a 7 percent return on sales and a 20 percent return on investment. Managers who "made the numbers" kept their jobs; those who did not were sent into the wilderness. A premium was placed on short-term profits. Long-range planning was sacrificed.

The managers found it hard to attain Cordiner's goals. One reason given was that Cordiner was less prepared to turn power over to the decentralized business units than he had seemed to be. By pressuring managers to disgorge large profits from their business units, Cordiner placed an undue burden on these profit centers. Sometimes they were too small; sometimes, as stand-alones, they had trouble coping. All of these factors turned managers against Cordiner, who, in turn, left the impression of being cold, aloof, uncaring toward his employees. He did not want GE to unionize, believing that if management did its job, unions would not be needed. Not unexpectedly, many top and middle-level managers picked up and left, weakening some of GE's business units.

For all the grand sweep of change, the push for profits, the investment of much capital in computers and nuclear power, the nurturing of the consumer field, Cordiner did not turn GE around. Revenues stagnated and in 1963 were $4.9 billion, a $200 million increase from 1962 and a $500 million increase from 1961. Not a lot of growth. When, in 1959, three senior General Electric executives were found guilty in a U.S. District Court in Philadelphia, Pennsylvania, of price-fixing, some accused Cordiner's stress on meeting the numbers of creating the kind of atmosphere in which such behavior became inevitable.

Corrective action was needed, and in 1963 the board turned to a man who had headed GE's Lighting business and done well there. After the tempestuous Cordiner era Fred Borch, a friendly, accessible type who sought advice and took a hands-on approach, was a welcome change. He became president and chief executive officer in December 1963 (and chairman in 1968).

Borch sprinkled capital investment in many areas and waited to see which ones flourished, which foundered. As Jack Welch aptly put it, he "let a thousand flowers bloom," pushing the computer and nuclear power businesses, getting into modular housing and the portable entertainment field, nurturing General Electric Credit. Aircraft Engines and Plastics were given a chance to grow as well. The trouble was that some of Borch's acquisitions, some of which were in the personal service and education field, were expensive and went nowhere. [8]

A feeling persisted that GE's magic had disappeared. Still in the throes of the electrical price-fixing antitrust suit of 1959, GE under Borch had been investing heavily in computers, commercial jet engines, and nuclear energy, leaving little time for the monitoring of its older businesses. The period between 1959 and 1966 was called "the Era of Profitless Prosperity." A capital goods boom helped GE grow in the second half of the 1960s. However, it remained much the same kind of company it had been throughout its history. In 1968 the traditional electrical equipment businesses—Power Systems, Consumer Products, Industrial and Electronic Equipment—provided 80 percent of its earnings.

When Borch assumed power, General Electric had five general product groups, 25 divisions, and 110 departments. To accommodate the boom of the late 60s Borch doubled the number of groups from 5 to 10, doubled the number of divisions from 25 to 50, and increased the number of departments from 110 to 170. The bureaucracy was mushrooming.

Toward the end of the decade Borch thought that he might set matters straight before he left for good. He sensed that GE was becoming sluggish because its managers had been forced to devote too much attention to making the company's newer businesses profitable. This was understandable: With so much invested in these businesses, the focus was naturally on them. As a result the traditional product lines were being overlooked.

Borch felt strongly that long-range planning had to be reshaped. For decades General Electric had used 5- and 10-year plans. When Ralph Cordiner decentralized the company, it became the responsibility of each unit to plan 5 and 10 years ahead. Borch looked at the plans of the units and found them wanting. The quality of the plans varied radically. Some were excellent; some were indescribably poor. Often they were financial projections designed to make the unit manager look good: During the first year or two, a period of heavy investment, the projection was that the business would not do very well. During the following 5 or 10 years the projection was that the business would do marvelously. Managers predicted great long-term profitability. The only trouble was that these long-range projections never came true. They especially did not come true for GE's three main pursuits (nuclear energy, computers, and aircraft engines).

A new technique was needed, one that would not neglect the old-line businesses and that would allow the company to make tough decisions regarding which businesses should survive, which should be jettisoned. Borch devised a new technique that he called "strategic planning": It called for using the most rigorous business analysis ever undertaken by an American corporation. Before launching the new technique, Borch set about to recast the 170 business units, combining them into structures that made more sense than the existing ones and trimming them down to a mere 43 newly named Strategic Business Units. The refashioning was needed, in part to aggregate authority farther up the corporate ladder, away from those decentralized, diffuse, and unwieldy units. Hopefully, the scaled-down units, bringing together businesses that had clearly defined competition and were natural allies in strategic planning for product, marketing, and facilities, would make the company less vulnerable to smaller and more specialized competitiors in GE's many markets.

Size was not a relevant factor in the reshaping of these businesses. Thus Aerospace, Aircraft Engines, and Major Appliances became SBUs at the group level. The Medical Systems, Appliance Components, and Chemical and Metallurgical businesses became SBUs at the division level. Tungsten Carbide Tooling and Engineered Plastics were forged at the department level. Another SBU emerged from a department with annual sales of only $25 million that manufactured commercial cooking equipment: It had its own competitors, its own markets, its own distribution system, and a discrete product line.

As it turned out, Fred Borch only had time to introduce the concept of strategic planning. It was left to his successor, Reg Jones, to implement the concept.

CHAPTER TWO

◊

"Looking After the Stepchildren"

Reg Jones. The man who chose Jack Welch. The man who became a foil to Welch. The man who believed fervently that he and Welch were cut from the same cloth, that they shared the same view of the world, that it had been the most natural thing in the world for Reg to select Jack as his successor. And yet how different Reg seemed. How hard it was to convince someone that these two men, one born in Stoke-on-Trent in England, the other born in Peabody, Massachusetts, were all that much alike.

Reg's journey through life began in Stoke-on-Trent on July 11, 1917. He moved from England to America at the age of eight. Though he spent little time in his native land, Jones retained the mannerisms and speech of an Englishman. Indeed, he looked and acted, not like the American businessman that he was, but more like a British banker or an Anglican clergyman. He spoke in forceful, methodical, clipped tones. The words came out ploddingly but with great moral authority. He had a patrician air. One wag noted that he pronounced his first name with a hard g—as in God. Even when he was America's most admired businessman, it was easier to think of him as delivering a lecture on philosophy or preaching from a pulpit than as sitting around a corporate conference table.

Despite the aristocratic image Jones came from humble beginnings. His father was a steel mill foreman. Two aunts of his mother who had been living in the United States returned to England one summer with stories of the good life in America. Reg's father brought his family to Trenton, New Jersey. He became an electrician and set up his own business.

Reg remembered his teachers in England as strict. He retained a vivid recollection of proctors in the back of the classroom waiting to straighten out an errant pupil. "We had total discipline. You even had the ruler on your hands or your bottom if you misbehaved or if you hadn't done your work."[1]

Three of Reg's high school teachers encouraged him to read the classics even though these were not required reading. He not only admired these teachers. He wanted to join their profession and thought of teaching social sciences at a high school.

In 1934 Jones entered the University of Pennsylvania in Philadelphia. At the time it was the only American university to offer a five-year program that qualified a graduate to teach in all of the then 48 states. Jones enrolled in the program. He was required to spend his first two years in Pennsylvania's College of Arts and Sciences, his final three years in the School of Education. He found the college and the School of Education disappointing, but he had a growing respect for Pennsylvania's Wharton School of Business. A number of his social science courses, such as political science, economics, and sociology, were taught at Wharton. "I was so impressed with Wharton because every time you showed up in class, they gave you a blank piece of paper and a 10-minute quiz. Every month you had an exam. [The professors] knew whether you were keeping au courant with your subject, whereas in the college and in the School of Education you rarely got an examination until the final. I just didn't see that the same drive was there to crack your skull open and fill it."[2]

Jones noted that all the School of Education professors did was teach John Dewey's educational philosophy, arguing that students should have free rein. Jones felt that the Penn professors were misinterpreting Dewey by advocating far more permissiveness for students than Dewey intended. During his junior year Jones applied to Wharton, and Wharton officials were happy to accept the virtually straight A student. They made clear, though, that he had to take all the required courses and would not be able to graduate in four years. No matter. Jones had planned to be at Pennsylvania five years anyway.

Jones's business acumen was soon in evidence. He held down three jobs at once. Tutoring became his cash cow: He could give lessons in nearly any subject. On the night before a final exam he hired a room in the Christian Association and ran a review session that began at 6 P.M. and continued for as long as there were customers. He paid someone to collect $2 from each person. Sometimes as many as 100 students appeared, earning Jones $200 a night. He also worked at the library five nights a week and put in hours with the Buildings and Grounds Department. Though he had a full course load in his fifth year, Jones earned twice as much then as he did during his first year at General Electric (when he earned $26 a week).

Upon graduating in 1939, Jones joined General Electric, entering its business training course. Three years later he began his career as a finance man by becoming a traveling auditor, though, having taken only five hours of accounting at Wharton, he had barely prepared for such assignments. He traveled widely, learning every aspect of the company's operations, and developed a knack for solving problems quickly. During the next eight years he gained the reputation of being one of the company's best auditors. All of the GE auditors were seen as zealots, as people obsessed with numbers, whose mastery of numbers meant control over the organization. In the next few decades, especially in the 50s, the finance men ascended into great positions of power at GE, and no one epitomized them more than Reg Jones.

In 1950 Jones became assistant to the controller of the Apparatus Department in Schenectady, New York. Six years later he was general manager of the Air Conditioning Division in Bloomfield, New Jersey. During this time Jones's problem-solving abilities became evident. The Air Conditioning Division was losing several million dollars a year, largely because of a faulty compressor design. The compressors carried a five-year warranty, but during that period they had to be changed as often as four times per unit. Jones urged GE's engineers to design a new compressor and to construct a modern manufacturing plant in Tyler, Texas. Soon the Air Conditioning Division stopped hemorrhaging. Eyes began to focus on Reg Jones.

Over the next decade Jones rose rapidly. In 1958 he was named general manager of the GE Supply Company Division, a distribution arm for appliances and electrical products. Six years later he became general manager of the newly formed Construction Industries Division. He headed these two divisions until 1967, when he was named head of the Components and Construction Materials Group. He became group executive of the Construction Industries Group in 1968 and later in the same year a vice president for finance. At first Jones thought of refusing the job: He enjoyed the operations side more. When he finally accepted the finance position, he enjoyed it so much that he refused further promotions for a while. Unlike many other executives, Jones was conversant with all aspects of the company, and that served him well. William H. Dennler, a GE vice chairman who retired in 1972, noted that "Reg made suggestions that were far beyond what you would expect from a financial man. Although he might be talking with others about spending money, he'd chime right in on marketing or on technical matters. In time, he got to be considered a good backup man on anything, . . . but he was the best financial man I ever met."[3]

Toward the end of his tenure Fred Borch took a hard look at some of General Electric's major businesses—those that were not doing well. Borch had been bothered that so much attention and cash had gone to three businesses in particular—at the expense of the rest of the company. In 1969 he asked Reg Jones to head up a study of these three—Nuclear Energy, Commercial Aircraft Engines, and Information Services and Systems (Computers). They had been losing money for years. It was the toughest assignment Jones had ever been given. Until that time GE was reluctant to sell any of its components. Selling off a business was considered an acknowledgment of failure. Yet Jones and the two other members of the Ventures Task Force were being asked to determine whether to sell off a GE business.

Jones and the task force decided to keep the Nuclear Energy and Commercial Aircraft businesses. The Computers business presented Jones with a terrible decision. The business had lost money for the last 14 years. Logic dictated getting rid of it. Yet it had been Jones himself who had recommended that GE enter the computer field. To become competitive GE had to develop a product line that encompassed both small and large mainframes. IBM, the supreme computer maker of the age, already had a full line of mainframes. Skeptics argued that even a $1 billion infusion of capital might not be enough to do well against IBM.

Jones determined that to become competitive with IBM General Electric needed a 15 percent share of the computer market—well over twice what it had. Growing through acquisition was not an option: The Justice Department informed General Electric that purchasing another computer firm violated antitrust regulations.

So Jones and the task force recommended selling the Computers business. It was an anguishing moment for him. He was asked why a firm that had successfully ventured into aerospace and nuclear energy had not been able to hack it in computers. Jones was depressed, but Fred Borch helped raise his spirits by suggesting that he try to find a buyer for the Computers business.

Jones ruled out IBM because it already had a full line. Honeywell expressed interest. Meetings were held. Joint studies were undertaken. Negotiations began. There was enough paperwork, Jones suggested later, "to fill a room."[4] Finally, in May 1970, a deal was struck. The terms—highly favorable to GE, which recouped most of its $400 million investment—turned Jones into a hero around the company. Indeed, the GE–Honeywell transaction went so smoothly that a number of business schools, including Harvard, conducted case studies of this classic corporate divestment.

The Honeywell deal catapulted Reg Jones into the GE limelight. Suddenly he became CEO material. As an ardent practitioner of the new art of strategic planning, Jones won wide respect. When the time came to select a replacement for Fred Borch, Jones was a strong candidate. He had none of Ralph Cordiner's abrasiveness or Borch's toughness. He seemed mellow by comparison. But he could be articulate and persuasive and hardheaded, and thanks to his accounting background, he had a wonderful ability to tackle business problems. Though Jones himself doubted whether he could serve as an ambassador for General Electric, he was politically sophisticated and world-minded and others thought he would be well able to represent the company in Washington and elsewhere.

Other candidates were mooted: Walter Dance, Jack Parker, and Herman Weiss. All three were vice chairmen, but none of them had Jones's breadth of experience within GE. During his 33 years in the company Jones had been in manufacturing, marketing, administration, and finance. He had something else going for him: Weiss had come from the Lamp Division, as had Fred Borch. Dance was an appliance man. Some felt that the lamp and appliance fellows had been running General Electric for too long. Jones's advent to power was a triumph for the finance men.

Reg Jones was elected president of General Electric on June 23, 1972. He was made chairman and chief executive officer the following December 15. Thanks to the economic boom of the late 60s, Reg Jones took over amid increasingly favorable circumstances. In 1971 GE had netted $471.8 million in profits on sales of $9.4 billion. The perplexing problems surrounding the Computers, Nuclear Energy, and Commercial Aircraft Engines businesses had been resolved. The Computers business had been sold. Profit margins as a percentage of sales were at the 5 percent level for the first time since 1965.

Economic factors beyond GE's control affected its balance sheet in the 1970s. While energy shortages were foreseen, high inflation was not. To protect General Electric from the ravages of inflation Jones took the company down a new path. Creating a long-term hedge, GE in 1976 spent $2.3 billion to buy the coal- and mineral-rich Utah International, Inc., which was mostly in Australia. That put GE in the natural resources business, mining coal, copper, uranium, and iron ore and producing natural gas and oil.

This surprise purchase raised eyebrows. Many were shocked. Why was General Electric buying a mining company? Why was it buying a company at all? That had not been GE's style. GE had nurtured its own businesses and had not tried to acquire outside interests. The Utah purchase was a major departure for both Jones and General Electric. It was a signal that no matter how conservative Jones had been, he wanted to shake the company up a little. He was trying to say: "We're not moving fast enough, aggressively enough. I'm going to show you that I am going to get things moving. So I'm going to take a lot of this company's cash and buy this business." Jones had no intention of converting General Electric into a natural resources company. He merely wanted to commit the company to change.

When he took over, Jones pledged that GE would resist focusing on only a few glamorous businesses as it had in the past. Now it would also pay attention to GE businesses that had been treated like stepchildren. He pointed to Engineered Plastics, Medical Electronics, Mass Transit, and Modular Housing as examples. He pledged too that Appliances, Electrical Apparatus, and Industrial Products—GE's core businesses—would not be overlooked. It was to deal with all of these businesses that Jones committed himself to implementing Fred Borch's concept of strategic planning.

The benefits of strategic planning soon became evident. Analysts "discovered" that an electromechanical business environment was changing into an electronic business environment. Thousands of GE employees who had only mechanical or electrical skills would now need to be trained to work in electronics. Strategic planning analysts also helped GE to take an increasing interest in global markets, and to treat its offshore competition, long considered irrelevant, with much greater respect. Reg Jones explained: "It was this understanding of our markets and competition and our products that we really got out of the strategic plans. The forecast that was made was not just a wish list. It was founded on a deep understanding of our strengths and weaknesses."[5]

With the new strategic planning technique in force Jones proposed that GE focus its resources on Medical Systems, Transportation, Plastics, and Power Generation. Yet he insisted on improved financial performance from all GE businesses. He paid special attention to Consumer Products, the venerable cash cow. Core businesses were harvested. Certain high-tech businesses received only restricted capital allocations. Escaping Jones's scalpel were Aircraft Engines and Plastics.

Notwithstanding some setbacks in the core businesses and a pair of recessions, Jones took General Electric through the 70s in grand style. In 1971, the year before he took over, the company's earnings were a bit above a million dollars a day—$471 million for the year. As of September 1979 General Electric was the world's largest manufacturer of electrical equipment and among the world's leaders in electronics, nuclear power, consumer goods, and aerospace. Between 1968 and 1979, GE's sales had more than doubled, to $19.6 billion, and its net income had tripled, to $1.23 billion. In 1979 GE had 401,000 employees and 562,000 stockholders. Funding the high-tech fields that were investigated in GE's laboratories, Jones made profits by selling CT-scanners, industrial plastics, and silicone products. He began to move GE overseas more aggressively, so that by 1980 the company was generating 40 percent of its earnings from offshore sales as compared with 30 percent a decade earlier.

Jones had a prestigious following among American business leaders. He became their spokesman in Washington. Facing the Carter White House, Reg Jones and businessmen in general had much to overcome. Businessmen—largely Republicans—had a negative image and were automatically viewed as adversaries of the government. Jones recalled senior politicians telling him that labor and consumer groups were far more powerful than businessmen because these groups each spoke with one voice. "You fellows in business are each coming to us speaking with many tongues, each of you looking for your own interests in your own industry, and the hell with the American economy and the hell with all other businesses. If you're ever going to be heard, you'd better get your act together." So Reg Jones became co-chairman of the Business Roundtable, an elite fraternity of business leaders who helped businessmen speak with one voice on the major issues of the day.

He became a familiar figure at the Carter White House. He was well liked by Carter's aides, who found him cool and convincing, quietly forceful, and self-assured. Jones reflected a new type of business-man in stark contrast with the types who railed against "big government" and steered clear of Washington. He believed that the way for big business to have influence in the Capitol was to be there, to talk with the politicians, to lobby as effectively as possible. No one did it better than Reg Jones. Stuart Eizenstat, President Carter's domestic affairs adviser, said of him: "I think he is one of the wisest, most intelligent, most informed people on public policy issues that I have ever met. He's always armed with the data, and he's extremely articulate in making his presentation. He stands very high in the White House. The president has tremendous respect for him. Anytime he calls, the door is open."[6]

Jones was asked to join the Carter cabinet on several occasions. The New York Times reported that he had been offered two cabinet posts—director of the Office of Management and Budget and chairman of the Federal Reserve Board.

Jones at the time did not confirm the reports, but when interviewed after retirement, he acknowledged that Carter had wanted him to join the cabinet. He had been offered positions "somewhat similar" to those the Times had reported. The offers had come, Jones pointed out, when he already had a retirement date in mind. He was convinced that if he left "prematurely," before a decision on a successor was made, "things could go awry." Was the lure of government a temptation? "It's always tempting," Jones acknowledged. But what bothered him about accepting a government position was that someone—an interim or actual successor as president of GE—would have had to be appointed to replace him. Either outcome would have undermined his effort to find the right successor.[7]

When Reg Jones retired, he was the most admired business leader in America. In both its 1979 and 1980 surveys of "Who Runs America," U.S. News & World Report reported that Jones was considered the most influential person in business. In May 1981 Fortune magazine found him to be the most popular CEO among his peers. That same year a Gallup poll named Jones CEO of the Year. He had boosted the name of American business in Washington. He had come to symbolize a new kind of chief executive officer, less antagonistic toward the government, more comfortable maneuvering through the corridors of political power.

The outgoing chairman had kept GE's management standards on a high plane as well. The *New York Times* called General Electric a "model of modern management techniques." The Harvard Business School generated 90 complimentary case studies. To business schools GE had been the model of how a company should be run: Long-range strategic planning, which Jones had overseen, had been adopted by the business community at large. General Electric's balance sheet appeared strong. In 1980, Jones's last full year as CEO, the company had sales of $24.96 billion, 11 percent higher than in 1979, and earnings of $1.5 billion, a 7 percent increase over its earnings for the previous year.

Jones liked to talk of the company's record of solid performance, of its earnings growth, which had been much faster than the growth in earnings of Standard & Poor's 400 stocks and the growth of the American gross national product. In his final remarks as chairman before the January 1981 General Electric Management Conference, where some 500 senior managers had gathered in the Belleview Biltmore Hotel in Belleair, Florida, Jones observed, "We had the pleasure of passing the billion-dollar mark in earnings, and we have a balance sheet that should give all of us confidence in our resources for the future."

"From Poker to Plastics"

The man who took over General Electric in the early 1980s had never dreamed of a career in big business. When Jack Welch was young, he gave little thought to what he would do when he grew up. At first his mother thought it would be nice if he became a priest. That may explain why she took him to church every morning. She eventually abandoned that idea and only wanted him to be a success, which meant landing a good job. If his father had a preference, he never voiced it. That was like him. He was a man who said little.

Jack Welch's parents named him John Francis Welch, Jr. Everyone, however, called him Jack. He was born on November 19, 1935, in Peabody, Massachusetts, across the city line from Salem, where he grew up. An only child, he was born when his parents, John Francis and Grace Welch, were in their early 40s. They had been trying for a child for 16 years. Jack's parents were the children of Irish immigrants. Neither finished high school. This did not keep Grace Welch from pushing education on her son. The residents of Salem were all like that: They had little money, but they valued schooling. Grace had a keen mind: She was so good at mathematics that she did tax returns for neighbors. The young Jack had a very happy childhood. Later he recalled with appreciation how much support and understanding he had received from his parents.

John Sr. was a train conductor on the Boston & Maine Railroad. He was a quiet man who refrained from ordering his son around. He let his wife take the lead in bringing up the boy. Jack once described him merely as "a good man, hardworking, passive."[1] John Sr. did instill in his son an interest in the outside world. "I was always interested in current events because my father was always bringing home all the newspapers from the train. I read every newspaper there was. So I was a news junkie and a sports junkie from the first day."[2]

Jack's father left for work every day at 5 A.M. When Jack was 10 years old, his mother began a daily routine that began at 6 A.M. Grace roused him out of bed to get him to church on time. It was not easy: "I'd moan and groan. She'd push me and push me and get me out of bed. Then I'd go in the car with her." Upon arriving at church, Jack put on the uniform of an altar boy. Grace sat in the front row. Forty minutes later she drove him back home. Then breakfast and finally off to school. Young Jack recalled going to church daily in deference to his mother, not some divine inspiration. "That was what you did. It wasn't a question of me being religious." Did he enjoy the morning drill? Clearly, he was less than enthusiastic. "I never thought about it too much. I was hoping for a fast mass with a fast priest." The masses were all in Latin. Years later Jack could still recite a few verses, but he acknowledged, "I don't know what it means." He observed Catholic ritual without taking it too seriously. But he maintained a belief in God.[3]

He and his mother drove to the train station in Salem each night to pick up John Sr., due in at 7:30 P.M. Often the train was late. Jack sat for hours talking to Grace. She was "really my buddy, really my friend as well as my mother."[4] John Sr. was able to provide enough income for a summer house and a new car. His son retained a memory of his father's railroad that never left him: the featherbedding practices that tolerated inefficiencies in work and duplication of effort. It was Jack Welch's earliest lesson in how not to run a business!

Grace was proud when Jack did well (as when he became captain of the golf and hockey teams in high school), and she smothered him with attention, as mothers do with only children. "She always felt I could do anything. It was my mother who trained me, taught me the facts of life. She saw reality. There was no mincing words. Whenever I got out of line, she would whack me one. But she was always positive, always constructive, always uplifting. And I was just nuts about her."[5]

Not only did Grace instill ambition in Jack. She also thought it crucial that he build up self-confidence. "She wanted me to be independent. She thought I should control my own destiny." It was Grace

who told Jack that his stammer, which persisted slightly into his adult-
hood, was no defect at all but merely a sign that his mind was racing
faster than he could speak. She could have unwittingly made her son
feel inferior for having this handicap. That she did not was perhaps the
greatest gift she gave Jack. He might have turned out shy and introverted, lacking in the self-confidence he needed to excel in business.
The trace of the stammer never gets in his way. Indeed, most of the
people who notice it feel a sense of awe that Welch managed to reach
the height of the business world despite it. One such person, Michael
Gartner, president of NBC News, admired Welch so much for over-
coming the handicap that he, probably jokingly, said: "He's so forceful
and dynamic, I wish I stuttered."[6]

Jack Welch's mother treated him as an adult very early, even to
the point of playing poker or gin rummy for money with him during
his lunch hours when he was only six years old. When Grace won, she
shouted "Gin" so that the neighbors heard. Nearly a half century later
Jack recalled being careful not to reveal his hand, keeping his cards
close to his chest. To a six-year-old, even the pennies were high stakes.
When Jack was 12, his visiting aunts and uncles turned to him if they
needed a sixth person for their card game. "I was like an adult sitting
there playing poker."[7]

Why did Grace treat her child as an adult? Welch thought that she
may have feared she would die young, as all of her brothers and sisters
had, and that he would then be unable to cope on his own. Although
other parents might accompany their children on outings, Grace sent
Jack alone on the train to Boston to attend ball games. When Jack and
his friends played street hockey at night, everyone else had a curfew.
Not Jack. Grace did not check up on him. "I just knew enough to
come home." Jack's mother died at the age of 66, when her son was 26
and able to cope on his own.

Like the other children of blue-collar families in Salem, young
Jack spent his afternoons playing baseball and basketball near a rock
formation known as "the Pit." Essentially a playground, it had a
baseball field and swings. "A scrappy place," Welch recalled. The first
signs of his fierce competitiveness surfaced at the Pit. Tempers
sometimes flared. This did not bother Jack. "It was a way of life. You'd
have fights down there. . . . Over a game or who said what about
whom. Anything." Jack and his pals also hung around the corner
grocery store. No good reason—it was just what youngsters did in

Salem. The store owner became annoyed when Jack and his friends blocked the door.

Jack could not be intimidated. "He was a nice, regular guy, but always very competitive, relentless, and argumentative," according to Samuel E. Zoll, a childhood friend who became chief justice of the district courts of Massachusetts. Jack once chewed Zoll out in the middle of a basketball game for letting a larger opponent score. What struck Zoll was Welch's lack of inhibition: "He never thought privacy was appropriate for such comments."[8]

Jack's high school days were cheerful. He had many friends, was one of the best students in his graduating class, and participated in varied extracurricular activities: He was class treasurer and active in sports (in addition to golf and hockey he played baseball). His best subjects were math and chemistry; he found languages—Latin and Spanish—troublesome. By high school he had reached a height of 5 feet 8 inches and was solidly built. Earning pocket money was crucial. He was always working. His first jobs were caddying and delivering newspapers. "I had every way in the world to get a dollar."[9]

Jack's mother kept urging him to attend a university. Her brother had studied electrical engineering in college and had landed a good job. He was the only family member to obtain a higher education, and his experience impressed Jack. "He was an engineer, so I decided to be an engineer." Simple as that.

Well, not that simple. While Jack's school record permitted him to consider the finest American schools, he knew that even if he were accepted at a university, he would have to find a source other than his parents for tuition. While a high school senior in 1953, to his good fortune, he was nominated for a Naval Reserve Officers Training Course scholarship on the basis of his academic qualifications. So were two of his classmates. The winner or winners (Jack was never sure how many of the three could win) would receive free tuition, room, and board at college. Four years of reserve officers training was a condition of the scholarship. John Welch, Sr., decided to pull strings so this his son would win. Watching him ("poor guy") scrounge around for contacts and sensing that he did not know anyone was a pitiful experience for Jack. Of the three nominees only Jack failed to win a scholarship. One of the two winners went to Columbia, the other to Tufts. Jack was "devastated," all the more so because "I thought I was as good or better than they were." Mingled with his disappointment was a feeling of pity toward his parents, who were bitter at not being able to help their son. "My mother was mad because we didn't have pull. I sensed this frustration over the whole thing. It was real. It was the first time I'd seen that happen."[10]

A sobered but determined young man applied to and was accepted by the University of Massachusetts at Amherst. Influenced in part by his uncle, he chose chemical engineering as his major. Later he made it sound as if the choice had been between that and studying medicine. "I liked math, and I liked chemistry, and I didn't want to be a doctor because I couldn't stand blood. I didn't like cutting up animals and things." Physics and electronics seemed too abstract. That was the appeal of chemical engineers: What they did, you could see and smell and feel. There was a practicality to the subject.[11]

Jack had a superb scholastic record at college, dean's list every year. He managed to have a good time as well. Of the 60 members at the sports-minded Phi Sigma Kappa, he was the only engineering student. He and the brothers got along wonderfully: Welch enjoyed the camaraderie of the card-playing, fun-loving "jocks." He often joined them in an all-night game of poker only to wake the next morning and trot off to class while they stayed in bed. The fraternity was on academic probation most of Jack's four years. He graduated in 1957 with a degree in chemical engineering.

Though it had been heartbreaking for Welch to enroll in a state school, he eventually decided that the loss of the scholarship was a blessing in disguise. He may have been rationalizing. Nonetheless, he convinced himself that winning the scholarship would have made his university career a personal strain. He would have been forced to attend a top-flight school, to mix with lots of other bright students, making it difficult for him to excel in his studies. In short, he would have had to live the kind of pressurized existence he did not want for himself. "I got much more nurturing than I'd ever have gotten if I had been just in the middle of the pack. UMass didn't have the best students. I took chemistry. I very quickly became very good at it."

One image haunted him for years—that of the math whiz who was a high school chum of his and went to MIT, had a nervous breakdown his first year and flunked out. He had been a much better student than Welch in high school. In contrast, "I became a golden boy at UMass." In retrospect Welch concluded that he had gained self-confidence from being among the best at a less rigorous school. He doubted that an MIT would have done that for him.[12]

Welch went on to graduate school. In 1958 he received a master's degree in engineering from the University of Illinois. In 1959, while attending Lenten masses, he met his first wife, Carolyn. They married soon thereafter; after a marriage of 27 years and four children, they were divorced in 1987. (In 1989 Welch remarried, this time to Jane Beasley, a mergers and acquisitions associate at the New York law firm of Shearman and Sterling.)

In 1960 Welch acquired a doctorate in chemical engineering at the University of Illinois. He wrote his thesis on the role of condensation in nuclear steam supply systems. The thesis encouraged him to believe he could master tough projects. "You go down 27,000 blind alleys. It doesn't work, you start again. You feel there's no hope while you're asking those questions, pressing, probing, pushing. But you have to get it resolved; otherwise you'd spend your whole life looking for the ultimate answer."[13]

Welch always knew that he would go into business. At first he thought of starting his own company, but he sensed that he could put his doctorate to best use within the framework of a company with vast resources. That was how he arrived at General Electric in 1960.

On the job interview circuit he came upon Daniel Fox, a chemical researcher at General Electric in Pittsfield, Massachusetts. Pittsfield was then home to 12,000 GE employees, including the 300 who were struggling in the plastics operation. At that time the plastics business was largely a support arm for other GE businesses. Its scientists experimented with chemicals, hoping to produce commercial products for GE, but it had barely made $100,000 a year. Back in 1953 Fox had invented a new plastic called Lexan quite by accident. Scientists at the GE Research and Development Center had been trying to develop an improved thin film insulating material for wire, but every material that seemed to work deteriorated when exposed to water. Fox remembered guiacol carbonate, a substance that had caused him frustration while he was in graduate school at the University of Oklahoma because it could not be broken down by boiling water. He mixed it with other ingredients in an effort to solve the wire coating problem. What he got was a "glob" so hard that he could not extract his stirring rod from it. The wire coating problem was eventually solved by other means.

The glob, however, was kept around the lab, Jack Welch recalled later, "like an inanimate mascot." Sometimes it was thrown down stairwells in futile efforts to break it. Its unique properties provoked first curiosity, then excitement. GE's Chemical Materials Department took over the product and sought ways to commercialize on its near unbreakability.

It was at that moment that Jack Welch dropped in on GE looking for a job. He had a full round of interviews set up for one fall day. He began by meeting the Chemical Materials people, who hoped to persuade him to work in their burgeoning Lexan factory. Impressed with the young Ph.D., the Chemical Materials researchers grew concerned that if word got around that this promising fellow was in the building, he would be snared by the Chemical Development Operation, where Daniel Fox worked.

Fox had been working on his own on PPO (polyphenoline oxide), discovered in 1956 by Allen Hay, a polymer that had excellent strength at high temperatures. With Lexan getting all the attention over at Chemical Materials, Fox and PPO, along with the entire Chemical Development Operation, attracted little notice. Welch, who had no idea of the tense rivalry that existed between the Materials and Development groups, was thrown innocently into the midst of it that day.

The Materials people kept Welch until 4 P.M., when one of them grudgingly let Fox meet him, informing Fox that the young Ph.D. had to catch a train back to Illinois in an hour. Fox discovered good qualities in Welch and did "a real sales job" on him. In the end he persuaded Welch to miss his train, stay overnight in Pittsfield, and come to work. "By early evening," Welch recalled, "I was a goner, infected by his enthusiasm, enthralled with his ideas, and impatient to work for him."[14]

Welch began his career at General Electric on October 17, 1960, as a process chemical engineer. His first task was to find a pilot plant for making PPO—and then to set it up. After locating a broken-down building in Pittsfield, he and a chemist hired on the same day as Welch spent the next year setting up the plant. Fox's magnetism made up for the primitive conditions and the Chemical Development Operation's low status. Welch called Fox "a mad scientist and a wonderful, wonderful person."[15] Fox's modesty was especially appealing: "Here he had invented Lexan and he was already pooh-poohing it and off to make this new thing (PPO) bigger and better. It takes a unique person to do that. Most people just stick to what they know."[16]

A year after he began, Welch almost quit. In October 1961 Welch was given his first annual appraisal, a highly positive one. He was, however, distressed to learn that he had also been given only the standard $1,000 raise, bringing his yearly income to $11,500. That was far too little. Welch did not want to work for this "skinflint," as he called his and Dan Fox's boss.

The size of the raise was not Welch's only gripe. The previous year, when Welch and his wife came to Massachusetts to look for a place to live, the boss had refused to pay for a motel room for the two of them. Welch had had to take a room in a rooming house and to send his wife to his parents' home. Welch also complained that instead of treating Chemical Development as a research and development center, the boss ran it as if he were an accountant. "We had one phone. When it rang, we passed the phone around with a long cord. He was just very, very cheap. But a good man."

Welch decided to leave. He found a job advertised in the *New York Times*; traveled to Skokie, Illinois, for an interview; and accepted an offer from International Minerals and Chemicals. He sent his wife, now pregnant, out to Skokie first. He planned to join her soon.

The future chairman and chief executive officer of General Electric was departing after being with the company for only a year because he had been given "a lousy raise." Though it seemed bizarre, Welch's boss planned a going-away party for him. The night before, however, a GE executive flew into town with an offer Welch could not refuse: If he stayed at GE, the company would make it worth his while financially. It would also apologize to his prospective employers for his change of mind and reimburse them for costs incurred. Best of all, he would no longer have to work for the skinflint. The whole experience, Welch recalled, was "very traumatic."

Back at work, this time as process development project leader for the development of PPO, Welch spent the next few years in the pilot plant with his five-member team, trying to turn PPO into a commercial product. It was not easy. The chemical did not seem to have much potential because it was very difficult to mold, but Welch persisted. In 1963 he was named manager of Polymer Products Manufacturing.

Then came the breakthrough. Welch and his team figured out that if they blended polystyrene with PPO, they could make a plastic that had excellent strength at high temperatures and was easy to mold. This thermoplastic resin was known as Noryl.

In 1965 Welch sold GE on the idea of letting him build a $10 million factory in Selkirk, New York, to produce the PPO blend. When the time came to appoint a manager for the plant, few wanted the job. The Lexan scientists at Chemical Materials were not prepared to risk good careers for a product that had not proved its commercial value. Lexan had sales of $25 million a year. Only Welch was eager for the job, and he begged his superiors to let him have it. They did. In 1966 he was named manager of the Polymer Products Operation. He had a title, a factory, but not much of a product. The following year, 1967, the Selkirk facility was in place.

Now the battle between the Lexan fellows and the Noryl upstarts intensified. Though Welch knew it was an uphill battle, he possessed an ability sorely lacking in others in the plastics operations: the ability to sell a product! Most of the others were technical people (Welch, for that matter, was too) who knew their way around a laboratory but had little experience at selling a product. Given a great deal of latitude by the home office, Welch sensed that if he could sell Noryl to GE's businesses, he might be able to sell it to outside customers as well. At the time all houseware products were made with metal. It had not yet dawned on anyone that substituting plastics for metals would make such products cheaper and lighter. Welch went around to GE's appliance makers and made this point. Their first reaction was cautious.

Welch had an idea: Traveling to the Research and Development Center in Schenectady, he suggested to scientists that they sheathe an electric can opener with Noryl rather than metal. Now he had a product he could sell! Showing the can opener around, he convinced people at GE that Noryl had many other applications, including car body parts and computer casings.

Welch was acquiring a reputation as a marketing genius. It became clear to his bosses that his skills should be used not just for the low-flying Noryl but for Lexan as well. Noryl brought in $1.5 million in sales a year; Lexan, $9 million as part of the $26 million plastics business. In 1968 Welch was put in charge of the Chemical Development Operation, giving him responsibility for Lexan and all of GE's polymers. In 1969 he changed Chemical Development's name to the Plastics Business Department. That year, he predicted that GE

Plastics' products had a potential sales volume of well over $200 million a year. In time his prediction would prove too modest.

Being put in charge of the Chemical Development Operation was a great turning point for Welch. He was no longer stuck with just Noryl. He could now try to sell the plastics product that appeared to have the greatest potential of all—Lexan.

Lexan, which was transparent, brought to life the concept of a truly unbreakable glazing material. In addition it was so tough that it could be used as a substitute for metals in numerous applications. It could resist high impact and great stress. Lexan's introduction started a materials revolution in which American consumers turned to lighter, cheaper products that had far greater performance qualitites than metal or glass. Windows glazed with Lexan sheet, for example, are 250 times stronger than glass. Because Lexan was virtually unbreakable, it was highly promotable.

Thanks to Lexan, Welch was able to push GE's Plastics business ever upward. A whole host of applications were found for Lexan. It became the premier plastic in the world. It appeared in automobile bumpers, baby bottles, football helmets. The helmet visors of the astronauts who landed on the moon in 1969 were made from Lexan. The pedestrian ramp leading to New York's Yankee Stadium was covered with Lexan.

Welch alone sensed the potential for GE's plastics products. He possessed the vision to convert its embryonic plastics business into a highly profitable enterprise. Aiding him was the hands-off attitude of the top GE brass, who were devoting their time and energy to other pursuits. Welch liked the freedom. "We were really the odd ducks. Nobody spent a lot of time worrying about us."[17] That gave Welch the chance to act "entrepreneurial" and to take "ownership." He could do pretty much what he wanted—follow convention or flout it. He chose to move in unorthodox paths.

The Plastics business had been dominated by companies like Du Pont. Plastics salesmen were technically oriented and low-key. They tended to be impersonal and indirect. Welch saw an opening. He saw no reason why his Plastics business could not act like any other consumer business and grab the customer by the throat or, if not that, at least try to shake his hand. In trying to sell raw plastics to a company, Welch sought out not just the purchasing manager, but also the researcher who had developed the company's final product. This was often the researcher's first encounter with an executive. Welch took him out to lunch, invited him back to Pittsfield, peppered him with questions.

This hands-on contact enabled Welch to customize his products to the demands and needs of the client. Using a strategy similar to one he would employ in the 1980s, Welch invited customers to help design products. He used color print ads and glossy sales films and even engaged the comedians Bob and Ray to do a radio ad. Pushing Lexan as a replacement for glass, he put together a television commercial with a bull in a china shop. Naturally, all the items but those made of Lexan broke. To show how unbreakable Lexan was, Welch employed the hard-throwing major league baseball pitcher Denny McLain: Welch positioned himself behind a Lexan screen, and McLain then threw fast balls at him. Lexan protected him!

In late 1971 Welch became general manager of the Chemical and Metallurgical Division, and in 1972 he was made vice president. In 1973 he became vice president and group executive of the Components and Materials Group.

Because he was so successful, Welch was given other businesses to manage apart from Plastics, including Medical Systems and Diamonds. These were older GE businesses. Welch and some of those around him took a rather dim view of the large bureaucracies that existed in them. Welch was eager to shake things up, though at times the businesses simply could not be moved. He made many management changes. Some worked, some did not. He tried to get people to ask a lot of fundamental questions about the businesses. Why did they have to sell the product the way they were doing? Why did it take 60 days rather than 30 to deliver the product? Welch generated a lot of energy, and though there were setbacks, he realized that this deep probing of businesses could work wonders.

"He developed that as a style," declared Robert Wright, the president of the GE-owned NBC Television Network, "and figured that it was always a road to knowledge if not success. It got things going. When you ask questions, you have to make decisions. You can't just sit around and talk a good game; You finally have to do something. Getting people to make decisions that would have been done by committees over a long-extended period of time was a fundamental part of that approach."[18] Wright had worked with Welch in the plastics operation starting in 1973, the year Welch was named vice president and group executive of the Components and Materials Group. That year the Plastics Department became a division.

Wright recalled Welch as a "very radical kind of manager." Welch was much younger than the other GE managers. Plastics under Welch was "like a high flier, a little business which was run by this fellow who had a very odd reputation, boisterous, demanding. Welch took a lot of chances. He believed that the business would be successful. Even when it wasn't, he was doing his best to cover for it."[19]

Wright found working under Welch exciting. Everyone seemed frenetic. People took out charts and graphs to show him and predict how much bigger the business would grow. Wright was not sure he believed all the heady predictions, but he thought to himself: "At least these people are turned on to something." Beyond that, they were beginning to sell Plastics. "All of a sudden," noted Bob Wright, "there was a tremendous demand for these products," and Welch was the reason. "It's hard for me to describe what a fantastic business that was and still is," Wright said. "If it had been a business by itself, it would have been much bigger than Apple Computer or other businesses that are acclaimed as being stars. I can't think of any business in the 1970s that came out of nowhere to be as strong, as well positioned, as profitable as that one. And basically it was [due to] Jack Welch. There were a lot of people killing themselves in there, but he was the one who should get the credit for that, deservedly so."[20]

In the wake of the Arab oil embargo—at the end of 1974—the Plastics business collapsed, as did other parts of the American economy. Orders dried up. Everything ground to a halt. No one expected it at the time, but the downturn lasted for a year. Wright recalled: "People were praying. Jack Welch's career was on the line. He'd built all these plants, and everything was kind of stopped for a period of time." Welch responded by trying to get employees to work harder. "He was very solemn," Wright recalled. "We didn't know exactly what to do. We never had a situation like this." Capital was being consumed, factories sat idle. "Jack felt, rightly so, that the whole company was looking at him, saying: 'Here's this bright guy. Look at his business. It's not doing very well. Maybe this guy's not a genius after all.' "[21] Then the recovery came. By the mid-70s the business was growing 30 percent a year. As America's concern for energy conservation increased, consumers turned from metals to plastics, which required less energy to produce.

Asked the secret of his success in Plastics, Welch smiled broadly and noted that he had been part of a small group competing against Du Pont and the other large plastics companies of the world while GE was not in fact a plastics company. That proved an advantage. "We were able to move quickly, and we had a lot of rope to hang ourselves with. We had support, rope, and resources. Guys in bigger chemical companies always used to tease me at meetings, how lucky I was because my bosses didn't read the chemical magazines, whereas at Du Pont the chairman, the vice chairman, the group executives, all read the same chemical magazines. So they got hell from everybody on every project they ever had. In our place, in its diversity, that wasn't the case. We were a garage shop working crazy hours, passionately. I hired every employee that we had. So we were all sorts of likenesses. We had a helluva time."[22]

Indeed they did. Welch made sure to instill a team spirit in everyone. "I remember when we got our first 100-pound order. We had the '100-pound' club. People would run down the hall, yelling that they had gotten an order. I remember when we got a 5,000-pound order. The roof almost came off. We bought beer and pizza. We had a celebration."[23]

In December 1977 Welch was promoted to senior vice president and sector executive of the Consumer Products and Services Sector and vice chairman of the GE Credit Corporation. He moved from Pittsfield to Fairfield. By that time the Plastics business, a $40 million operation in 1968, had reached nearly $500 million in sales. It had grown an average 50 percent a year in sales during that period. Four years later, in 1981, it became a $1 billion business and one of General Electric's fastest-growing industrial divisions, a serious competitor of Du Pont and Dow Chemicals. In 1980 the Plastics Division was renamed Plastics Business Operations; three years later Plastics became a group. By 1992 GE Plastics was a $5 billion business.

CHAPTER FOUR

◊

"The Great Airplane Interview"

It began, as many business decisions do, with the drawing of a chart. Out came the pencils and the graph paper. Out came the pack of cigarettes. Reg Jones drew a very large rectangle. Then six vertical lines within that rectangle. Along the top of the rectangle he wrote the years 1974 through 1980. Along the left side he listed five categories. Having constructed the 35 little boxes, Jones mulled over what categories to choose. The chart was his private secret. It was early. Very early. No need to make anyone think that his doctors had given him some bad news. No reason to give the impression that a major change was soon to occur. Jones chose vague categories. Phrases like "Structure of the Corporate Executive Office" and "Key Process Role Changes." They were good disguises for the real purpose of the exercise. As he peered over the chart and its title, "A Road Map for CEO Succession," Jones felt no obligation to come up with names. It was far too soon for that. He waited another three years before nailing down a final list of candidates. One of them would emerge as his successor. One of them would take on what many considered the toughest job in American business, running General Electric.

The year was 1974. Jones had been in the job for only three years. At 57, he had no intention of stepping down in the near future. The last two CEOs at General Electric had retired at the age of 62, before the usual retirement age of 65. Yet no one was forcing Jones to leave the job early. So why engage in such an exercise at this time? Why resort to secret charts? Why devote even as much as five minutes to a decision that did not need to be made for years?

◊

The answer has much to do with Reg Jones. Everything about him suggested that he liked to plan ahead, that he hated to rush. He sat erect. He had a formal air. His words came out ponderously, grudgingly. I'm not at all sure what businessmen are supposed to look like: I do, however, have an image of them as being terribly frenetic, tense, pushing themselves until they collapse. That is not Reg Jones. The idea that he would drive himself and others to reach unconscionable deadlines seems strange, almost perverse. His whole demeanor appears to say: "Plan ahead." When he reached for the pencils and the graph paper, that is precisely what he was doing.

Knowing that one day he had to give the job up, Reg Jones wanted to make sure that he went about it the right way. So the chart became his road map to help him make the right moves. It would force him to stay on schedule. Reg Jones was proud of that chart. For years he kept it in his files. When he sat in his office at GE Capital in Stamford, Connecticut, in June 1991—17 years after he drew the chart—he had been retired as chief executive officer just over a decade. He had been given the Stamford office because he had been CEO—to advise if and when called upon. I asked him at one stage when he had concluded that Jack Welch should replace him. Before he answered, he thought for a moment and then searched through some files. He quickly found the once secret chart. He gazed at it for a minute or so with a satisfied look. He seemed to be saying to himself: "Yes, that was a clever thing I did, picking Jack Welch. I really got it right."

Jones has often been asked why he began thinking about a successor so long in advance. The most important answer has to do with the nature of General Electric: It was indisputably one of the most complicated and prestigious business institutions in the land. For that reason alone, much thought had to be put into choosing its next chief executive officer. The passing of the baton to a new chief executive was a critical moment for this major corporation. Its very future was at stake.

So Jones felt he needed time, lots of time. After all, such decisions had rarely been taken at General Electric. Though it had been around since 1892, it had changed leadership only six times. (Charles Coffin, its first chief executive, had run it for 30 years!) GE had always prided itself on being a meritocracy. Accordingly, it was rich in executive talent, making the choice of a leader that much tougher. Reg Jones knew that a lengthy contest would be brutal, knew that the candidates would have to go through their paces before the board of directors as if the past counted for nothing, as if they were performers under a circus tent.

Jones could have short-circuited the race: He could have gone to the board at the last minute and declared, "This is my decision, take it or leave it." Meritocracies, however, do not make such critical decisions in haste. The candidates had to feel that they had been given a fair and full chance. The board had to be given adequate time to consider them. Such a selection process would, Jones believed strongly, produce the best choice. Given General Electric's talented executive bench, the process would be tough. In fact, when the race was over, a few of the losing candidates left GE to become CEOs elsewhere!

When the succession contest at GE ended and the business school professors had a chance to analyze it, some of them concluded that Reg Jones should have shortened the contest. It was not essential to turn the contest into the survival of the fittest. In response to these critics, Jones smiled, certain that he had acted wisely. Yes, he stated, he knew that the business school fellows thought his succession contest had the candidates hanging by their fingernails for an unreasonably long time. But the damned thing had worked, hadn't it? Look at the results. Look at the man who had been chosen. Look at what Jack Welch had done for GE in the last decade. Was anyone willing to state that selecting Jack Welch had not been Reg Jones's wisest decision?

Still, the exercise was intriguing because it was so rigorous, so complex, so lengthy. It would have been natural and logical for Reg Jones to have favored a carbon copy of himself. After all, as he approached retirement as chairman and chief executive officer of General Electric in the late 70s, he was picked by his peers as the most admired business leader in America. Surveys published in the media attested to that. If Reg Jones was number one in the hearts and minds of other American businessmen, should he not target someone just like himself? Not necessarily, he thought: "I felt and still feel very strongly that no chief executive officer should look for a clone. I think it's very important that the succeeding CEO be different from his predecessor because corporations need change. There's a dynamism that is missing if the successor is just a clone of the predecessor."[1]

Jones insisted that he had no one in mind at first. Once he had begun his chart in 1974, Jones asked the Executive Manpower staff to prepare a preliminary list of candidates. Staff members tried to beg off. "That's 10 years down the road," they asserted. Jones told them to proceed nonetheless. He wanted the list by the end of the year. The Executive Manpower staff named 96 candidates.

Of these candidates, 44 were automatically disqualified on the ground that they were 55 years old or over. Jones must have known that he would not make the final decision for as long as five years. He did not want to choose someone who would have only a few years to run the show. He wanted someone younger than 60. That left 52 candidates. Of these, 34 were considered not to be of CEO caliber, reducing the list to 18. A recently hired executive was added to the list of candidates. He raised their number to 19.

What struck Jones when he looked over the list of candidates was the absence of one name: Jack Welch. Welch was then just 39 years old and still in Pittsfield. However, Jones was aware of Welch's exploits in Plastics. A decade after his retirement Jones remembered how curious he had been about why Welch had been overlooked. And he remembered the answer he got: "They said his extreme youth was the key. He didn't seem to fit the GE mold. They said also that he was different from the typical middle manager. He was a bit of a maverick." The members of the Executive Manpower staff believed that another 10 years had to pass before Welch could be considered for CEO. After all, GE had always chosen men in their 50s as CEO. Jones disagreed and ordered that Welch's name be added to the list, which now named 20 candidates.[2] Of those, 9 were "not highly rated against the specs," reducing the list to 11 candidates.[3]

By early 1977 Jones was ready to move a select group of candidates into a position where they could be seen and tested. The original Jones "road map" had called for a president who would be named in 1978 or 1979: He would serve as chief executive officer and Jones's heir apparent until Jones was ready to step down. Jones abandoned that idea in favor of one that encouraged competition for the top post and allowed the board time to familiarize itself with the candidates. Jones developed the concept of sector executives, a new level of management. He appointed six sector executives who reported directly to the Corporate Executive Office. Jack Welch was one of them. The other five were John F. Burlingame, 58; Edward E. Hood, Jr., 50;

Stanley C. Gault, 53; Thomas A. Vanderslice, 47; and Alexander M. Wilson, 54, president and CEO of Utah International. Except for Wilson, the sector executives became in effect the finalists for the job of CEO, along with two others (Alva O. Way, senior vice president for finance, and Robert Frederick, senior vice president for corporate planning and development). As head of Utah International, Wilson became a sector executive, but because of his lack of experience at GE Jones did not consider him a candidate. Later Jones tried to give the impression that he had named the sector executives to impose more order on the strategic planning process and not to create a succession contest.

However, Edward Hood, who in 1992 was vice chairman of General Electric, remembered debating the strategy with a Harvard Business School professor. The professor argued that GE had become so large and diverse that it had to create this new layer of management. Hood said, "You've got it upside down."

"What do you mean?" the professor asked.

"It has nothing to do with control. It has to do with succession planning."

The professor looked at Hood as if someone had turned on a light bulb.[4]

Jack Welch stood out at General Electric for one reason alone: He was one of its few successful entrepreneurial types. He was credited with being the key force behind the hugely successful Plastics business. After moving to Fairfield in 1977, he again performed a miracle, turning GE's moribund Medical Systems business into a huge winner. It was Welch who encouraged large investments in CT-scan technology, making General Electric a world leader in medical imaging. And in building up GE Credit, Welch was instrumental in moving General Electric away from the less profitable manufacturing areas into the fast-growth financial services field.

Welch did not want to move from Pittsfield to Fairfield, though that was the road to leadership at GE. Jones brought him to Connecticut as senior vice president for Consumer Products and sector executive for Consumer Products and Services. "I needed to see more of him," Jones commented. "Jack objected to coming. He resisted initially. He liked the freedom. I understood all that, but it was important that these people come."[5] Welch was content in Pittsfield, where his children attended high school. In his post as vice president and group executive of the Components and Materials Group, Welch had been running a series of businesses that he found most appealing: Plastics, Diamonds, Electronic Components, Appliance Components, and Medical Systems. "What could I do sitting down there [at headquarters] in a corner office that I couldn't do all from where I was? . . . The structure and the bureaucracy gave me great difficulty. Don't forget, I grew up in this pea patch."[6]

Yet the path to the most senior positions in GE lay, not in pea patches like Pittsfield, but in Fairfield. And to Welch GE's headquarters seemed to lack a team spirit. "Headquarters are strange places in corporations. They don't make anything. They don't sell anything. And so they don't have a focal point. . . . The ability to celebrate is [lacking]. You don't work all night, get a big order, and go out and have a pizza party."

Eventually Welch got used to the surroundings and resigned himself to his new life. Colleagues quickly took note of his qualities. Edward Hood was struck with how quickly Welch could read a business situation. "He placed a very large premium on winning. He was never satisfied with the status quo."[7] Dennis Dammerman, GE's senior vice president for finance in 1992, worked as Welch's liaison to GE Credit from Welch's first day in Fairfield. At first Dammerman was concerned that his explanations of how GE Credit functioned would be too complex, but Welch caught on quickly.

Welch's vigor made an immediate impression on Paul Van Orden, who had arrived in Fairfield in 1977. Van Orden had been managing the Audio business in Syracuse, and when Audio and Housewares became one division, he moved to headquarters to head it. After Van Orden's first day of work with Welch he reported to his wife that Welch had "enormous energy. I remember meeting Jack for breakfast. We had some changes I wanted to make. I just felt if he were sitting there and I looked away, I might look back and there'd be only a pile of ashes on the chair. He literally consumed himself with energy. It was almost hot. That Irish, red, excited kind of look."[8]

Welch was excitable all right. Van Orden recalled entering a staff meeting soon after Welch took over the Consumer Products Sector and finding Welch white hot in anger. "He was flushed, we were going around the table making business presentations, and the next guy walked up, and Jack just started ripping the business presentation to shreds. After about three minutes he stopped and remarked: 'Wait a minute, I apologize. It has nothing to do with your presentation. I just got a phone call, and it got me upset, and I'm taking it out on you and I shouldn't be. So I'll just sit here for a moment.' He was having a soft drink—he went over and got the bucket of ice, he put it on the floor beside him, and he started eating the bucket of ice, and it was kind of semicrushed. But he ate the whole bucket of ice. He just literally consumed the bucket of ice in about the next half hour."[9]

Welch made mistakes. One occurred in 1978, when he approved the development of a washing machine code-named L–7. The machine used harmonic vibration to save energy (the tub did not spin). GE, never a major force in the laundry room, had great hopes for this machine. Though the four-year project cost $30 million and produced a machine "the size of a Titan booster" (according to a former employee), the machine did not work. William E. Rothschild, a GE strategic planner, noted that it "did everything but wash clothes." Welch saw the project through. Rothschild and others blamed him for the fiasco. All Welch could say was that "I was new to the business, the case was persuasive and well documented, and I supported it. It's not the only failure I've had."[10]

Welch was a tough boss. GE managers used to hide from him employees whom he did not like, fearing that he would fire them if he saw them. These employees even had a nickname: They were called "mummies." Welch was impatient with underlings who failed to follow orders. Once, he ordered his general managers to cut inventories immediately. A month later, at a meeting he called to check on their progress, he was exasperated to learn that no one had implemented the order. Recessing the meeting, Welch said that he wanted action. He got it speedily.[11]

Early in 1978 Reg Jones was ready to intensify the succession contest. He began a series of what he called "airplane interviews" with the candidates. Jones borrowed this idea from his predecessor, Fred Borch. Each of the candidates was summoned to meet with Jones separately. None knew why, and each was sworn to secrecy. With much satisfaction Jones later described how the meetings went: "You call a fellow in, close the door, get out your pipe, and try to get him relaxed. Then you say to him, 'Well, look now, Bill, you and I are flying in one of the company planes, and this plane crashes. [*Pause.*] Who should be the chairman of General Electric?' Well, some of them try to climb out of the wreckage, but you say, 'No, no, you and I are killed. [*Pause.*] Who should be chairman of General Electric?' And boy, this really catches them cold. They fumble around for a while and fumble around, and you have a two-hour conversation. And you learn a great deal from that meeting." What Jones learned, more than anything else, was who was prepared to work with whom and who disliked whom.[12]

Welch was taken completely by surprise at being summoned to see Reg Jones. If any other candidates had been called in to see Jones, they had not said so. So Welch went in cold, not knowing what the point of the meeting was. Jones asked him what advice he had for advancing the company. More entrepreneurship, more risk-taking, Welch replied. In polite language he told the CEO that the place had become too "buttoned-down, too formal, too ritualistic." With the company growing so large, should a president be appointed in addition to the CEO, Jones asked? No, replied Welch, that would rob the CEO of needed power. The company should have "a single head," with perhaps a couple of vice chairmen. Jones felt that Welch's answers were thoughtful. Not interested in dialogue, he merely sat back and listened, taking notes. At the first interview the candidates were asked to say who, beside themselves, were their three choices, without ranking them. When Jones asked Welch to evaluate the other candidates, the sector executive again turned diplomatic. "A very good list," replied Welch. Jones asked who was the best qualified. "Why, me, of course," answered Welch.[13] Jack forgot one important rule of the game: He was supposed to be dead!

Three months later Jones called the eight men back for another round of airplane interviews; this time, however, each had been advised in advance, and so the men brought copious notes. Jones recalled that second round: "You call the fellow in and say, 'Remember our airplane conversations?' 'Oh, yeah,' and he starts to sweat a little bit. 'Now,' you say, 'this time we're out there together, we're flying in a plane and the plane crashes. I'm done, but you live. Now who should be the chairman of General Electric?' " Specifically, Jones asked each candidate to supply three choices, one of whom could be himself, for GE chairman. A few did not nominate themselves, but others did. Those who did were then asked what major challenges GE faced and what they would do about them. Jones also asked the candidates to comment on what GE's strategic aims should be and how to achieve them.

If Welch harbored thoughts about buying and selling various business units, he kept them to himself. But he did express serious interest in "moving forward." Jones was suitably impressed. "He had tremendous drive. He had very good ideas as to how we had to move and get ahead of the game—where we could make changes that would be beneficial." Recalling that second airplane interview, Jones thought it unsurprising that Welch did not mention a personal ambition to make large acquisitions. For GE to have considered buying a business as large as RCA in those days was, as Jones put it, "beyond the realm of even speculation." Antitrust sentiment remained strong in Washington.

Ed Hood recalled that at both interviews, when Jones asked him his choices for GE leadership, two of his three choices were Welch and Burlingame. Hood learned later that he, Welch, and Burlingame had included each other on their lists. Welch vaguely recalled that he had chosen Hood and Burlingame.

Robert Wright, the president of NBC News, explained why the field eventually narrowed to Welch. "Ed Hood had been shipped around to a lot of different places, and because he had been shipped around, he hadn't been able to demonstrate [sufficient achievement]. The Aircraft Engine business [for which Hood was responsible] had not really caught on fire, unfortunately for Ed. It caught on fire after Jack got the job [as CEO]. . . . If the Aircraft Engine business had caught on fire five years earlier, maybe Ed would have had the job. Jack's business [Plastics] was a star, and Ed's business was still consuming zillions of dollars of capital and not producing." John Burlingame was not a "viable candidate," as he had not been associated with a successful business. Thomas Vanderslice "publicized himself perhaps a little too much. He got anxious, and Reg just decided that he was too aggressive."

Precisely when did Reg Jones decide that Welch was his choice? Not until after the two airplane interviews in the spring of 1978. Choosing Welch as the next CEO of General Electric required nerve. Robert Wright noted that Reg Jones was handing over a large company with a rich history and many seasoned managers to a "sort of wild man." Welch, Wright added, "had such an erratic history. . . . And he was a lot younger and hadn't really demonstrated his abilities outside of the principal business he came from. I thought it was a pretty ballsy move by Reg Jones."[14]

Some General Electric people thought Welch was not mainstream enough to become CEO. GE was a fine, well-run, highly established, traditional company headed by America's most admired CEO. A frequent *Fortune* cover story. A company whose traditions made it profitable. Inside GE Welch was considered too rough, too impatient to succeed the smooth, diplomatic Jones. Welch's style seemed ill-matched to the "buttoned-down" company. Moreover, he had worked mostly in nontraditional GE businesses—Plastics and Medical Systems in particular. GE's traditional focus had been the electric industry, large steam turbines, transformers, appliances, and lighting. Aware of how eager Welch had been to shake things up in Consumer Products, some fearful GE executives sensed that Welch was more likely than any of the other candidates to overhaul the company. Why, they asked dolefully, let this maverick from Pittsfield "fix" a company that was not broken?

Welch seemed as improbable a CEO outside the company as inside. During the summer of 1978 Richard Vancil of the Harvard Business School met Welch through a friend at General Electric. Welch was then a year into his job as sector executive. He had been charged with recruiting graduates from the Harvard MBA program. In the fall of 1978, at Vancil's request, Welch talked to Vancil's students about the informal processes of management in a large organization. The students loved him and found him exciting. Part of their excitement came from knowing that Welch was in a hotly contested race for CEO. Vancil asked his students whether Welch would win: "My students concluded that Welch did not fit their stereotype of GE's CEO and the job would probably go to someone more conventional. Welch was a maverick, he let the students know it, and they loved him for it, but that's what happens to mavericks. I didn't know the other candidates either, but I shared my students' view."[15]

The conventional wisdom was that Reg Jones would choose a clone of himself; that he would reject Jack Welch as too countercultural, unorthodox, and change-oriented for the structured, orderly GE. And yet, as hard as it was to admit publicly, Jones knew that GE needed someone at the helm who would act aggressively. None of Welch's other so-called defects bothered him especially. Not his relative youth (Welch was 42 years old early in 1978); not his lack of experience in running any of General Electric's core businesses. Welch had one credential that past General Electric CEOs had lacked, his technical background, and this appealed enormously to Reg Jones: "Here was a Ph.D. in technology and a man who had worked in some of the most technical sectors of General Electric. In a business as complex and involved in as many diverse high technologies as General Electric, you have to have someone periodically as CEO who is most comfortable discussing technical issues. And Jack brought that. In that sense he was really different. . . . I thought it was really important that we have someone who looks at issues differently. . . . The business has changed. Along with his ability to plan, his understanding of technology, his dynamism, and his quick grasp of new businesses, he was one of the first executives to understand the significance of global competition. He had an interest in the international area that was absolutely first-rate."[16]

Once Reg Jones had decided that he wanted Jack Welch to be his successor, he needed to sell Welch to the board. He devised a clever tactic that would give the board time to get to know Welch. In August 1979 Jones went to the board and recommended that three vice chairmen be appointed—Welch, Burlingame, and Hood—and that the three be elevated to the board. The board agreed.

That same month, soon after naming the three new vice chairmen, Jones revealed to some members of the board that he favored Welch. He gathered together the five members of the board's Management Development and Compensation Committee, which was responsible for major personnel shifts. Jones told the committee his reasons for selecting Welch, Burlingame, and Hood as vice chairmen.

But he went beyond that, "beginning even at that early date to shade their thinking that while they might see Jack as the youngest, as perhaps different from the typical GE executive, I had the strong feeling that he had the capabilities that were needed for this assignment."[17]

Members of the committee questioned Jones. Some asked him why he had not selected persons other than the three to be vice chairmen. The discussion, as Jones recalled, was "quite extended." The two outgoing vice chairmen—Walter D. Dance and Jack S. Parker—differed about Jones's selection of the trio. (Dance and Parker stayed on until the end of the year, then retired.)

In the next, final lap, lasting 15 months, Jones made sure that the board had the chance to meet and judge the three. To make sure that each of them was given a fair opportunity, he told his secretary to keep detailed records of every contact that the three made with the board. Jones assured them that there would be a "level playing field" and that each of them would have an "equal shot" at presenting himself to the board.

What of the other candidates? When it became clear that they had not won the top job, Vanderslice, Way, Gault, and Frederick left GE. Vanderslice became president of the General Telephone and Electronics (GTE) Corporation; Way assumed the presidency of the American Express Company; Gault took over as CEO of Rubbermaid; Frederick did not leave immediately, but headed up the international sector for a while, then departed in 1982, becoming CEO of RCA.

Jack Welch became a company vice chairman on September 1, 1979. He cannot put his finger on the moment when he knew that he wanted to become CEO, but it was not long after he moved to corporate headquarters. Once he got into the work at Fairfield, he grew increasingly confident that he was qualified to run General Electric: "All the competitive juices probably came out. I saw my peers close up. I had assessments of everything, I saw the job more clearly. And I wanted it. I thought I could do it. I thought I could really make a big company move with the speed of a small company. I really had that—whatever you want to call it—dream." He decided that it would be better to say as little as possible about his ambitions to others at GE. "My objective was to be cool. I probably wasn't very cool. But my objective in life was to clearly not show it. Some people showed it very badly during that period and were rejected by Reg [Jones] because of some of that."

Although some portrayed Welch as a dark horse and others thought he had no business even being considered, he had all the confidence in the world. When asked if he thought of himself as a long shot, he roared back with a loud, forceful no. He added that he had been "kind of shocked" when he discovered that others thought his chances were slim. He sensed that his critics disliked his style more than his youth. Years later he thought their attitude "outrageous." He felt perfectly qualified. [18]

In November 1979 Jones held his annual meeting with the board's Management Development and Compensation Committee, which was followed by a dinner for the entire board. Jones was the only "inside director" at the meeting. As he did every year, Jones rated the top two dozen GE executives. He also recommended who was to replace whom should calamity suddenly strike one of those executives. Again he spoke about the three vice chairmen, and again he leaned toward Jack Welch as his successor. "Here too I began to say, 'I want you to get to know the youngest of these perhaps more than you have because you've spent more time with the other two.' So it was evident even that early that I was saying to them: 'You better pretty seriously consider Jack Welch.' "[19]

The more the board saw of Welch, the more it liked him. Welch, Hood, and Burlingame were present at every board meeting, at every board dinner, at every social event, every presentation. Board member Gertrude Michelson recalled one presentation that Welch made to the board. The topic was broadcasting. "You quickly saw that he was extraordinarily bright and very competitive, not in an unattractive sense. Jack spoke about the advantages of this company, what he thought it was worth. Then the bidding got to be quite high. I was impressed more than anything else with his ability to walk away from the deal. It got too rich to be sensible, and because he is so competitive, it would have been very easy without being intellectually dishonest to rationalize that deal. But he didn't. And here he had gone out on a limb to the board: [He had told us] that he had a good chance to do it. Then to have to say 'I think we should walk away' is not something anyone relishes. It takes a strong, self-confident person. He was more natural, more himself than most people are in that situation. He didn't want to spill soup on his tie, but he wanted you to know who he was. That was a very appealing quality for leadership. To be self-confident, to be honest with yourself."[20]

Jones happily sensed that the board was coming around to his choice. Referring to Welch, board members whispered to Jones: "Is that guy sharp!" Or, "Did you see how quickly he responded to this question at the board meeting?" Or, "Look at the vision he showed in this presentation." Welch's great virtue to board members was the fact that he alone among GE's higher echelons had demonstrated an ability to "grow" businesses. First in Plastics, then in Medical Systems, finally at GE Credit.

In November 1980 Jones again convened the board for his yearly personnel review. The session was held at General Electric's New York offices rather than at Fairfield. Jones wanted to avoid having someone listen in while senior executives were being rated. This time it was clear that the board wanted to make Jack Welch the next CEO and to retain Burlingame and Hood as vice chairmen. A month later came the big announcement. Jack Welch would succeed Reg Jones as the head of GE. Jones had the task of telling all three men what the board planned to do. To Welch he observed simply, "You're going to be chairman-elect. I'm going out on April 1. And you're taking over." Welch replied: "Thanks. I'm going to really give it my best."

What title should Welch be given? When Jones took over, he had been named president and had used that title for the first six months. A few board members thought calling Welch president for just three or four months (before Jones officially stepped down the following April) made no sense. The board took no vote that day. This was not an official meeting. Jones wanted the formalities concluded within a month. There would be a board meeting, Welch would be officially selected, then the press would be told.

On December 19 Reg Jones chose the 47th floor boardroom of GE's New York offices to make the board's decision public. Earlier in the day the 20 members of GE's board had formally selected Welch as the next chairman and CEO of General Electric. Jones read out a typed statement declaring that Welch would succeed him the following April. "I am the most happy man in America today," Welch pronounced.[21] The *New York Times* explained that Welch had been chosen because he had "molded himself into an aggressive manager of fast-growth businesses within the vast General Electric." At 45, Welch was the youngest chairman in GE's history. The year before, he had earned $572,000 as vice chairman. His salary package as CEO would be $904,000. This was not an occasion on which Jack Welch would quit over not getting a big enough salary raise! (Welch's salary package grew to $975,000 in 1982, to $2.6 million in 1989, to $2.9 million in 1990, and to $3.2 million in 1991).

Of the decision to keep on the 50-year-old Ed Hood and the 58-year-old John Burlingame as vice chairmen, Welch declared: "We all came to the party as good friends. It's my goal to create an atmosphere of sharing both the good and the bad, where they can grow and I can grow, and we continue to have a good time."[22]

Asked that day about GE's prospects for 1981, Welch talked in optimistic terms. "We really have businesses positioned, through planning and the allocation of capital resources, to have a wonderful year." He acknowledged that GE was likely to face growing competitive threats from Japanese consumer appliance manufacturers. "But if you look at our strategies in major appliances, we're clearly putting ourselves in a position of quality far better than before. If we get the competition, we'll be able to handle it. If we don't, we'll be in a better position than most of our domestic competitors."

Reaction to Welch's appointment was enthusiastic. "It's an absolutely super choice," beamed GE-watcher Robert McCoy, vice president of Kidder, Peabody, Inc. "Like Jones, he is a unique personality. He knows how to produce numbers, and people like to work for him. He is good at identifying niches in markets, and then throwing lots of aggressive young people in to run the business, giving them money and letting them go."[23]

In January 1981 Welch appeared before a group of General Electric officers in Belleair, Florida, and noted that two weeks after the big announcement he still felt elated. He then added somberly: "Beyond this very real emotion, I do understand the responsibility. I'm confident of my strengths and, more important, I'm gaining a better understanding of my limitations every day."

After Jones retired, he looked back at the succession process and sought to give the impression that he had always wanted Welch and that he alone had been the driving force in choosing Welch.[24]

Evidence exists, however, that Jones may have had other choices before Welch and backed Welch only after the board had vetoed his previous selections. During a roundtable discussion on CEO succession sponsored by *Chief Executive* magazine, Jones's airplane interviews cropped up. Walter Wriston, a GE board member and a participant in the roundtable discussion, noted: "That's a great story, but it's not the way it happened."[25]

Wriston hinted that Jones had not had Welch in mind throughout the succession contest and had proposed several others first whom the board had vetoed before it finally came around to Welch. Wriston, in an interview with the author, noted that some board members believed that John Burlingame would make a better CEO than Welch. "It's fair to say that all of us [on the board] had come to the conclusion that it would be Jack fairly early on. . . . One school of thought said that John Burlingame—he was 59 or 60—can go in and make the transition and give Jack a couple more years to sandpaper the edges; then we'll go forward. That is the safe way to go. I argued that was the wrong way to go because all you did was lose momentum for three or four years and trying to regain momentum is a helluva lot harder than keeping it going when you've got it—though I had the greatest respect for Burlingame. Unfortunately . . . so much of life is when your mother has you. . . . Others on the board [who supported Welch] said the world is changing at a velocity that you can't believe, and we need somebody who can go in—not say that what we've been doing for the last 20 years is wrong, because it wasn't, but say, 'I have to change this to live in the new world,' and that's Jack. . . . The process by which it [the succession] gets done is half bureaucratic, half magic, half serendipity, half something else. At the end of the day the 'Comp' committee and the board were enthusiastic in favor of Jack."[26]

What did the candidates think of the selection process? Ed Hood found it withering. "Frankly, while it produced a good result, in the end it was debilitating. People inevitably became polarized and competitive to a fault. The agenda of some other people, not all, was to shine even at the expense of their peers. That's just a natural phenomenon when you set up that kind of situation." Candidates sought to take credit for actions, sometimes deservedly, sometimes not. Mostly,

Hood thought, the process went on too long and too many candidates were involved. He would have narrowed the contest down to two or three people; seven candidates were just too many.[27] Did Welch object to the long, drawn-out succession contest? Not really. "I thought it was pretty quick. . . . I thought it had some advantages and disadvantages. Obviously the final result pleased me. The fact that we got three of us who could work together well pleased me. I had respect for both Burlingame and Hood. And finding that chemistry was an important outgrowth of the process."[28]

CHAPTER FIVE

◇

"Storm Signals"

In business the meek did not inherit the earth. The tough-minded did. Fortunately, Jack Welch was a combative type. For the business arena had grown larger and increasingly competitive, girdling the globe with a new array of enterprises with international pretensions. When competition was strictly domestic, when only the American marketplace counted and the rest of the world economy seemed inconsequential, companies like General Electric could triumph far more easily than in 1981. The 70s, however, brought changes. It was no longer possible to think of the "rest of the world" as microscopic and irrelevant.

Welch's great achievement was that he recognized the changes taking place before others did. His gut instinct told him that to survive in the rapidly shifting environment General Electric, as well as the other giants of American business, required a whole new vision, a whole new set of strategies. Many businessmen, at General Electric and elsewhere, scoffed at such talk, dismissed the warnings, and argued that all was well, that the signals across the horizon were illusory. They insisted that the storm Jack Welch worried about was a phantom.

These businessmen argued that their businesses were not ill, and sometimes, as in the case of GE, they were right. But, as Welch understood better than most, their arguments missed the point. In an environment with only a few important domestic competitors it had been possible for a GE to do well in the 70s. When that environment shifted, however, to include foreign competitors, trouble loomed

◇

ahead. Yet, most of the people at General Electric fervently believed that the 80s would be the 60s and 70s all over again, that with a little more push, a little luck with the economy, GE could prevail as it had for so many years, that in time it would bring some of its less active businesses back on line and all would be well. Unlike Jack Welch, they refused to read the portents of change.

The strongest signal came from overseas. America had once dominated the most important markets of the world economy. Steel. Textiles. Shipbuilding. Television. Calculators. And automobiles. Slowly, at first imperceptibly, others, most notably the Japanese, began grabbing away customers, luring them with higher-quality products at cheaper prices. Smokestack America was crumbling, and one dismal sign was the plight of the steel industry, which lost $3.2 billion in 1982. In parallel, the Japanese had grabbed 20 percent of the American market. What was happening in steel was felt as forcefully in the American car industry.

By the 70s Japanese-made Datsuns, Hondas, Toyotas, and Mazdas were streaming through American ports at the rate of 6,000 cars a day. As of the spring of 1981, the Japanese controlled 23 percent of the American car market. The Detroit carmarkers, once kings of the market, were reeling. In 1980 alone they lost $4 billion. The problem of the car industry was that it had not read the signals correctly. It had not understood that smaller, better, more fuel-efficient Japanese cars were a threat. America's consumer electronics industry also failed to read the signals coming from across the Pacific. By the time it understood that Americans had a voracious appetite for videocassette recorders, it was too late. Twenty percent of American homes had VCRs in 1985; six years later 70 percent did. And the Japanese had cornered the market from the start.

As Detroit went, so went the nation: One out of every five American workers was employed directly or indirectly in the making, servicing, or selling of cars. Such industries as steel, glass, and rubber were heavily dependent on a flourishing Detroit.

With the arrival of the 1980s the American economy looked increasingly unhealthy. Inflation, only 3.4 percent in 1971, had climbed to 18 percent in March 1980. Since inflation made it hard to keep costs down people were led to ask why they should invest in new products. Even if new products did get made, they would not be cheaper or better than what the Japanese and others overseas were producing.

Other signs of distress were in evidence. The price of oil, only $1.70 per barrel in 1971, had peaked at $39 per barrel in 1980. Auto and truck production, which reached 8 million vehicles in 1971, slid to a mere 6.4 million by 1980. Still the highest in the world, American productivity had outpaced that of the West Germans and the Japanese in 1979, but it had been slowing since the 60s. In 1979 the United States ranked only 10th in annual per capita income ($10,662) among members of the Organization for Economic Cooperation and Development. That great industrial power, Switzerland, led the list with $14,967 per capita, while the per capita income of such other economic giants as Denmark, Sweden, and Luxembourg also surpassed that of the United States. Not surprisingly, America headed for a recession that began in early 1981. (The prime lending rate hit 20.5 percent in August.)

America's economic salvation lay in improving the quality and reliability of its products and in bringing costs down. Yet American productivity, which had risen nearly 3 percent a year in the 50s and 60s, now grew less than 1 percent annually. Economists asserted that if the United States had maintained its earlier productivity growth during the 70s, inflation would have been cut in half and the average annual income per American family would have been 25 percent higher in real, not inflated, dollars.

The United States had to become not only more productive but also more aggressive in competing for business around the world. World trade had stood at $2 trillion in 1981 and was expected to grow dramatically over the decade. Yet thousands of American companies were not exporting. Only 1 percent of American firms accounted for 80 percent of the country's exports; 9 out of 10 American companies did not export at all.

All of these factors had important effects on General Electric, most of them negative. For those who had led the company through the 70s, it was anguishing to acknowledge that despite Reg Jones's gleaming balance sheets, GE was heading for the shoals. In the fall of 1991 Jones readily stated that the increasingly competitive business environment had been a major reason for selecting Jack Welch. Yet he found it difficult to acknowledge that GE's businesses had needed an overhaul by the late 70s. While admitting that he had experienced some anxieties as he was preparing to step down, he emphasized that "nothing was losing money at the total business level." Unlike his predecessor, Fred Borch, he had encountered "no crushing problems." Moreover, GE had possessed enough cash and marketable securities to pay off all of its debt, so the company was "in a very strong financial position at the time."[1]

Bathing in a glory reserved for few other captains of American industry, Reg Jones could be forgiven for striking such an ebullient note. No other company had received such a warm reception from the press, due in no small measure to the nation's love affair with the man at its helm. Could such a company be heading for a fall? The very thought seemed preposterous.

But one could look behind the media's romance with Reg Jones and see signs that Mr. Edison's company was not delivering the goods. As late as 1970 fully 80 percent of General Electric's earnings came from its traditional electrical and electronic manufacturing businesses. With manufacturing on the slide, even Jones understood that the time for GE to diversify had come. He began the process, but only slowly. In 1980, Jones's last year, the traditional GE businesses still accounted for half of the company's earnings.

Moreover, most of GE's businesses were clearly troubled, earning less than they should have earned. Some, such as Consumer Electronics and Semiconductors, were admittedly in competitive industries. Power Systems had been suffering because the nation was using less electricity. GE's two global businesses, Plastics and Aircraft Engines, were far less productive than their Japanese competitors. The company had made several unsuccessful attempts to globalize. Taken as a whole, GE was a dull, unexciting organization. "Just another GNP company" was the harsh phrase used to sum up its lethargy.

That lethargy permeated GE's 1980 annual report. Reg Jones wrote that GE had turned in a "solid performance" in 1980. Overall, its sales and earnings had reached new highs despite adverse economic conditions in American and overseas markets, despite a decline in profits for industry in general. And yet the storm signals could be seen in the sluggish earnings of a variety of GE businesses. Those earnings had been "pretty decent," according to Paul Van Orden, the former executive vice president, but they had not grown at the enormous rate that had been expected.

Between 1976 and 1980, net earnings had risen from $261 million to only $407 million in the Consumer Products and Services Sector, from $160 million to only $315 million in the Industrial Products and Components Sector, from $61 million to only $141 million in the Power Systems Sector, from $202 million to only $373 million in the Systems and Materials Sector. The net earnings of GE's natural resources operations, largely Utah International, were $181 million in 1976 and only $224 million in 1980.

Critics of GE's performance in the 70s contended that GE had added financial and industrial services to its mix of businesses because it lacked new products; that it spent too much of its resources on nuclear reactors, jet engines, and consumer products; and that it did not work aggressively enough to save its computer business and its integrated circuit business. They argued that salvaging those businesses might have brought GE into technology far earlier, far quicker. The critics of GE also lashed at it for not converting its products from electromechanical to electronic components fast enough. Above all, they charged that GE had been too afraid of risk. Robert H. Hayes, professor of business administration at the Harvard Business School, commented just two weeks before Welch took charge: "A lot of U.S. companies are finding that people without a technological background are unskilled in understanding the nature of technological risk. They substitute a degree of caution and risk aversion because they can't stomach the risk. But you can't quantify and reduce all the risks in technology. You need animal spirits. The survivors who have [them] dominate the industry. GE is doing a lot of questioning right now about whether it may have become too monolithic. The giant is twitching a bit and trying to change."[2]

When Reg Jones stepped down, no one wanted to say a harsh word about him. He had brought so much respect to General Electric. Only after he left office did some GE executives suggest that the "legend," as Jack Welch sometimes referred to Jones, had not been— quite so legendary. Paul Van Orden, who worked in Fairfield from 1977 until his retirement in December 1990, felt no inhibitions in talking about the Jones era: "An honest appraisal would be that Reg had begun to devote a significant portion of his time to the public policies issue. He was somewhat less attentive to the goings-on in the business. He relied to a large extent on a competent, corporate staff structure. So nobody sensed that anything was greatly wrong."[3]

In the early 90s, flushed with earnings that towered over those Jones had produced, exuberant at being part of the greatest success story in American business, GE executives looked back to the 70s and contended that General Electric's supposed virtues had not been virtues and that its vaunted corporate structure, which had supposedly excelled at command and control, had in fact been a straitjacket. In the 70s no one had an unkind word for Reg Jones's strategic planning system. According to James P. Baughman, GE's manager for corporate management development and director of the Crotonville Management Development Institute, it had been "the finest flower of the preceding 15 years."[4]

Business schools had praised this "finest flower," but GE's executives of the 90s looked down their noses at the strategic planning technique for not being supple, for slowing things down, for not helping managers to spot trouble quickly enough. These executives recalled how planners wrote memos read only by other planners. The emphasis placed on formality and on strategic planning and control had stifled the entrepreneurial spirit that a company like General Electric needed. That stifling of entrepreneurial spirit bothered Jack Welch more than anything else.

The original idea of the strategic planning process and the new bureaucracy that had come in its wake had appeared sound. *Bureaucracy* was not considered a dirty word. "In fact," noted Gertrude Michelson, "in a way it represented organization, orderliness. You had a boss, and he had a boss, and somebody else had a boss, and you went through the channels, you wrote memos—that was the way an orderly business was run."[5]

Yet General Electric had grown so immense and so diverse that nearly everyone seemed to be a manager of some sort. Of GE's 400,000 employees, 25,000 had the title of "manager." Some 500 of these managers were senior managers, and 130 were vice presidents or higher. Required to "manage," this flock of supervisors engaged in little else but reviewing what their subordinates were doing. In theory such reviews seemed necessary to keep the enterprise moving in the right direction. In practice, however, managers wound up spending an inordinate amount of time filling out routine reports and selling their plans to managers on a higher level than their own.

When Fred Borch and Reg Jones reclustered the business units into 43 Strategic Business Units, the command-and-control function was supposed to improve dramatically. But the addition of a new layer of finance and planning staffs resulted in a situation in which executives commanded and controlled one another, leaving them with no time to determine how a business was performing. The planning system, Jack Welch asserted, "was dynamite when we first put it in." But the format was cumbersome. "We hired a head of planning, and he hired two vice presidents, and then he hired a planner, and then the books got thicker and the printing got more sophisticated and the covers got harder and the drawings got better. The meetings kept getting larger. Nobody can say anything with 16 or 18 people there."[6]

The paperwork was endless. Dennis Dammerman, senior vice president, finance, remembered ordering the shut down of a GE computer that had been grinding out daily reports for no apparent reason. The computer had produced a stack of paper 12 feet high, which meant that Dammerman had to strain his neck to see the top of the stack. The reports contained product-by-product sales information—down to the penny—on hundreds of thousands of items. Executives felt compelled to analyze the reports, to talk about them to one another. This left little time for studying the big picture.

Richard Burke, vice president for manufacturing at Major Appliances in Louisville, recalled the pitfalls of strategic planning in the 70s. "I was in the turbine business. It was the first time I got involved in one of these big strategic plans, and we had this big thick book. There was a whole bunch of stuff that was mandatory to fill out that had to go to Schenectady and then up to sector, then up to vice chairman before it went up to Reg [Jones]. These were 3-, 5-year, even 10-year plans. Functional reviews. I remember one night I got up in front of our general manager meeting and somebody asked me about the future, and in 10 minutes I articulated the strategic plan for the business. Some guy said, 'I think you just gave us a strategic plan.' I got to thinking: 'Goddamn it, I did.' And I had been filling this whole damn book up for a lot of bureaucrats up there."[7]

The whole system had simply become too bureaucratic. Jim Baughman, sitting in his office at General Electric's management development center in Crotonville, along the Hudson River in New York, recounted some examples of this stultifying bureaucracy: "We had nine turbine departments going to market rather than one. We had gas turbines, steam turbines, and combined cycle turbines. And small, medium, and large of each so that you had small gas, medium gas, large gas; small steam, medium steam—all to the same customer base. We sold billions of pounds of plastic into the automobile industry; and billions of light bulbs into the automobile industry; and millions of electric motors into the automobile industry. And yet the sales staffs were going to the automobile industry as if they didn't work for the same company. We were missing chances to combine our hits.

"Extreme decentralization had created micro profit and loss units that really weren't of critical mass to play in the markets we were in. It had also created many, many layers of approvals, and functional boundaries where engineering would design something, throw it over the wall, and manufacturing would say: 'Who the hell designed this?' They'd figure out how to make it, throw it over the wall, sales would say: 'Where in the world did this come from? We can't sell it.' Service would say: 'How the hell are we supposed to fix this?' There was no horizontal flow. So we had hierarchic boundaries that slowed down the decision process. Things took too long. We had boundaries between the businesses. Where we should have been going to market as a team, we were going separately. We also had the 'nih' factor—'not invented here.' If we didn't think of it, it wasn't important. And we had a very domestic orientation. All of these things were signs. You'd see it in the slowness of decisions, in plans rather than actions, in turf battles, in lack of synergy where you'd want more synergy."[8]

Indeed, strategic planning had become an unhealthy force in the company, attaching more importance to style and structure than to substance. Its most characteristic feature was the memo. Memo writing became a way of life, and managers fired memos at one another with such frequency that executives might have mistakenly concluded that their main task in life was simply to read! For all its flaws, the system did assure that nothing went terribly amiss. But little more. Paul Van Orden noted that the presentations had become formalized, ponderous, laborious, without much give-and-take. "I can remember guys coming around and overseeing appropriation requests. Some of the staff felt they were checkers. They would mosey around in your businesses and prepare lists of questions for the vice chairman and the chairman to ask in the review process. There was nothing greatly wrong in this. But it was not prone to search out and really try to do something fundamental with some of the sick businesses."[9]

While insiders at GE voiced such thoughts at the time among themselves, few put such carping on the record. Later, when General Electric had turned itself around, when many of the problems had been addressed, it became fashionable, indeed almost obligatory, for the GE people to speak openly about all that had bogged down the company in the 70s. The company's culture back then exhibited a nervousness, a skepticism, an apprehension that GE could not remain a great institution in the 80s unless employees began to recognize what was happening outside GE. Bill Lane, manager of executive communications, wrote in *Monogram*, GE's internal employee magazine, that the problems were there for people to see but that almost no one wanted to: "Load growth fizzled with the energy crisis, and the marketplace was invaded by new competitors from abroad, some of whom had a pipeline into their national treasuries and were spared the onerous imperative of earning a profit. But the crash didn't come overnight. It was visible, plainly visible, on the horizon for years, but the backlog of orders acted as an anesthetic. We were number one in share and [were sitting in] the most comfortable deck chair on the *Titanic*."[10]

When Jack Welch became General Electric's eighth chairman and CEO on April 1, 1981, he felt as if he were sitting in the most comfortable deck chair on the *Titanic*. Had he been like other new chief executive officers, he might have decided that it was better not to rock the boat, better not to tinker with a good thing. Maybe it was his relative youth. Maybe it was his "winning is all that counts" mentality. Whatever it was, Welch could not lie back. In a statement to the board of directors and share owners that month, he commented: "A decade from now we would like General Electric to be perceived as a unique, high-spirited, entrepreneurial enterprise . . . a company known around the world for its unmatched level of excellence. We want General Electric to be the most profitable highly diversified company on earth, with world-quality leadership in every one of its product lines."

Although Welch had a strategy in mind that would turn the place upside down, he spoke warmly about Reg Jones and took a sanguine view of General Electric in public. "Mr. Jones left us a healthy company," Welch wrote to share owners in the 1981 annual report, "one with a strong balance sheet and a record of sustained earnings growth."

But a decade later Welch was able to express a more critical view of his predecessor's era. "I could see a lot of businesses becoming [like] Consumer Electronics, lethargic. American business was inwardly focused on the bureaucracy. [That bureaucracy] was right for its time, but the times were changing rapidly. Change was occurring at a much faster pace than business was reacting to it."[11]

Unlike many other business leaders, Jack Welch welcomed the major changes in the business environment. He was too eager for a good fight, too intent upon looking reality in the eye, to turn away. To him the business arena was one more playing field where opponents met and clashed, where the losers lost because they stuck their heads in the sand and the winners won because they assessed their opponents' strength and the playing field accurately.

At the beginning of the 1980s so much was new: high-tech industries and global competitors were sprouting up; higher-quality products and new standards of productivity were appearing. And it was all happening at a much faster pace. Jack Welch was the first head of a major U.S. corporation to sense what impact these changes would have on his company. He was also the first to develop a carefully defined plan to deal with the changes.

While others were saying that GE was in good shape, Welch recognized what most business leaders recognized only later about their companies—that to stay alive and to prosper, General Electric required a major restructuring. At that time restructuring was a novel idea and the word *restructuring* had not yet come into vogue.

Restructuring. Not just stripping away a little bureaucracy here or divesting a few businesses there, but a thorough reshaping. So sweeping that the new General Electric would resemble the old one only in name. It was to be one of the great shifts in American corporate life. To restructure Jack Welch needed both vision and guts, and he paid a price for his boldness. A large number of former GE employees and some current ones had accused Welch of being heartless, insensitive, brutal.

The veterans were contemptuous of any tampering with the General Electric mystique. One hundred and three years of history, from Thomas Edison to Charles Coffin, from Gerald Swope to Reg Jones, had created a corporate culture that cried out: "Hands off!" The institution—a collection of factories, offices, and, dare one forget, people—was one of America's abiding corporate success stories. Why tamper with success?

Jack Welch knew why. If others were annoyed at him for daring to alter what history had wrought, he was equally annoyed at those who thought that General Electric's past should dictate how he behaved today and tomorrow. Welch, for that reason, had little use for GE's traditions. They only got in his way. (When Joyce Hergenhan, vice president for public relations, proposed that an official corporate history be written, Welch took one second to shoot the idea down.)

General Electric was not immutable. Unlike Michelangelo's statue of David, it was not intended to be merely admired. Chipping away at it was no sacrilege. It could and indeed should be altered as circumstances required.

Welch began with the premise that General Electric had too many diffused businesses that could not succeed in the long term. He immediately undertook a careful study of the strengths and weaknesses of all the GE businesses. He wanted to move fast, but he also wanted to make sure that he had a firm grasp of the businesses before he made decisions. "I didn't have a great beginning move," he stated, sounding as if he had been about to start a game of chess. The first year, he knew, was critical. "I was succeeding a legend whom I admired. And I wanted to change what he had done."

Welch knew that the change he envisioned could not occur with a bureaucratic structure that worked slowly. Somehow he had to recast GE's vaunted management so that it responded more quickly to changes in the environment. In short, the bureaucracy had to become lean and agile.

For 15 years GE had been the leader in strategic thinking in American business. When Welch became chairman, one of his first acts was to dismantle a good deal of the strategic planning staff. He did not abandon the notion of strategic thinking, but he wanted the planning to be done in the field, not at corporate headquarters in Fairfield. So he changed the location of the strategy reviews. When asked what his approach to cutting out red tape at GE would be, Welch answered:

"That's a loaded question. General Electric was voted in a *Fortune* poll to be the best-managed company in America, so one can't go in here looking to change a great deal. There are some things that we can do better, like shorten the time for decision making, but we're not going to cut out the review processes that have made our company so strong. We are not going to be short-circuiting the system."[12] Welch did not short-circuit the system, but he knew that he had to change GE's crowded, top-heavy structure, which had 29 pay grades, 12 layers of management, and 600 profit and loss units. It also had a 30-member Planning Department in Fairfield.

From the very start Jack Welch was determined to give General Electric a high-tech image. He wanted to turn the company away from its past, away from its dependence on electrical manufacturing businesses. He wanted to push GE into the arenas with the greatest earnings potential. Just before Welch became CEO, GE had taken important steps down the high-tech road. It had earmarked $500 million for the "factory of the future" project; and it had spent $235 million to buy Intersil, a producer of metal oxide semiconductors, and $150 million to buy Calma, a leading firm in computer-aided design and manufacturing technology.

Welch wanted to accelerate these changes. Hoping to generate new excitement about factory automation and to place himself clearly in the corner of GE's high-tech businesses, Welch waited only 24 hours after becoming CEO to spell out GE's plans for the factory of the future. In that factory, computers would instruct machines to perform as many jobs as possible—ranging from the design of a part, to assembly, to final inspection. This would improve quality and productivity in the workplace.

On April 2, 1981, GE announced that it planned to manufacture and sell an industrial robot as the first product of its new factory automation business. Controlled by dual microprocessors, the robot would have a sense of touch that could detect missing components or substandard parts and could repeat the same motions within one-thousandth of an inch. The robot had been developed by an Italian company called DEA. The DEA robot was intended to assemble small items such as automotive parts. GE called the robot Allegro.

GE's ambition was to replace Fanuc, the Japanese company that dominated the world market in industrial robots and machine tool controls, as the leading distributor of factory automation products. GE wanted to become a kind of supermarket for such products, at which clients could acquire whatever computerized equipment and automation advice they needed in one visit.

Forecasts were made that the factory automation market could reach $25 billion a year. GE hoped to capture at least 20 percent of that market within the decade. GE was a natural player in this game: It had sold factory automation products for years. Among them were drives that varied the speed of alternating-current machines, programmable controllers that turned on machine lights, and numerical controls that told machines how to cut, drill, or shape precision parts. Indeed, no other company had assembled as many pieces of the factory of the future as GE had.

Juices began flowing at GE. According to James A. Baker, who headed the Technical Systems Sector, "Carrying through the concept of the 'factory of the future' is kind of a holy grail in this company."[13] Making a larger commitment to this concept than any other American company, GE appeared to have an edge: It had the largest industrial sales, distribution, and service networks in the world.

The restructuring of General Electric began with a small step. Welch waited until the late summer to carry it out. In the 1981 annual report, Welch's first since becoming CEO, he referred to the step as a "major" company reorganization. The "highlight" was a change in the organizational table of Reg Jones's sectors, the first such change since Reg Jones had initiated them in 1977. Welch announced on August 4, 1981, that he was introducing two new sectors in order to underline the importance of high-growth and high-tech businesses to General Electric. To explain these actions he wrote a six-page, single-spaced memo to all GE officers. Welch later took the excessive length of that memo as a sign of his relative youth.

The first new sector, Technical Systems, embraced all of GE's electronics efforts. Under this roof were placed such high-tech GE businesses as Industrial Electronics; GE components that designed and produced integrated circuits; and the microelectronics-intensive GE businesses, which included Mobile Communications, Aerospace, and Medical Systems. The second new sector, Services and Materials, was supposed to nurture GE's high-growth businesses. Into this sector went GE Credit Corporation, GE's Information Services, and the Engineered Materials group.

During that same month of August the politicians in Washington looked for ways to spur investment as part of an attempt to strengthen the sagging economy. Specifically, they hoped to aid the capital-intensive companies in order to make those companies more productive and to create more jobs. What they came up with—the 1981 Tax Act—landed Jack Welch and General Electric in one of the company's most anguishing controversies of the 80s. The provisions of the act seemed benign enough: They allowed faster write-offs for capital investment through investment tax credits.

"Do you understand what this legislation means?" GE's lobbyists asked members of Congress with a mixture of bewilderment and hidden glee. Yes, the politicians replied, when clearly they did not. The lobbyists tried in vain to warn Congress that the legislation might backfire and become a damaging political issue once the public learned what the politicians were in fact doing for corporations like GE. For, with the passage of the act, General Electric would be able to avoid paying federal income taxes simply by freeing up funds for investment.

Despite the public relations risks General Electric plunged full steam ahead. It undertook a multibillion-dollar investment in its own factories and, through GE Credit, it provided billions of dollars in equipment that it leased to other companies. As a result, in keeping with the provisions of the 1981 Tax Act, GE was able to avoid paying federal corporate taxes for the most part. It took tax credits of $104 million in 1981, $176 million in 1982, and $35 million in 1983. It paid only $185 million in federal corporate taxes in 1984 and only $285 million in 1985. In time, the nonpayment of taxes, a perfectly legal act on General Electric's part, did backfire.

CEOs who had taken over companies in their late 50s or 60s may have looked upon getting the top job as a reward for long service, a brief stopping-off point before retirement. For that reason alone, these older, more traditional CEOs had little incentive to seek change. But Jack Welch had none of their conservatism. He was at least 20 years away from retirement. He had much to do before then. The first real shot in his revolution was fired in December—after he had been CEO eight months. In a speech at the Hotel Pierre in New York City on December 8, 1981, he was supposed to update a group of financial community representatives on how General Electric was doing and what its immediate plans were. He felt a need, however, to go beyond that, to explain in more detail why he thought it necessary to take far-reaching steps at GE.

To explain the General Electric strategy Welch cited a letter to the editor that he had come across in the latest issue of *Fortune* magazine. The writer, Kevin Peppard, director of business development at Bendix Heavy Vehicle Systems in Elyria, Ohio, captured Welch's thinking about strategic planning for a company like GE. Peppard observed that Karl von Clausewitz, the 19th-century Prussian general and military historian, had written in his classic *On War*, published in 1833, that men could not reduce strategy to a formula because chance events, imperfections in execution, and the independent will of opponents automatically doomed detailed planning. Peppard suggested that the Prussian general staff under the elder Helmuth von Moltke, who had been triumphant over Denmark, Austria, and France in the 1860s and early 1870s, perfected Clausewitz's concepts in practice: "They did not expect a plan of operation to survive beyond the first contact with the enemy. They set only the broadest of objectives and emphasized seizing unforeseen opportunities as they arose. . . . Strategy was not a lengthy action plan. It was the evolution of a central idea through continually changing circumstances." Welch noted that in running General Electric, he planned to adopt the notion that strategy had to evolve and not be etched in stone.

Welch's most essential task, as he saw it, was to boost the value of General Electric's stock. On December 19, 1980, the day that Jack Welch was elected chairman and CEO, the stock was $14.50. It closed that year at $15.31.[14] In 1981 the stock hovered between the mid 20s and the mid 30s. To raise the stock's value Welch had to alter GE's image as a company composed of hundreds of different businesses, going in hundreds of different directions. That image had instilled little confidence on Wall Street. Welch sensed that GE needed a new organizing focus to repair its image.

At the Hotel Pierre he outlined the concept that became a hallmark of his tenure as chief executive officer at General Electric. The concept was known as "Number One, Number Two." Welch began by predicting that inflation would become the major enemy of American business in the 80s. It would lead, he said, to slower worldwide growth. It would mean that "there will be no room for the mediocre supplier of products and services—the company in the middle of the pack. The winners in this slow-growth environment will be those who search out and participate in the real growth industries and insist upon being number one or number two in every business they are in—the number one or number two leanest, lowest-cost, worldwide producers of quality goods and services or those who have a clear technological edge, a clear advantage in a market niche.

"Where we are not number one or number two, and don't have or can't see a route to a technological edge, we have got to ask ourselves [management theorist] Peter Drucker's very tough question: 'If you weren't already in the business, would you enter it today?' And if the answer is no, face into that second difficult question: 'What are you going to do about it?' The managements and companies in the 80s that don't do this, that hang on to losers for whatever reason—tradition, sentiment, their own management weakness—won't be around in 1990. Think about the fact that in the high-growth period between 1945 and 1970, almost one half the companies that would have been on a Fortune 500 roster disappeared either through acquisition, failure, or slipped quietly off the list due to lack of growth. We believe this central idea—being number one or number two—more than an objective—a requirement—will give us a set of businesses which will be unique in the world business equation at the end of this decade."

The Number One, Number Two strategy could only work, Welch insisted, if General Electric adopted certain "soft values." The most important of which were what he called "reality," "quality/excellence," and "the human element."

Reality meant that General Electric people had "to see the world the way it is and not the way they wished it were or hoped it will be." Quality and excellence meant "stretching beyond our limits, to be, in some cases, better than we ever thought we could be." The human element meant that people dared "to try new things." Adhering to these values would, Welch argued, produce a more high-spirited, adaptable company, one that was more agile than enterprises far smaller than GE. He talked too of offering "ownership" to the managers of number one and number two businesses and providing them with "the freedom and flexibility" to win the 80s.

Jack Welch's blueprint for the 80s and the 90s was the need to be the leader in your business, to be agile, to keep only businesses that were pulling their weight. He skipped specifics, preferring not to mention how much suffering many of his employees would be forced to endure in order to put that blueprint into action. He had been in the job only eight months. It was still too early to dwell on the convulsions about to take place at GE.

Welch was so enthusiastic about his new strategy, so certain of its merit, that he assumed his auditors would catch on at once. They did not. As questions came from them, Welch grew increasingly frustrated. They had not caught on. They asked instead about how General Electric would do in the next quarter. They wanted numbers, not philosophy. They wanted to walk away with a sense of whether GE's balance sheet was improving, not with the words *reality* and *ownership* ringing in their ears. Welch was crushed. "I knew I wasn't hitting a chord with them. My agenda and theirs were passing in the night." He began yelling at them to relieve himself of some of the frustration. Nothing worked. The speech, he recalled sadly, "was literally a dud."[15] At first he blamed himself. The he concluded that the auditors had been at fault. He would not let their disdain hold him back. He vowed not to let them get under his skin. "The hell with them," he murmured. (A decade later he found the indifference of the Hotel Pierre audience ironic. How much had changed since then, he said. In subsequent years, after the views he had expressed at the Pierre had proven out, after the business community had acquired a great respect for the Jack Welch Approach-to-Business, audiences digested every word of his philosophy and then went back to their offices and tried to put it into practice at once.)

Few in the business community thought much of Welch's ideas at first. The traditionalists argued that it was no time to be revolutionary. No wonder. What Jack Welch was trying to do was on a scale that had never before been tried on the business scene. No one had sought to reshape such a venerable, diversified American business institution so drastically. As Welch prepared to unhinge General Electric from its past, he benefited from having the board firmly in his corner. Walter Wriston, one of the most influential men in American business at the time and a GE board member since 1962, made a point of telling his acquaintances, "We've got the greatest new CEO." Word of Wriston's bubbly support quickly filtered back to Welch, who was elated. Asked how the board had reacted to the Welch revolution, Wriston, retired now as chairman of Citicorp, said, "We stood up and cheered." Wriston has to qualify as Jack Welch's greatest fan. "The Scriptures say, 'For everything there is a season.' Jack is the right season for today's world."[16]

One strong boost came from another GE board member, J. Paul Austin, the chairman of the Coca-Cola Company. He had cornered Welch at a dinner party one night when the board was visiting a GE plant in the West. "I had my best blue suit on and my white shirt," Welch remembered proudly, "the newest tie my wife had gotten for me. I was looking very corporate-like. Paul Austin came over to me and said, 'Jack, I want to tell you one thing. You got here with a game plan that was you. Don't ever lose you in this game. Don't ever lose it.' "[17]

CHAPTER SIX

"Number One, Number Two"

Unpopular, the object of suspicious, fearful employees, Jack Welch pursued his vision. Some snickered that he was out of his mind, that he wanted to move too fast, that he did not need to restructure the company at all. Others thought little of his candor, of his profanity, of his irreverence toward GE's past. If Welch learned of these rebukes, he did not let them stand in his way.

He was determined to send a new message to Wall Street: that General Electric was not some messy conglomerate with all sorts of scattered and unrelated businesses; that the company had purposes and a focus; that if his vision were implemented quickly, General Electric would make significant progress toward its goal of being the most competitive enterprise in the world. He knew the questions that were being asked about General Electric: Was the company committed to investing heavily in a high-tech future? Would it remain committed to the factory of the future even if that caused earnings to slow down in the short run? How was it going to adjust its 280,000-strong work force in the United States—one of the largest in the country—to an automated factory? Talk about being number one or number two in a market might sound impressive, but was GE truly ready to shed mature, old-line businesses that were no longer faring well? And what about Welch's dream of making the company entrepreneurial? How would he nudge the old elephant to overcome the inertia its history and tradition encouraged.

Welch had answers to all of these questions. But he had to convince Wall Street that he was transforming the lumbering, gigantic

◇

GE. The company did not seem to be centrally focused. It was producing such diverse products as nuclear reactors and microwave ovens, robots and silicon chips. It was involved in time-sharing services and Australian coking coal. On the one hand, that diversity made excelling in every field nearly impossible. On the other hand, it gave General Electric earnings protection from economic downturns. GE had recorded 26 quarters of earnings increases in the midst of several recessions. Still, investors had trouble understanding what General Electric produced—and how it would do in the future.

In early 1982 General Electric had an AAA bond rating and possessed almost $1.5 billion in cash and liquid securities. Its earnings for 1981 had been $1.65 billion on revenues of $27.24 billion—making it by far the largest broadly diversified company in America. But its stock was stuck in a slump. In the early 70s it had sold at 22 times earnings per share; in early 1982 it sold at only 8 times GE's estimated profits for 1981. In 1981 it hit a low of 25 ½ and a high of only 35.

Welch hoped that Wall Street would take notice and begin to "understand" the company if its earnings rose impressively. Hiking GE's revenues, while a worthy pursuit, was not easy and depended on factors that were often beyond the company's control. It seemed wiser to achieve higher earnings by getting rid of GE's weak holdings, driving out unnecessary costs—and paring the number of employees.

Welch began the campaign to boost earnings by developing a new central focus at GE: The company would keep only businesses that were number one or number two in their markets. Those businesses would be the "leanest," as Welch said at the Pierre, the "lowest-cost, worldwide producers of quality goods and services or those who have a clear technological edge, a clear advantage in a market niche." To become lean—and "agile," another favorite Welch word—General Electric's businesses would have to slim down. To eliminate bureaucracy—and many employees. Fully 70 percent of the 350 businesses under General Electric's wings were either the first- or second-ranked in their markets. While being one of the top two market leaders was critical, it was not sufficient. Welch insisted that the business had to be in a high-growth industry, and in the early 80s that meant either high-tech or services, not the traditional manufacturing businesses.

To help perform the radical surgery that Welch knew was essential for GE, he needed a senior planning man. One day in the fall of 1982 he telephoned Michael Carpenter at the Boston Consulting Group, where Carpenter had worked as a consultant for nine years. British-born, trained at Harvard Business School, Carpenter had almost been hired by General Electric twice in the recent past, and BCG executives who had come to work for GE always talked highly of him. This time the GE chief was not going to take no for an answer. Carpenter recalled his astonishment at learning the General Electric CEO wanted to talk to him. "I picked up the phone. I remember his words to this day. He said 'M-m-m-ike, it's t-t-t-time to sh-sh-sh-it or g-g-g-get off the pot about General Electric.' He stuttered rather more at the time. He doesn't stutter at all today, but that time he stuttered."[1]

Although General Electric strategic planning process had a stellar reputation Carpenter wanted no part in dealing with that process—or in overseeing it. "If you want me to come down and run a planning process," he replied to Welch, "I don't want to come. Because I have never worked for a major company and seen a strategic planning process that works. They're usually a complete waste of time." In saying this to Welch, Carpenter was dismissing the model for American management in the 70s. Unfazed, Welch then explained what he wanted from Carpenter: "We've got to restructure the portfolio. We've got $5 billion in cash. We have to make some acquisitions. I need somebody who can meet the challenge on that front." He offered Carpenter the post of vice president for business development and planning. Carpenter accepted.

When Carpenter sat down with Welch for the first time after joining GE, the new planning executive played devil's advocate with regard to acquisitions. "You know, Jack," he said, "95 percent of acquisitions don't work." Welch, however, wanted his strategy to work and urged Carpenter on. One strategy they adopted was to buy businesses that would enhance those in which GE was already strong. For example, to strengthen its financial services operation GE acquired Employers Reinsurance in 1984. Another strategy was to buy undervalued or underperforming businesses in which value could be created.

Given the new stiff, competitiveness of the business environment, General Electric had to own and nurture only businesses that would be, in one of Welch's favorite words, "winners." Winning meant turning in large profits. No longer would GE have the luxury of holding on to businesses that were sometimes profitable, sometimes not. After World War II the boom periods of the 50s and 60s allowed a company like GE to coast through squalls that affected some businesses but not others. The 80s and 90s, thanks to mounting overseas competition, had, not squalls, but devastating hurricanes that threatened to bring all businesses down at once.

Welch's strategy for GE was unusual: He wanted all of GE's businesses to dominate their markets. Yet he presided over a large, diversified portfolio of businesses—350 in all, clustered in 43 Strategic Business Units. Very few other American companies could boast so large a portfolio, and those that could were not as strong as GE across the board. Welch was saying: "Let's compete only in businesses that we have a chance to tower over."

The GE veterans had a natural disdain for the Welch vision of keeping only the best GE businesses. They had faith that the glories of the past would somewhat return, that the company's massive size and strength would see it through difficult times, that General Electric was a national monument and thus could not be toppled by cataclysmic forces.

Jack Welch knew better. He had looked the company over and sensed that it was time to recast this disparate giant into a more coherent whole. Crotonville's Jim Baughman remembered meeting Welch the day after Welch became chairman. Welch told him: "I want a revolution in GE. Let's go for it."

The revolution had to overcome the tradition of regarding GE businesses as children that the parent company would not disown if they failed to do their chores. Welch wanted to change the rules of the game. Within the GE family, performance would be the new criterion. A "son" who failed to do his chores—to become number one or number two in his field—would be disowned.

Welch believed that he had no choice. He knew that his decisions would be heart-wrenching. But the elephant had to become a gazelle. The fat had to come out. GE had to be made sleek and aggressive. Welch understood that this could be done by reshaping the company and putting it on a major diet. He would be alone among American business leaders in downsizing a company that was not in crisis. The conventional wisdom had been that laying people off should be the last resort of a company that had already suffered serious financial reversals. For that reason, downsizing carried the stigma of defeat, of throwing in the towel. Because it signaled both a serious decline in the company's fortunes and an evasion of social responsibility, downsizing was to be avoided if at all possible.

Firing people was not easy in the 60s and 70s. The worker enjoyed many protections. One of the principles that the labor unions had etched into the soul of America in the 20th century was the right of every individual to hold a job. The corollary was that no one could be fired unless discovered to be a serial murderer or worse. Politicians in Washington believed that a person's work was more important than a corporation's bottom line; so they lobbied hard to preserve jobs back home. The prevailing view among corporate managers was that a sense of job security made a worker more productive.

Yet Welch believed that keeping the worker in place had become a failed strategy. General Electric's main competition now came from overseas companies whose workers were achieving higher productivity rates. To match and surpass those rates GE needed to rationalize its businesses by upgrading equipment—and slimming down employee rolls.

The effect would be to put thousands of General Electric employees out of work. If that bothered Jack Welch, he did not show it. He was convinced that this massive surgery was needed to make GE better. He did not ask: Is the revolution worth the pain and suffering I am inflicting on these people? He did not ask whether he owed these people continuing job security. No doubt, given a choice, many of those laid off would have preferred to keep their jobs even if this meant that the company would make smaller profits. That was not an option for Jack Welch. His job was not to make people happy but to make the company as profitable as possible.

And so a heavy price was exacted from the General Electric community. But because those who were told they must go left quietly, without major strikes or protests, their pain and suffering seemed transient, ephemeral. Any guilt or shame felt by Welch and the senior echelons would pass.

A revolution it would be. To achieve it Welch had to change the way everyone at General Electric had behaved for years. Until Jack Welch took over, nearly everything and everyone involved with the company had been home-grown. From the very beginning down through World War II General Electric had developed and built up its own businesses for the most part. "We were vertically integrated to the nth degree. We depended almost entirely on internal financial resources, internal technical resources, internal human resources,"

recalled Jim Baughman.[2] That had always been considered one of GE's great strengths. After more than 100 years of accomplishment came enormous pride. The pride, however, nurtured a kind of do-it-yourself culture. Nearly everyone had joined the firm at an early age and risen through the ranks. GE employees talked mostly to other GE employees. They learned to bristle at anything "not invented here."

Jack Welch's revolution formed around a new principle: Nothing was sacred. The company had to stop looking inward. It had to step out into the new world, and that meant shedding businesses and managers and employees that were not producing; it meant bringing in new businesses and new managers and new employees that could produce. This was the essence of restructuring. A bold, new strategy. General Electric had shed businesses before, but not with the same purpose in mind that it had now: This time it was divesting in order to reshape the entire company. It was adopting a wholly new approach: It would grow from without. At first Jack Welch shied away from publicizing what he was doing. His annual reports were peppered with references to acquisitions and divestitures. GE, however, did little boasting in the media or inside the company. Restructuring was too new, too removed from the traditional way that major corporations did business. Perhaps most important, it was causing too much pain to its victims.

Good reason existed for downplaying the whole exercise. Dennis Dammerman, senior vice president, finance, recalled "that it would have been controversial for a company at that time to have stood up and said, 'We're not going to think of the company in terms of 350 businesses anymore—we're going to think of it in terms of 13 (some of which are inside the circle and some are outside).' "[3] At first there was "just disbelief," remembered Paul Van Orden, former executive vice president. At Crotonville, where he spoke occasionally, Van Orden was inundated with questions about the Number One, Number Two strategy. Why was it necessary to be number one or two? What was wrong with being a good number three or four? The latter question usually came from people in third- or fourth-ranked businesses. "The guys in these businesses can make nice money and get nice investment returns," those people argued. "What the hell's wrong with being in that position? Is it unstable? What the hell is the argument?"

Welch argued that in many cyclical businesses it was precisely the number three, four, five, or six business that got hurt during a cyclical downturn. Number one or two businesses were not going to lose market share. Because they had a leadership position, they could employ more aggressive pricing. Because of that position, they had the resources to bring out new products. Often, he noted, businesses that thought they were third or fourth had been ranking themselves only against domestic competition and were in fact seventh or eighth.

Paul Van Orden remembered how difficult it was for some at GE to confront the new strategy, because it "established a hard cutting edge for people to measure themselves. We had some traditional GE businesses that didn't stand up very well under those kinds of conditions. There was a feeling that they were really not part of the family. It was the beginning of a whole discussion about loyalty, being a part of the family, establishing new criteria to judge the businesses. A lot of people said, 'We're not number one or number two, but aren't we a cash cow?' [Under the old system] not many businesses got thrown out. You're growing, you're kind of a cash cow. It was a cultural shock for a lot of people, and there was a lot of grousing."[4]

Some felt that using his Number One, Number Two yardstick, Welch just might sweep away a business that in another decade could be a great winner. This point was made by Mark Markovitz, an engineer with GE in Schenectady, who, in a letter to the editor in *Fortune*, wrote: "Jack Welch's predecessors—Ralph Cordiner, Fred Borch, and Reginald Jones—nurtured the Aircraft Engine, Gas Turbine, and Plastics businesses when they were small or money-losing operations. What chance of survival would they have had under Mr. Welch's No. 1 or No. 2 test?"[5]

Early in 1982 Welch took a pad and pencil and sketched three circles for Jim Baughman. "Look," he said, his voice becoming forceful, "these are the businesses that we really want to nourish. These are the businesses that will take us into the 21st century. They are inside the circles. Outside the circles you have businesses that we would prefer not to pursue any further." One circle contained GE's core businesses; the second, high-technology businesses; the third, service businesses. The businesses inside these circles would get the company's resources. Those outside would not.

The Welch vision had become even more concrete, more focused. Now anyone who wanted to know what General Electric was all about could simply look at the circles, look at which businesses were inside and which were not.

Fifteen businesses went into the circles, businesses that Welch deemed to have the best chance to be big winners in their fields over the next decade. Being placed outside the circles did not automatically mean a permanent stay in purgatory. In fact General Electric adopted the motto "Fix, close, or sell" as its strategy for dealing with businesses outside the circles. "If it was possible to fix a business," Jim Baughman explained, "and bring it back inside the circles, OK. But the chances were we would sell it to someone who liked that business more than we did."[6]

The Three Circles concept was Jack Welch's compass as he navigated through the early 80s. He used the concept as a framework for bringing clarity to the organization. At times Welch and his associates played down Welch's doodles by saying, "Oh, that was just an organizing principle so that we would be better understood," as if Jack Welch could doodle without General Electric feeling the shock waves. The truth was that Welch's Three Circles sent shivers through the organization. Those lucky enough to be inside the circles liked the security of being there. But those relegated to the purgatory outside the circles were distinctly uncomfortable. They did not like Jack Welch's doodling at all. It seemed to be sending them this clear message: "I put you outside my circles, not to encourage you to work harder so that you could get inside, but because I am putting you on the chopping block!"

Within the Services circle were Credit Corporation, Information Services, Construction & Engineering Services, and Nuclear Services. Within the High Technology circle: Industrial Electronics, Medical Systems, Engineering Materials, Aerospace, and Aircraft Engine. Within the Core circle: Lighting, Major Appliances, Motor, Transportation, Turbines, and Contractor Equipment. Outside the circles were Microelectronics, Broadcasting, Small Appliances, Switch Gear, Wire and Cable, Central Air-Conditioning, Ladd Petroleum, Mobile Communications, TV & Audio, Large Motors & Generators, and Large Transformers.[7]

I asked Welch whether intuition or some more concrete business measurement guided him in placing businesses inside or outside the circles. He replied: "I'm looking at the competitive arena. Where does the business sit? What are its strengths vis-à-vis the competition? And what are its weaknesses? What can the competition do to us despite our hard work that can kill us a year or two years down the road? What can we do to them to change the playing field? In a business you lay out the world competitive arena, the market size, the players in each pool, the global share, so you get the playing field defined. Then you ask somebody: What have you done in the last two years to improve your relative position in that? What moves have you made? What moves has the competition made in the last two years to change the playing field in its favor? What dynamite move could you make in the next two years to change the playing field in your favor, and what are you most frightened about that [the competition] might do to change your game? That's all you really need. If you have a game that's vulnerable, somebody can move fast, get you. And you don't have a checkmate play or another move. You've got to get out of that game."[8]

During 1981 Welch had tried to move swiftly in order to push GE in the proper direction. In his letter to share owners in the 1981 annual report Welch could not say that the company was in potential trouble. Rarely are leaders of American businesses so candid with share owners. Welch did, however, hint at the problems: He wrote that GE would be "strengthening our core businesses and developing new, fast-growing businesses. We are revitalizing our cash-generation core businesses."

The need to advance heavily into high-tech and service businesses was clearly on his mind when he wrote: "Our major focus is on developing strong positions in the more vital sector of the world economy: engineering materials, information services, financial services, construction services, medical systems, and natural resources." Elsewhere in that annual report he wrote that market leadership was a "central requirement," but he did not mention the need to shed many of GE's businesses. Why stir unnecessary alarm? Without doing so, he had earmarked a record amount of expenditures for research and development ($1.7 billion) and for plant and equipment ($2 billion). And he had given a boost to GE's factory automation project.

Power Generation was one of General Electric's core businesses. The decision Jack Welch would make about the fate of this business would be important to GE's overall future. Power Generation (or Turbines, as the business is also called) had been the largest and most profitable business at GE for a hundred years. During that period electricity load growth was strong and a feeling persisted that it would continue forever. Although the market was fundamentally strong, the 1973 oil embargo and the virtual collapse of the domestic utility market had hurt it severely. In 1973 GE delivered 60 gas turbines. The following year it sold only one. While at that low level, the Power Generation business was severely shaken by a worldwide recession that caused its market to plummet further.

Jack Welch had to decide what to do with this cyclical core business. In 1980 Power Generation had earnings of only $141 million on sales of $4 billion. That year it contributed 15 percent of GE's revenues and 9 percent of its total earnings. Had Welch insisted on a rigid application of his Number One, Number Two approach, he might have found good reason to dump GE's Power Generation business.

Given the lowly state of the business in 1981, Welch could have put Power Generation outside the Three Circles. Had he done so, it would have been difficult to adopt a "fix, close, or sell" strategy for the business. It was not possible to "fix" anything. One could only hope that the market for this cyclical business would return. Welch decided to keep the business, to restructure it drastically. During the 80s nine plants were consolidated into four. The Schenectady work force, which numbered 29,000 in 1981, has been reduced to 13,000.

David C. Genever-Watling, senior vice president of GE Industrial & Power Systems, recalled how Welch thought of Power Generation during the spring of 1981: "He knew it was going to come back. It had to. Electricity consumption on a global basis had to continue to grow. The analysis was: 'I'm going to hate [Power Generation] the next eight years. But 10 years from now, I'm going to love it.' Because the market's going to come back. Jack Welch is accused frequently of being a shortsighted, next quarter leader. This is the perfect example that he is far from that. He had to make a 10-year bet to hang on to this business and spend $800 million on it. He had to believe that he understood what was going to happen in the fundamental dynamics of the world's economics. With Consumer Electronics he said: 'Fundamentally, I hate this business.' In Power Generation he said: 'Fundamentally, I love it. I just hate the current market. And I'm going to hang on to it until the market comes back.' "[9]

After his first full year as CEO Welch reported to share owners in the 1982 annual report that GE was financially stronger than it had been the year before "despite deep and prolonged worldwide recession." Its earnings of $1.817 billion were 10 percent ahead of its earnings in 1981, though its sales, $26.50 billion, were slightly lower.

It was during 1982 that General Electric moved decisively away from dependence on its original manufacturing businesses and began to invest heavily in a future focused on high-tech products and high-growth service businesses. It moved a larger share of research and development funds into the high-tech side. A prime example of the stress on high-tech was the GE medical product program aimed at developing nuclear magnetic resonance (NMR). This new diagnostic technique allowed observers to "see" into the body without resort to X rays. In the mid-70s GE had become the world leader in the $4 billion diagnostic-imaging market when it developed the "fan beam" CT-scanner. It was hoping to keep its lead with NMR. To deepen its commitment to high-tech efforts General Electric spent $130 million on an expansion of the corporate R&D center in Schenectady. That expansion included the construction of an advanced electronics laboratory.

The service side took on increasingly important dimensions at GE. The great success story on that side was GE Credit Corporation, which went from a lowly $77 million in earnings in 1978 to earnings of $205 million in 1982. The high cost of owning business equipment created opportunities for GE Credit, which, with over $12 billion in assets, was the largest diversified finance company in the United States. It offered leasing, business financing, and other services. GE Credit was a major contributor to the success of the Services and Materials Sector, whose revenues in 1982 were 10 percent of the GE total but whose earnings in 1982 were 22 percent of the GE total.

The reaction to Welch's first efforts at restructuring was strident. He was nicknamed "Neutron Jack"—an allusion to the neutron bomb, which eliminates people but leaves the buildings standing. Welch hated the nickname and thought it unjustifiably implied that he had been unfair to his employees. The nickname was used to define Welch in the media as a heartless soul who cared only for the bottom line and was not concerned about the welfare of his employees. "I think it was a harsh term," he said softly, but with anger apparent in his voice. "Mean-spirited. They call me 'Neutron Jack' because we laid off people even though we gave them the best benefits they had in their life."[10] Deep inside Welch felt that he was indeed a caring person, but one who understood that the only way to build General Electric in these perilous times was to create a lean, agile company and not to turn GE into a welfare society. The welfare society would eventually stagnate. The lean and agile GE had a chance to make it.

Welch could not fathom why the critics blasted him. He was not Attila the Hun. He was just trying to improve his company's balance sheet. For Welch, the fact that he had provided a soft landing for those laid off should have impressed the naysayers. It did, but only to a certain extent. I doubt that Welch could have done anything—short of reversing his decision to lay off so many people—that would have disarmed his critics.

What turned the critics off was Welch's seeming indifference toward what he was doing to his employees. It was indifference, however, that allowed him to wield the knife without remorse. Welch was not incapable of displaying compassion, but compassion was irrelevant when you had to be the executioner.

In the early 80s restructuring was big news. Closing plants was big news. Firing large numbers of workers was big news. Such big news that in February 1982 CBS's "Sixty Minutes" assigned Mike Wallace and a team of producers to look into General Electric's decision, made the previous summer, to close a metal steam iron plant in Ontario, California.

The plant was due to close at the end of February, a week before Wallace's report would air. Although the plant had been making a profit, GE felt that a greater profit could be made by manufacturing steam irons overseas. In 1981 the plant had turned out over 4 million metal irons. GE insisted that metal irons would not sell anymore and so it had to manufacture plastic irons. It would do so in Mexico, Brazil, and Singapore.

In 1982 no federal law required advance notice before a company closed a plant. (A federal law passed in 1990 required sixty days advance notice before a plant employing over 50 people was closed.) So the 850 employees at the Ontario plant would have had no recourse if GE had given them a one-week advance notice. During the 70s corporations routinely gave only one week's notice before closing plants.

The "Sixty Minutes" report included a significant amount of footage praising GE for acting generously toward its employees. Jack Welch was vice chairman when the decision to close the Ontario plant had been made. But it was his decision that GE should air its positions on the "Sixty Minutes" program rather than seem evasive. His view was that GE had a valid argument and that no reason existed for issuing a mere "No comment." Accordingly, Frank Doyle, senior vice president for external and industrial relations, presented GE's views on camera.

The point that Mike Wallace tried to make in his report, which aired March 7, 1982, was that many American products were no longer made in the United States because American corporations were finding it more profitable to shut down their U.S. operations and open overseas plants. Wallace began by introducing his viewers to the Ontario plant, an hour's drive from Los Angeles. General Electric had purchased the plant 50 years earlier and had been making metal irons there ever since. For most of that time it was the only big employer in Ontario.

Overhauling the Ontario plant so that it could make plastic irons would have been too expensive and taken too long, according to GE. The local union disputed that claim: GE was switching to plastics just to make a larger profit. Frank Doyle, then the GE senior vice president, told Wallace: "The jobs those people are doing are vulnerable in any case whether we move overseas or not because if the United States manufacturer cannot deliver to the American consumer a quality product at good cost, then our foreign competition will invade those markets and take those jobs in any case."

Wallace interviewed Mary Macdonald who, like her father and brother, had worked at the Ontario plant all her life. Mary had worked there 23 years. She was also president of the union local. "It hasn't been just a job to people," she explained. "People have applied for jobs in that plant and waited two or three years to get them. It was a job that you could have pride in. We had a product we could have pride in. A person, when they were finally able to get on in that plant, they felt that they were secure and then they could go and build a secure life for themselves. It's a hard thing. It's an emotional thing because we feel that the plant doesn't belong to General Electric. It belongs to us, the people in the community."

Wallace painted a depressing portrait of those who become unemployed: They would be forced to work at half the wages they had earned at GE (which paid them $8 an hour). They might have to wait years before they found a job and even longer before they got back to their pay scale at GE. Unemployment, Wallace said, quoting anonymous studies, could lead to wife beating, separation, divorce, even suicide.

Mary Macdonald told Wallace: "How far can this country go in taking jobs out of the country. It's not the American workers challenging the Mexican workers or the workers from Brazil or Singapore. Basically we're all being exploited for the sake of profits. When does it stop? When does this whole thing end about challenging what is enough profits? And who has to be thrown in the street? Or thrown to the dogs in exchange for that profits?"

A man named Dick Prestone, with 21 years at the plant, stood before an audience and declared that he felt betrayed. "We are people. We have families. We have obligations. We live in the community. We want our right to work. Why don't we have that right to work? Corporate has not made Ontario the iron capital of the world. You people have. We have done it through our work, through our sweat. Now they're saying, 'We don't need you anymore.' We say that's unfair."

Wallace interviewed a GE spokesman who argued that a business had to . . . stay in business—"which means make a profit. It does not mean that the business is not concerned about the impact it has on the public and its employees."

GE debated how much advance notice to give the Ontario plant. At first some executives feared that announcing too early would have serious negative effects: Key people might quit; the productivity of those who remained behind might slacken; and activists would have ample time to protest.

The union tried to force GE and the mayor of Ontario to find a plant buyer that would make metal irons. That effort failed. Employees tried to buy the plant themselves. That did not work. The employees were ready to take pay cuts. GE was not interested. However, it did help the employees to get over the trauma of the plant closing by contributing substantially to a state-run job center on its property where job interviews were held and job skills were taught.

Finally, a local machinery manufacturer bought the plant. The manufacturer planned to take a year to retool it and then to hire 250 people who had worked for GE in the plant.

Wallace closed by saying, "There really isn't a good guy and a bad guy in this story. GE is doing business just about like everyone else. The bottom line isn't people. It's profits."

The "Sixty Minutes" report produced immense sympathy for workers who had been laid off for no other reason than a profitable company's desire to make bigger profits. It was difficult for many to understand General Electric's argument—that these workers were in danger of losing their jobs under any circumstances unless they produced high-quality, low-cost products. That appeared to be what they had been doing. GE received a reasonably sympathetic treatment from CBS on other counts.

The layoffs were a painful experience for Welch and seemed to contradict his approach to business in the 1970s, when he had had the reputation of being a wild-spending maverick who knew how to "grow" businesses. He hated his image as a "downsizer."[11]

CHAPTER SEVEN

◇

"A Company That Doesn't Pay Taxes"

The first major step in GE's downsizing came in January 1983. It received little attention within the company. But the outside world took notice. That month GE announced that it would sell Utah International, the natural resources company, for $2.4 billion to the Broken Hill Proprietary Company, Ltd. (BHP), an Australian industrial and natural resources company. Wall Street got the message. Something exciting was happening at General Electric. Its stock, long inactive, hit $50 a share, nearly twice the price a year before.

Selling Utah seemed odd at first glance. It had turned in decent profits, $318 million in 1982 and $284 million the year before. Yet Welch sensed that trouble lay ahead since Utah's main market, coking coal for steel, was depressed. GE kept one part of Utah—Ladd Petroleum—as insurance for GE's plastic needs.

Now the strategy was taking shape and Welch was gaining a certain self-confidence, though he had only begun to reshape the company. The shedding of Utah also fitted into his strategy of pruning a whole array of unprofitable overseas GE businesses—"popcorn stands," he called them disparagingly. Once the pruning was over, Welch planned to reshape the remaining GE businesses into truly global competitors. Over 75 percent of GE's competition was now foreign, whether Japanese or American.

◇ ◇ ◇

Nowhere did the layoffs have a greater effect than in Schenectady, the birthplace of the General Electric Company. GE's presence in that city had turned Schenectady into one of America's most important manufacturing centers. In the immediate years after Edison arrived in Schenectady, his Machine Works had grown into a city within a city: It covered a square mile of downtown with streets, factory buildings, warehouses, a hospital, and its own police and fire services. General Electric had once employed 29,000 people in and around Schenectady.

The ax fell in the mid-80s. In June 1986 the company announced that it was moving its gas turbine manufacturing division to South Carolina. The following November it announced that it was closing a large motor manufacturing plant. A total of 3,500 General Electric workers lost their jobs during this period.

For Fran Ahl, a spray painter in the Large Steam Turbine Generator facility in Schenectady and a veteran union man, the memories were still vivid. "It seems like in 1986 we had one piece of bad news after the other. The first came when Gas Turbine was moved to South Carolina. Those people were like family. The news was devastating to them. They couldn't believe it. I got called for union board meetings at 12, 1 o'clock in the morning. Every time we'd get called, I knew it was bad news. The wire mill went out. The Motor Department went out. The foundry went out. I saw people who were losing their jobs crying in the union hall. They said they had two or three kids and couldn't pay the mortgage."[1] Some in the plant wanted to strike in support of the laid-off workers. But union leaders argued that this would not bring the work back. Moreover, a prolonged strike might lead General Electric to close down the remaining Steam Turbine facility. "We had to work with the company, not against it," said Fran Ahl. "We had to learn to trust one another." Jim Carter, general manager of manufacturing in Schenectady, felt that the union's moderation saved Power Generation from even worse erosion. "We were within a week of taking the Generator business out of Schenectady. We said, 'We've got to take 30 percent out of the cost of generators,' and the work force responded to that. The world was changing on us, and we had to deal with the fact that it was changing. Otherwise the competition would have cleaned our clock."[2]

Downsizing without long strikes was no easy trick. General Electric had to find a way to win the unions over. Labor relations had been prickly ever since the bitter nationwide 1969 strike, which had lasted four months. Many employees still assumed that GE executives were antiworker. During bargaining sessions General Electric's executives had exhibited little generosity. Jack Welch and Frank Doyle, the two men who conducted GE's negotiations with the unions in 1982, knew that they had an uphill fight. They had to show a warm spirit toward the unions.

Trying to be candid and generous at the same time, Welch and Doyle informed the unions that a major restructuring was soon to occur. GE planned to include benefits in the new contract that would make the restructuring as smooth as possible. "We felt," said Doyle "that without [a generous contract] the chances of executing a radical downsizing were going to be much tougher." Included in the contract was GE's promise to provide six months' advance notice before closing a plant. Complaints were voiced that Welch and Doyle had overspent on the 1982 contract, providing far too generous amounts for work transfer and plant closing benefits as well as health care benefits after layoffs. Doyle estimated that those benefits cost GE hundreds of millions of dollars each year. One dividend of the generous settlement, Doyle explained much later, was that "it gave enormous credibility to our assertion that these plant closings had to take place, because if they didn't, why pay for them?"

The unions grumbled, disliked what was happening, but in the end complied. Bill Bywater, president of the International Union of Electronic, Electrical, Salaried, Machine and Furniture Workers AFL-CIO, represents 150,000 members, 37,000 of whom are General Electric employees. Bywater expressed understanding, not bitterness, toward Welch. "Whether we like it or not, automation is the direction we're going in. We have no choice but to go along with" the Welch restructuring of GE. Bywater practically congratulated General Electric for increasing its productivity with only half of its original work force. Even more surprising was his warm praise for Jack Welch. "He's a brilliant man. One of the smartest company guys I've ever dealt with, if not the smartest."[3]

Roger Creal, an executive officer of the local union for Appliance Park in Louisville, found it painful to watch helplessly while fellow workers were laid off. The blue-collar force had dropped from 24,000 in 1973 to 9,500 in 1991. An employee in the range facility for 28 years, Creal was philosophical. "It's just something you have to learn to live with. If I continued to resist [the bosses] with the old organized labor philosophy, that is a self-destruct because it's either some jobs or no jobs. If the competition has the latest innovations or the greatest assembly techniques, and we don't have them, we will not survive. So what we do together is to try to cut our losses. It never becomes easier to eliminate jobs, but it's a necessary part of the business, and we try to do it with as little impact as possible."[4]

Welch was thrilled that GE's treatment of laid-off workers appeared to have gone so well. "I was quoted in *Fortune* in bold letters, and *Fortune* expected to get a big blast. I said a lot of people could be angry, that will happen, but none can say they were treated unfairly. They didn't get a letter, and we didn't get a letter. That's a tribute, not to me, but to lots of people down below in this system who had the resources to treat people fairly." Welch was right in saying that people were given generous benefits in their severance packages. But it seems doubtful that a person who lost his job at GE would write a letter of complaint to *Fortune* magazine! The only realistic recourse such a person had, in fact, was through the union, but the union representatives had little enthusiasm for curtailing Welch's downsizing or writing to *Fortune*.

In his first five years Welch had gotten rid of 130,000 jobs representing a 25 percent reduction in the GE work force, a larger reduction than had occurred at GE during the Great Depression of the late 20s and the 30s.

Asked if he was disappointed that GE had dwindled to only 330,000 employees, Welch said he was not. "Because if I had 400,000 employees and we were doing the same revenues, we'd be losing money. I wouldn't have good jobs. I wouldn't have a good union settlement. I wouldn't have the benefit plans. I wouldn't have the pension fund. I wouldn't have made lots of people who worked here a lot better off financially. Lots of GE people who never thought they'd make a million dollars made a million dollars. And lots of other people who are here in other jobs are getting good wages."[5]

Despite the discomfort of being associated with the downsizing, board members had nothing but praise for GE. Gertrude Michelson took the pickets outside her Greenwich Village home in stride. Walter Wriston had only praise for the arrangements for the transition of the laid-off workers. "We did just about everything a compassionate human being would do to make it go smoothly. We told everybody precisely what was going to happen with quite a lead time. It was done extremely well."[6]

Welch appeared to have convinced the public that he was on the right track. The media described him as a powerful, potentially exciting force in American business. A front-page piece in *The Wall Street Journal* told of how Welch had been "preaching a new gospel" with regard to management. It was a gospel that focused on the monster called "foreign competition." Because of foreign competition, companies like GE could no longer be conservative, could no longer treat their assets as if they were mere investment portfolios, looking for short-term profits at the sacrifice of long-term gains. Welch understood that innovation was required. The article quoted William Summers, of the management consultants Booz, Allen & Hamilton, Inc., as saying that "GE is trying to instill in its managers a sense of urgency when there is no emergency."[7]

Welch produced another strong year for General Electric in 1983. Earnings in 1983—$2.024 billion—were 11 percent ahead of earnings in 1982, but sales had grown only 1 percent, to $26.8 billion. In his first few years as CEO Welch tried to discard all of the units that showed no great growth potential. Little ones went along with the big. By the end of 1983 Welch had sold off 118 businesses. Among them were Pathfinder Mines, Central Air, and Mining Products in 1982 and Data Communication Products, Trapper Mine, eight radio stations, and two small television stations in 1983. The most important dispositions were the sale of Utah International, Family Financial Services, and the Housewares business. Utah, as noted, was sold for $2.4 billion to the Broken Hill Proprietary Company of Australia. FFS, a second-mortgage subsidiary of General Electric Credit, was sold to the Philadelphia Saving Fund Society for $600 million. Welch created much curiosity when he revealed in the 1983 annual report that GE had studied 100 candidates in depth, hinting at further, possibly major, acquisitions: "With our increased cash reserves from the sale of Utah and other dispositions, plus improved working capital turnover, the question has been raised: What will we do with the money? The short answer is: It's not going to burn a hole in our pocket. Some have wondered why we haven't made the big acquisition. Frankly, the temptation—and in some ways the easiest route—is to pay too much too fast. A large acquisition may, in fact, take place."

All was not rosy in 1983. Welch's dream of creating the factory of the future was fast fizzling. Calma, GE's great hope for bringing computerization to the factory floor, had fallen short of expectations. When it was purchased in February 1981, it had been the second-largest computer-aided design firm in America, supplying a wide range of software and hardware for parts designers, circuit designers, and architects. In 1982 its market share had been at a high of 12 percent. To boost that share it cut prices and invested much money in marketing. At first the effort paid off. Then trouble occurred: Products showed up late to market and did not perform reliably. Calma sales executives and engineers defected to rival start-ups. By the end of 1983 the vaunted revenue growth had dissipated. (In 1984 GE fired 15 percent of Calma's work force; the following year Calma had lost nearly half of its market share and was only in fourth place.)

Rushing products to market affected the factory automation project as well. GE had promised that by the end of 1983 it would introduce a new state-of-the-art numerical control device that simulated machine motions as they were programmed on a computer screen and warned of potential accidents such as the collision of tools. Unfortunately, in its haste GE introduced the device before many software bugs were eliminated. In 1983 GE's sales of numerical controls dropped 30 percent, to $60 million, and GE's losses on these controls reached almost $10 million. In the 1984 annual report Jack Welch could only admit to a "management execution miss."

The CEO did not give up. Welch still hoped to revive the sale of complete factory automation systems. In 1983 he brought in a new general manager, Frank Curtin, who produced a business plan that promised to bring in $600 million a year from factory automation contracts by 1988. GE advertised heavily with 15-page color supplements in trade magazines. "Stop waiting and start automating," future customers were urged. To comfort nervous clients who feared product unreliability, GE made the undeliverable pledge to guarantee the performance of the factory projects it took on. Most of the expensive parts of the factory of the future were computers and large machine tools, neither of which GE made. Thus GE had given the false impression that it planned to guarantee the performance of other manufacturers' products as well as its own. (In 1984 GE quietly withdrew its offer of performance guarantees.) By the close of 1983 GE had lost $40 million on the factory automation project, and two years later, $120 million.

GE's board tried to take a philosophical attitude toward the project's downfall. Walter Wriston noted: "Management said to us, 'It's a big market,' and it is. They said, 'We have the skills to do it,' and that was true. They also said, 'We'll lose money,' and they did. I suspect we'll look back [someday] at the beginnings of this business and say it was a success. How big, I don't know."[8]

Frank Doyle, senior vice president for external and industrial relations, explained that "factory automation was a big idea. We thought we had the wherewithal to be the full-range supplier of factory automation. But people don't buy an entire factory system. What they buy is programmable control ware, machine ware. If you're running a factory, you want to buy the piece parts. So being a full systems supplier never had the market value that we thought. Also, a lot of hard automation doesn't give you the kind of production capability that is currently [in the early 90s] seen as the way to go. In fact if you can take out hard automation and put people back, in some ways you will get a much more flexible factory system, shorter production lines, less accumulation of inventory, and faster cycle time."[9]

The epitaph on factory automation came from Welch himself. He took the blame. He kept telling his subordinates not to be frightened of taking risks—and of failing. He had done just that. "We picked the right market, but we couldn't have executed [the strategy] much worse. I endorsed everything [the factory automation team] did wrong. Somehow or other they got ahead of themselves in their execution. Until we automated our own dishwasher manufacturing, we really never knew what it was ourselves. We stumbled and fell and tried this and tried that, and then it finally worked. The automated business is doing extremely well, and programmable controls have turned out to be a real winner. It won't be a multibillion-dollar business in 1990 [as GE had predicted], but it will be a billion-dollar one making $80 million to $120 million."[10]

Later, much later, when senior GE executives discussed GE's flop in factory automation, they managed to praise Jack Welch rather than indict him. They esteemed his courage in admitting to making an error and in getting out of the project as quickly as he did. Rodger H. Bricknell, general manager for continuous improvement, Marketing & Product Management, at GE's Power Generation business, pointed at Welch's willingness to admit errors as one of his great strengths: "He's willing to write the slate clean every day. He's willing to say: 'I know I drove you one way yesterday, but I was wrong. Now I have some new information, the environment has changed, and that was a wrong program.' That's an enormous strength that's helped the company tremendously because some people just don't have the strength of character to say it was the wrong program and I was wrong. As for factory automation, we now know that we overautomated. We became inflexible in terms of the products that we were producing. We drove long cycles to change product design."[11]

The sale of the Housewares business to Black & Decker for $300 million in 1984 proved the most anguishing divestiture for General Electric employees. Giving up on toasters and irons and fans was selling off the company's heritage. These were the items that had made the company a household name across the land. The business had been deemed an essential part of GE's portfolio because anytime a housewife bought a toaster or a coffee pot or a steam iron, the company's public exposure was enhanced. GE had had substantial, profitable positions in Lighting and Major Appliances, and as Reg Jones noted, "I'd always felt we needed Housewares to fill the gap between the two, so that Mrs. Consumer could go into a retail establishment and see the General Electric line."[12]

Had the business been wonderfully profitable, its more unpleasant aspects might have been overlooked. But since it was a scrawny financial performer, the heartaches stood out. Paul Van Orden, who ran the Housewares business in the late 1970s, recalled what a source of consumer complaints it was: "Blankets burnt, mixers broke down. The toaster oven is an abomination, it's an oxymoron. It doesn't toast very well, it doesn't broil. You can't get the meat brown. It bakes OK if all you're trying to do is frozen potatoes. Housewares had a lot of exposure and a certain amount of pizzazz. You could bring out some new products, but it never had particularly high-quality products. It was the source of a lot of dissatisfaction."[13]

Welch's decision to sell Housewares was not universally welcomed, but he was surprised at the negative reaction. Housewares had been a mainstream GE business in the past. Crotonville's Jim Baughman recalled the controversy: "People said, 'How can you exit Housewares? How can you do that? It's a GE tradition.' Welch's answer was: 'In the 21st century, would you rather be in toasters or in CT-scanners?' It was a question of trading up in the world game."[14]

Housewares had been good for the GE of the past. It had no part in the GE of the future. As Joyce Hergenhan, vice president for public relations, noted: "Our strengths were lost in a business like Housewares. You come up with some great new hair dryer, let's say, and within two months all over the Far East people would be coming up with a lower-priced knockoff of the same thing. GE's strengths are technology, its technological resources, its financial resources, and a business like Housewares didn't play to those strengths at all. Anybody with a garage could knock off one of those products, whereas most of our big technological advances and investments have been in those businesses that benefit from our technological strengths and our financial strengths. We have the ability to take the hundreds of millions of dollars and the years that are required to come up with a new generation of jet engines, a new generation of gas turbines, a new-generation plastic, or a new-generation medical diagnostic imaging machine. These businesses have certain common things: . . . high technological content, high development costs, staying power."[15]

Reg Jones and Jack Welch got into a small wrangle when Welch asked Jones what he thought of selling the Housewares business. Jones suggested that doing this could harm GE's franchise with the consumer, which would in turn damage GE's Lighting and Major Appliance businesses. Welch then quoted from a marketing survey he had initiated. The survey suggested that shoppers would go on purchasing GE's lamps and appliances even after GE no longer sold housewares. As it turned out, Welch was right: Exiting Housewares had no impact on other GE businesses. In this case being number one or two in the market was not enough. Housewares had achieved dominance in its markets. Yet it had a major drawback in Welch's eyes: It was not a business with great growth potential.

Welch's efforts to increase GE's productivity through downsizing and factory rationalization were hampered in the early 80s by the high value of the dollar. Having invested several billion dollars in plant machinery and automation and cut GE's work force by 25 percent, Welch was pleased to find that the company's annual productivity increased 4 percent a year—four times the rate for American business as a whole. But the numbers were illusory.

"We were climbing up a down escalator," said Welch. "We'd invest to get three to six productivity points a year and then get blindsided by a 10 to 15 percent appreciation in the dollar." GE's exports fell from $4.3 billion in 1981 to $4 billion in 1985 because in effect the artificial strength of the dollar was giving its overseas competition a 30 to 50 percent subsidy. "For every step we climbed as a result of our strong investment in productivity," said Welch, "we were sliding back two steps because the exchange rates were aiding our foreign competitors."

GE's strategy for dealing with the high value of the dollar was to invest heavily in its businesses: $330 million in automation and facilities in its Transportation business, hundreds of millions in new and renovated factories for its Major Appliance business, and machines that would allow its Lighting plants to produce lamps faster and more economically than anyone else. Its five-year investment in these businesses reached more than $2 billion.

By 1984 GE had also sold more than 150 operations in transactions valued at $4.9 billion. Though Welch's philosophy and approach had become more sharply focused, the results were mixed. Revenues remained nearly flat due to the recession, the high value of the dollar, and the ongoing restructuring process. Between 1981 and 1984, revenue rose by only $737 million—from $27.240 billion in 1981 to $27.947 billion in 1984—but earnings increased nearly 15 percent a year. In 1984 GE reported a net income of $2.28 billion, up 13 percent from 1983.

Welch had moved the company increasingly into high-tech and service businesses. In 1980 GE's core businesses brought in 40 percent of its earnings. Four years later they accounted for only 34 percent. However, the high-tech component accounted for 31 percent of total earnings (compared with 25 percent in 1980) and services accounted for 24 percent of total earnings (up from 21 percent in 1980).

By the end of 1984 GE's businesses were frequently dominant in their markets. If not, they were making strides toward dominance.

Lighting was the largest manufacturer of lighting products in the United States, producing more than a billion light bulbs in 1984. The Major Appliance business produced electronic refrigerators that beeped if a door was left ajar, dishwashers that could be programmed to "remember" when to start, and microwave ovens that fitted under a kitchen wall cabinet. *Fortune* magazine named the newly renovated dishwasher plant in Louisville one of the 10 best-managed factories in the United States. More than $235 million had been invested to upgrade the refrigeration manufacturing processes; another $750 million, to modernize other segments of Major Appliances.

Motors remained the world's leading supplier of electric motors. These varied from fractional horsepower motors for home appliances to motors for heavy industry with several thousand horsepower. Power Generation was the leading supplier of gas turbines; it was also the top supplier of steam turbine gear propulsion sets and shipboard generation equipment for the U.S. Navy and of steam turbine generators for the world. More than half of the electrical power in the United States was being generated by giant General Electric power-makers.

Construction Equipment provided all of the electrical circuit protection and distribution equipment for the new Hoosier Dome in Indianapolis. It also provided contractors, original equipment manufacturers, and industrial customers with electrical distribution products for residential, commercial, and industrial construction. Medical Systems was the worldwide leader in diagnostic-imaging equipment used by physicians in diagnosis and treatment. Its CT-scanning and X-ray equipment were selling well. The U.S. Air Force had selected Aircraft Engines' F110 jet engine to power F–16 fighters; the U.S. Navy had chosen the same engine for its F–14 aircraft.

GE's Aerospace had built a new over-the-horizon radar system designed for the U.S. Air Force. The system provided air surveillance over the Atlantic, to 1,800 miles. New GE solid-state radar systems had been installed in Alaska. GE was also a leading developer of satellites, training simulators, aircraft controls, and other high-tech systems and equipment that met defense, space, and aviation needs.

GE's Materials business enjoyed world leadership in developing high-performance plastics as alternatives to metal, wood, and glass. Its Engineered Materials business continued to develop applications for silicone sealants, industrial diamonds, and other proprietary products. Cutting tools, edged with GE diamonds, were used widely in building and highway restoration. GE had allocated $500 million annually to automate the plants of its Industrial Electronics business. Though veering away from fully automated factory systems, the business continued to offer automation equipment.

GE Credit ranked as the nation's largest diversified finance company, with assets of $18.5 billion. It was an industry leader in leveraged leasing, leveraged buyouts, and retail credit agreements for national manufacturers. On July 1, 1984, it widened its financial services with the $1.1 billion purchase of Employers Reinsurance Corporation, one of the three largest property and casualty reinsurance companies in the United States. At that point GE formed GE Financial Services as the parent for both the newly named GE Capital (formerly GE Credit) and Employers Reinsurance.

The Nuclear Services business helped customers obtain top performance from their nuclear plants by training employees to refuel and service those plants efficiently. It also supplied customers with advanced fuel designs, engineering analyses, and equipment improvements. In 1984 the Nuclear Energy business bought Reuter-Stokes, Inc., an international supplier of high-tech nuclear instruments.

These businesses inside the circles accounted for 92 percent of GE's profits and 87 percent of its sales. GE was either a leader or one of the leaders in all of these businesses. Yet 20 other GE businesses—outside the circles—were dragging the company down. Though these 20 had more than doubled their revenues since 1974, their combined earnings—amounting to only $54 million in 1983—had shown no increase in a decade. The 20 businesses, including Large Transformers and Television Set Manufacturing, were put on notice: Dominate your industry, or get ready to be closed or sold.

In March 1985 GE suffered one of the worst blows of Welch's tenure, a blow to its reputation and to its pocketbook. On March 26 General Electric was indicted by a federal grand jury on two sets of charges: one set contended that GE's Aerospace business had filed $800,000 of incorrect costs on employee time cards; the second set contended that GE had lied to the government about work it had done on a nuclear warhead system. The indictment occurred in Federal District Court, Philadelphia, Pennsylvania. The 108-count indictment charged that GE had defrauded the U.S. government of at least $800,000 between January 1980 and April 1983.[16] GE's work on the nuclear warhead system was the result of a $40.9 million contract that the Air Force had awarded to GE in 1977 to overhaul fuses on intercontinental ballistic missiles.

Two days after the March 26 indictment Air Force Secretary Verne Orr requested a voluntary refund of $168 million for funds that had been paid to GE, but should not have been, for aircraft engine spare parts between 1978 and 1983. That same day Orr informed GE that, in light of the Aerospace indictment, the company had been temporarily suspended from receiving new defense contracts.[17] At that time, as one of America's largest defense contractors, GE received 20 percent of its revenues from military work.

According to the indictment, GE changed some employees' time cards without their knowledge and had other employees submit blank time cards that were then filled out incorrectly. This, the indictment charged, was done by two GE managers.[18] The alleged misconduct involved the plants of GE's Re-entry Systems Department in Philadelphia and King of Prussia, Pennsylvania. That division had accounted in 1984 for 3 percent of GE's 1984 sales of $27.9 billion.

At first General Electric denied that the company or any of its employees had committed any criminal wrongdoing. GE did say that it was prepared to reimburse the government for any improper charges that might have been made in filling out employee time cards.[19]

(On July 16 three former GE senior executives in the Aerospace business were indicted on charges of defrauding the Defense Department of $800,000.)[20]

Three days after the indictment, on March 29, Welch wrote a letter to all GE employees that attempted to put the front-page media coverage of the GE scandal into perspective. Noting that 100 of the 108 counts of the indictment related to 100 times cards, he pointed out that this represented a small part of the 100,000 time cards filed during that period. "While it is entirely possible," he wrote, "that, during the course of performing several multimillion-dollar contracts, charging errors did occur, there was no criminal wrongdoing on the part of the company or its employees. The company has not been convicted of any crime."

It bothered Welch, therefore, that the Air Force had suspended GE from receiving future defense contracts. That decision, he wrote, was "highly unusual and out of proportion to the disputed issues." He added, "In any large organization—and GE with its 330,000 total employees is a very large organization—people may make errors in judgment. These must be viewed in relation to the extremely good reputation of our company and its people."[21]

The Air Force appeared satisfied with Welch's handling of the scandal, for on April 18, three weeks after announcing the company-wide suspension on GE's receiving defense contracts, Secretary Orr lifted that suspension with the exception of GE's Re-entry Systems Department of the Aerospace Division, which remained excluded from bidding on defense contracts.[22] For two months after the indictment was handed down, GE clung to its denial of wrongdoing. It suddenly changed its position after Roy Baessler, a manager on the Minuteman work, acknowledged to investigators that he had knowingly participated in the scheme to cheat the Pentagon. On May 13 GE pleaded guilty to the charges in a federal district court. Although the company may not have benefited from Baessler's cheating, it had little choice but to plead guilty. Once an employee said he did it, GE's case in court was irrevocably weakened.[23] GE was fined $1.04 million and ordered to repay the overcharges.[24]

The time card accounting system scandal had its roots in 1980, when GE's Re-entry Systems Department in Philadelphia suffered cost overruns on a $47 million project to refurbish Minuteman missiles. GE had agreed in one contract to a fixed price for part of the work. This meant that it could not legally pass along any added costs to the Pentagon. If such added costs occurred, the company faced possible losses. To reduce those losses GE managers decided to shift the overruns to contracts under which the government would pay the added costs. Their method was to falsify workers' time cards without the government's knowledge.[25]

On May 14, a day after GE's about-face in court, Welch distributed Policy 20.10, which laid down new standards for the company's conduct toward the U.S. government. No such written standards had been issued previously, though a tacit understanding had existed that

GE expected its employees to follow the law. The new document read in part that it was "the objective of the General Electric Company to excel as a responsible and reputable supplier to the United States government. In furtherance of that objective, no employee shall, in connection with any transaction with the United States government, engage in any conduct in violation of law or otherwise inconsistent with the standards of honesty and integrity necessary to achieve that objective."

GE required every employee involved in government contracting to read Policy 20.10, to sign it, and to turn it over to a supervisor. A compliance board was created, an ombudsman was appointed, and employees were given an 800 telephone number to call if they wished to report alleged misconduct without first raising it with their supervisors. Policy 20.10 was part of GE's campaign to repair the damage its reputation had suffered from the worst scandal involving GE since three senior executives had been convicted of price-fixing and went to prison in 1959. Each story in the media added to that damage. "Scandal Rocks General Electric" was the headline in a *Time* magazine piece on May 27. The article noted that "an unsavory side" of GE had been exposed the week before in a federal district court in Philadelphia.

It was not until mid-September 1985 that the Air Force lifted the suspension of the Re-entry Systems Department of the Aerospace Division from receiving defense contracts. Secretary Orr lauded GE for being "forthright in uncovering, investigating, and reporting to appropriate governmental agencies potential past violations of government procurement regulations. This cooperative self-policing effort provided a means for effectively discovering and resolving problems promptly and constructively."[26]

In October one GE official was acquitted of charges that he lied about the case to a federal grand jury. Two months later a GE manager and a former GE manager were also acquitted. A former GE official dismissed by General Electric in May after admitting that he had violated company policy, pleaded guilty and testified on the government's behalf. The perjury charges against Roy Baessler were dropped.[27]

The Philadelphia defense scandal was significant as much for what it did not do to General Electric as for what it did do. While the company's reputation had been damaged, the damage did not last long.

Moreover, the damage did not affect the senior echelons of GE, most especially its chairman. No one had screamed, "Let's get Jack Welch. He's the guy to blame." The public went along with GE's contention that the fault lay at junior levels of the company and that the company as a whole should not be held accountable.

How did Welch cope with the scandal? Although "it drove [him] crazy," he put the episode into perspective. He noted that no one in the business community would imagine that GE's leadership had done something wrong, "would think that we would cut a corner. The facts are that in government contracting most people really do know—not the media, they don't want to know—that time-charging is complicated and these things are not fundamental bad behavior. There's a person down there [in Philadelphia] who was sloppy. Nevertheless it drives you crazy why people would risk their careers and their lives. But it happens. The argument that we're 300,000 people and there's no police force is a reasonable one to most people. If one of our top people was involved in some scheme and I was in on it, it would change the whole cast of it, but there isn't anybody alive who thinks I'd cheat for anything. There are a lot of characteristics about me, but not that. It wouldn't even enter anyone's mind. We wouldn't do it and we wouldn't tolerate it, and our board wouldn't tolerate it. None of us wants any part of it." Then, sadly, he addressed the prospect of future GE scandals: "It's going to happen at least five more times in the next several years, minimal. I know somebody's doing something right now I wish to hell they weren't doing."[28]

How had GE managed to deflect the bad publicity generated by the defense scandal? Board member Walter Wriston thought that "millions of people across the country open their refrigerator door, and the light goes on, and they see GE. That monogram stares them in the face every time they turn on the light."

Aha, it's an American institution.

Agreeing, Wriston noted: "We bring good things to life. We don't talk abut the fact that we make Gatling guns. We just bring good things to life. And the result is that the public perceives GE as bringing good things to life. The lights work, the refrigerator keeps the beer cold, the washing machine gets the spots out of your pants. And the concept of some guy ripping off the government on work parts is sort of an esoteric thing that doesn't affect me and GE because my relationship with GE is the light bulb."

Beyond that, GE's board members sympathized with Welch. "The thing that tears his guts out is some low-level fellow or woman ripping off the company," said Wriston.[29]

GE was also getting a good deal of bad publicity for not paying its taxes. The issue had been simmering, but by the mid-80s the spotlight began shining on the company for committing a perfectly legal act! As its own officials had predicted when Congress adopted the 1981 Tax Act, the provision permitting profitable companies like GE to write off large tax concessions did not sit well with a public that cared, not whether GE's behavior was legal, but whether it was seemly. The act had enabled GE to avoid paying any federal corporate taxes between 1981 and 1983 and to pay just $185 million in 1984 and just $285 million in 1985.[30]

Though Congress had passed the act, some of its members, undoubtedly reacting to mounting anger back home, grew agitated. Some members asked, "How could GE not pay any taxes?" They had obviously forgotten what the act said. Newspaper articles recounted which corporations paid taxes and which did not. "From a public relations point of view, it was a disaster," recalled one analyst. "For Joe Lunch Bucket, who pays a third of his income in taxes to the government, to see that the big GE pays almost nothing made him outraged."

Throughout 1985 General Electric undertook a public relations campaign explaining that it had done nothing wrong. A company communiqué issued on February 25 noted that in 1984 GE had in fact paid $1.012 billion in a host of taxes, including social security; state, local, and foreign income taxes; and property, franchise, sales, and use taxes. Since 1981 it had paid $5.6 billion in state, local, property, and other taxes.

GE also sought to convey how much good had come out of the tax concessions. Since 1981 GE had invested $7.8 billion in its own factories and GE Capital had invested $10.2 billion in equipment leased to other companies. That $18 billion in capital investment had created or preserved an estimated 250,000 jobs, contributed to the national economy, and helped America to confront foreign competition.

Writing in the 1985 annual report, Welch noted that the 1981 Tax Act had created misunderstanding. That did not deter him. "While we accept the reality that a system in which profitable corporations do not appear to pay taxes is politically unacceptable, we will continue to speak out on the critical need for incentives for productive capital investment." Bitterly ironical, in a speech to the Commercial Club in Cincinnati on October 17 Welch stated: "I represent a company that doesn't pay taxes."

With Congress debating what to do about the controversial tax concessions, Welch argued forcefully in his speech that the investment incentives should be left alone. He noted that the 1981 Tax Act had enabled GE to both help other businesses and to modernize and automate its own factories and thus to become more competitive in world markets. That competitiveness had brought GE a $2.6 billion trade surplus the year before.

Why, he asked, when the linkage between the 1981 tax policy and productive investment was so clear, did all of the tax reform proposals abandon the incentive to invest? "Is it because of political overreaction to anecdotes about corporations dodging taxes? . . . I suspect the fundamental reason for this is the human tendency to say, 'I'm paying taxes, so why shouldn't GE?' . . . By what yardstick can the investment that created 250,000 jobs and billions in exports be considered anything other than smart national policy?

" . . . You and I, with our faces toward each other and our backs to the threat, are arguing over whether GE should pay more taxes or some other company less. The threat, to all of us, is not in this room—or in this country. It is foreign competition. . . . There's a world trade war raging, and we're fighting a civil war."[31]

Congress was deaf to Jack Welch's pleas. On January 1, 1986, the investment tax credit was repealed. Few at GE were repentant. "We don't apologize for what we did," said Dennis Dammerman, vice president for finance. "We did what Congress expected us to do at the time. Much of the benefit of those tax savings was passed on to our capital-intensive customers in terms of their pricing. Did we like the publicity? No." But, he noted, "We don't today pay any more federal income taxes than we have to. We've been pretty successful at that so far."[32]

One defender of GE's behavior was Wall Street analyst Nicholas P. Heymann, vice president at County NatWest Securities. "This company was in the business of making money, not of paying welfare. If they were able to be smarter than the average fox in taking advantage of the tax code, more power to them."[33]

Six years after the controversy, Welch still insisted that GE had acted wisely, indeed shrewdly. "That's what it was all about, becoming more competitive. That's why we're $60 billion today versus $26 billion or $24 billion. That's why other companies who didn't invest didn't [improve as GE did]. I'll look anybody in the eye—I never was embarrassed by that. I thought it was a dumb bandwagon, media-driven campaign with no thought behind it. Jobs were being created. It was just plain stupidity. It was a clever thing to bash us with. But it was wrong. We were right."[34]

On one level, Welch was correct. GE had been aboveboard, never coming close to breaking the law. And it had, by virtue of its investments, created many jobs and helped the American economy to grow. But being right was not enough. A company the size of General Electric can withstand a great deal, but it cannot withstand a bad press. Unfavorable media reaction eats away at its balance sheet in a host of undetermined, ethereal ways.

GE had a way of preventing the unfavorable media reaction. It could have avoided the huge temptation that Congress had offered it. It could have paid some of the unrequired taxes as a gesture. Such a gesture would have tamed the media by making it much harder for journalists to take GE to task. Welch did not seem to understand that. He thought the media had been unfair. But he lost sight of what was his own best interest. Anything would have been better than to admit, even in an effort to be amusing, that he represented a company that didn't pay taxes. Few found him amusing. He had a chance to avoid this damaging situation. He missed it.

CHAPTER EIGHT

◇

"Making a Quantum Leap"

T hroughout much of its history General Electric had grown from within, as though it believed that buying an outsider rather than nurturing its own businesses was not playing fair. Jack Welch discarded that notion. He wanted to "grow" General Electric's highest-growth businesses, and he would do whatever that took: If buying outside businesses could help, he would buy—and be proud of building a bigger GE. Not simply for the sake of making GE bigger. Earnings were what mattered to him. Acquiring businesses that could bolster GE's earnings became a part of the new GE culture. In 1982 Michael Carpenter, vice president for business development and planning, warned Welch that acquisitions were difficult, but Welch was not deterred.

By 1985 the Welch revolution was well in stride. Annual sales were beginning to increase impressively, reaching $28.29 billion that year and making GE the 10th-largest company on the Fortune 500 listing, up a notch from the year before. Most important, its earnings shot up 2 percent in 1985, to $2.336 billion, making GE the fifth most profitable company in America. The improved earnings were due in no small measure to the $5.6 billion worth of businesses that Welch had sold off since taking over. The largest of these businesses was Utah International, which had been sold for $2.4 billion. Welch hinted strongly that he would be glad to grab a large company if the fit and the price were right. He had patience. His planners were looking carefully at the big fish all the time, but he had patience. For a long time he made no move.

◇

Then, in the mid-80s, Jack Welch cast his eyes on RCA. The Radio Corporation of America. Like General Electric, RCA was one of America's most famous corporate names. RCA started the National Broadcasting Company in 1926, entered the record industry in 1930, and was the first company to market a television set. RCA also had interests in defense electronics, consumer electronics, and satellites.

Until the early 1980s the idea that a General Electric would contemplate grabbing off NBC or, for that matter, CBS or ABC was preposterous. The three major television networks had always been considered monoliths whose owners would never part with these highly visible, highly profitable properties. In the 70s, however, the networks came under new pressures: Fresh viewing choices arose, including cable television, that threatened to cut into their perennially large audiences. Cable was a recent, but fast-growing, phenomenon. Though only 15 percent of American homes had it in 1976, 46 percent had it by the mid 80s and 60 percent had it by the end of the 80s.

ABC was the first network to exhibit vulnerability. It was taken over by Capital Cities in March 1985. Soon after that, Ted Turner made an unsuccessful attempt to capture CBS.

By the fall of 1985 it seemed inevitable that someone would try to grab NBC as well. Sometime that year the idea of a merger between General Electric and RCA struck Jack Welch. The more he dwelt on the idea, the more natural it seemed. The merger would of course be ironic. For General Electric and the Radio Corporation of America were not strangers. In fact General Electric had helped to found RCA just after World War I. In the 30s the two companies split apart, sundered by government edict. So their coming together in the 80s was like the reunion of a parent and a child who had been forcibly separated by an outsider, but years later were permitted to reunite.

The 1985 merger between General Electric and RCA had its origins shortly after World War I. It was in 1919 that Franklin Roosevelt, then assistant secretary of the Navy, encouraged General Electric to help create the Radio Corporation of America. It was formed so that the United States would no longer have to depend on foreign firms for its international communications, as it had during the war. GE, which held patents on long-distance transmission equipment, became

RCA's first major shareholder. For the next 11 years GE and RCA were bound up with each other, working together closely in developing the first crystal set radios, which RCA began to sell in 1922. These came with headphones and antennas and sold for $25.

RCA was in the hands of a brilliant, caustic son of Russian immigrants—David Sarnoff. With Sarnoff's encouragement General Electric, RCA, and Westinghouse set up the National Broadcasting Company radio network in 1926. Sarnoff acquired the Victor Company, which employed the logo of a dog whose head was cocked as he listened to "his master's voice" coming from the Victrola. Thanks to that dog, Nipper by name, RCA's recognition grew rapidly. In 1932, however, federal trustbusters coerced GE into selling off its RCA holdings. The memory of General Electric's early alliance with RCA has endured: The musical notes of the famous NBC chimes—G–E–C—stand for the General Electric Company!

In time, General Electric and RCA became fierce rivals. Each became a leader in communications, space technology, and the electronics industries. For almost four decades the two enterprises stood out as the symbols of American high technology—until they lost their edge to unexpected competition from the Japanese and other foreigners. In the 60s and 70s RCA strayed from its original focus by acquiring Hertz Car Rental and C.I.T., a consumer finance and leasing firm. It also entered the greeting card, frozen food, and carpeting businesses. Spending billions of dollars for these sidelines, RCA left the development of the hottest consumer product of the 80s—the video-cassette recorder—to the Japanese. RCA's earnings in 1981 were down to a mere $54 million.

RCA's crown jewel, the NBC television network, which for many years had been number two to CBS in prime time and in news, plummeted in the mid-70s. Symbols of its lowly stature were such prime-time misses as "Supertrain," a comedy-adventure set on a passenger train, and "Waverly's Wonders," a sitcom starring Joe Namath.

During the early 80s some sunlight penetrated RCA's darkened domain. In 1981 Thornton F. Bradshaw, president of the Atlantic Richfield Company, became the fourth RCA chairman in six years; in quick order he unshackled the $8 billion conglomerate from Hertz (selling it for $587.5 million) and C.I.T. as well as Random House and Gibson Greeting Cards, enabling RCA to concentrate on broadcasting, electronics, and telecommunications. Undoubtedly

Bradshaw's most significant decision was to appoint Grant Tinker the head of NBC in 1981. The task given to Tinker, who had developed "The Mary Tyler Moore Show" and other CBS hits, was to revive a network that had slipped badly in the ratings. CBS had dominated the ratings for 19 straight years, and only in the 1975–76 season had ABC grabbed the lead. The last time NBC had won the ratings contest outright was in the 1954–55 season. Tinker's predecessor, Fred Silverman, had taken over in 1978, when NBC's earnings were $122 million. Three years later they had dropped to only $48.1 million.

Performing miracles at NBC in the early 80s, Tinker improved the network's ratings with such shows as "Hill Street Blues," "Cheers," "St. Elsewhere," and "Family Ties." Tinker also supported Brandon Tartikoff's idea for a half-hour comedy with Bill Cosby in 1984. Tartikoff was president of NBC Entertainment.

In 1984 NBC's earnings of $248 million accounted for fully 43 percent of RCA's $567 million total. The next year NBC's earnings climbed to $376 million. RCA had turned around enough to whet the appetite of people like Jack Welch. For the past three years General Electric had increased its cash reserves by selling off unprofitable operations. That allowed Welch to consider a major acquisition. Welch had his corporate planners look at prospective targets. They examined a company's growth rate, its market, and its book value. When the computers spewed out those with the best records, the list was winnowed to only 50 possibilities. One of the companies under study was RCA. GE's top business planner, Michael Carpenter, recalled that "RCA repeatedly jumped out as being an undervalued company relative to its potential. We did a helluva lot of work understanding RCA. We understood it cold at the time we got into discussions."[1]

By the spring of 1985 RCA was described by the newspapers as a potential acquisition target. Mentioned as suitors were the Times Mirror Company, Gannett, Gulf & Western, MCA, Westinghouse— and General Electric. Media companies seemed attractive to Jack Welch. "I wanted to be in the network business," he said. "I liked its great cash-generating characteristics and that there was no foreign competition."[2] The prestige accruing to a TV network owner was another attraction, no doubt.

At one stage in 1985 it appeared that General Electric might wind up with CBS. Ted Turner, the founder of Cable News Network and in those days perceived as an upstart, cast his eyes on Bill Paley's network, much to the chagrin of the CBS brass. Eager to stave off Turner, CBS's president and CEO Tom Wyman dined with Jack Welch one night in March, told him that CBS was under attack, and asked bluntly, "Would you come to my rescue?" The idea obviously intrigued Welch, for he called an emergency session of senior General Electric executives to consider it. One of those executives was Robert Wright, who had known Welch from their days in the Plastics business in the 70s and since then had developed specialties in broadcasting and in deal making. Wright gave Welch a thumbs-up to go for CBS. The only trouble was that Tom Wyman never got back to Welch. (CBS kept Ted Turner at bay, bringing in Larry Tisch, who eventually took control of it.) The experience encouraged Welch to think that if not CBS, then perhaps some other broadcasting enterprise might be worth seeking. As Wright recalled, "We said at the right price it's worth a shot."[3]

Jack Welch was clearly on the prowl. In the fall he appeared before students at the Harvard Business School.

"If you could change the past," a student asked him, "what would you do differently?"

Quite a question. Why would Welch, having taken General Electric so far in the past 4½ years, want to do anything differently?

The GE chairman thought it over a moment and then, to the surprise of his listeners, confessed, "I don't think I've moved fast enough or incisively enough."

In that single sentence was the hint, the hint of what Welch had been planning to do for months. His eyes were big. He wanted to make The Big Purchase. He was ready to take General Electric down a road it had never traveled before. He had always hated it when GE was described as a conglomerate, the implication being that it was one of those corporate giants that bought and sold businesses willy-nilly and were more hodgepodge than focused. Yet Welch was confident that he could buy and sell and remain focused. His goal was not to make GE bigger. It was to add to the company's earnings and value. The right Big Purchase could, in his view, do just that.

With such thoughts in mind, in early November Jack Welch picked up the phone to Felix Rohatyn, a Wall Street merger specialist who was a partner in the Lazard Frères investment banking firm. Rohatyn was friendly with Thornton Bradshaw of RCA. Welch evidently made it clear to Rohatyn that General Electric was interested in

acquiring RCA. Whether Rohatyn transmitted that message to Bradshaw remains a mystery. Rohatyn did play matchmaker, and the three
met in his New York City apartment on November 6. Bradshaw
showed up in his tuxedo. He was on his way to a Navy League dinner.
The three men talked for only 45 minutes. General conversation.
Welch avoided any direct mention of his desire to buy RCA. Instead
the topic of consumer electronics was tossed around. So was the difficult position large American companies were in because of Japanese
and Korean incursions into their markets. Welch remarked later that
he had felt he was on the same frequency with Bradshaw. General
Electric's CEO was ready to move.

GE's business planners went into high gear. They had already
studied RCA thoroughly. They were aware that RCA had not been a
stellar performer, that it had lost its competitive edge. Their research,
while concentrating on the numbers, could not have missed the fact
that RCA's executives had been attending too many seminars; they had
not been driven by the profit motive as GE's executives had been.
Still, the synergies were appealing. Michael Carpenter, General Electric's senior planning executive, recalled thinking that "it looked pretty
attractive. Here was a very similar company to GE in terms of the way
it's managed and the businesses. It's undermanaged to a significant degree. The opportunity for combining corporate staffs is such that we
could save several hundred million dollars in operating costs."[4]

GE's planners again looked at every detail of RCA as if for the
first time. "They had every base covered and 15 I would never
have thought of," recalled board member Walter Wriston.[5] Then, after Thanksgiving, "we came back thinking this is the right thing,"
Welch noted.[6]

General Electric in 1984 had sales of $27.9 billion; RCA in the
same year had sales of $10.1 billion. RCA's Electronics business gar-
nered $4.8 billion; its Transportation business, $1.4 billion; its Entertainment business, $3 billion; its Communications business, $400
million; and lesser businesses brought in $300 million.

On December 5 Welch met Bradshaw again, saying that he
wanted to buy RCA. The RCA board met three days later and, with
only its president and CEO, Robert H. Frederick, dissenting, voted
9–1 to pursue the GE talks. Frederick was a former General Electric
executive. Negotiations began the next day. An air of secrecy prevailed
among the 12 GE and RCA senior executives who mapped out how to

implement the merger over the next few days and nights. "I couldn't even tell my wife where I was," recalled Jack Bergen, vice president for corporate affairs at RCA.[7]

For RCA staffers, selling David Sarnoff's baby, the home of Nipper, was hard to swallow. Would the RCA brand name be subsumed under the General Electric logo?

Among the dissenters was Lester Bernstein, the former editor of *Newsweek*, who had been RCA's vice president for corporate communications from 1973 to 1978. He asked bluntly why RCA should be sold. It was hard to understand why a $10 billion company that was doing better and better financially could not make it on its own, particularly since NBC and the company's defense-related businesses, which were RCA's most lucrative operations, faced no foreign competition.

A highly defensive Jack Welch brooked no criticism of the deal. Cynics pointed out that the merger reflected GE's failure to develop new businesses on its own, that GE was getting a bunch of big names but little else. When two *Newsweek* reporters appeared for an interview, Welch asked them what they thought of the deal. They raised doubts. That made Welch's blood boil.

"Are you business reporters? Then it's not just another merger to you. Look at what we've got in the size of these two companies, in the strengths of these two companies." Welch then ticked off the industries in which the new GE–RCA giant would be number one. "You now have an enterprise that is totally unique—in the world."[8]

Conscious of how large a step the merger was, Jack Welch wanted to proceed cautiously. "We've got to make sure to sell this thing in," he told his planning team. "We've got to make sure that people see why it makes sense. We've got to work hard on the communications." At first Welch wanted to tout the merger as a triumph for General Electric. To have the press release announcing the event read as if GE had taken a "quantum leap" that gave it a great boost. However, Tom Ross, senior vice president and head of public relations at RCA, warned that being too smug might encourage the Washington antitrust authorities to spoil the show. Better, Ross urged, to wrap the merger in the American flag, to proclaim that the GE–RCA union would have a better chance of standing up to the Japanese. Lukewarm about this advice at first, Welch eventually took it, and so General Electric's communiqué declared that the merger was "an excellent

opportunity for both companies to create a combined company that
will improve America's competitiveness in world markets."

December 12, 1985. Jack Welch called a press conference at the
General Electric building in Manhattan, and journalists showed up in
droves. It was Jack Welch's boldest move. And General Electric's. Crotonville's Jim Baughman called it the biggest countercultural step Jack
Welch's GE had ever taken. GE and RCA had agreed that GE would
purchase the communications giant for $6.28 billion—or $66.50 a
share. It was the largest nonoil merger ever. General Electric ranked
ninth among America's industrial firms; RCA, second among its service firms. Together they formed a new corporate power with sales of
$40 billion, placing it seventh on the Fortune 500, a step behind IBM
but ahead of Du Pont. RCA's shares closed at $59.25 on December 12,
the day the merger was announced, down $4.25 from the day before.

The merger was a friendly, all-cash transaction. That was no problem for GE, which had almost $3 billion in cash and a $1 billion line
of credit in place. RCA, thanks in large part to its recent divestitures,
had nearly $1 billion in cash and equivalents. However, Welch said
that GE would take on $4–5 billion in bank debt to pay for the deal.
That would not overly leverage the company, as the ratio of its debt to
its total capitalization would be only 30 percent. "This is going to be
one dynamite company," boasted Welch. With some Wall Street analysts putting the value of RCA's businesses at $90 a share, GE ap-
peared to be getting a great bargain. The merger would take a year to
complete: As military contractors, the two companies would require
antitrust clearance from the Justice Department (little fear existed that
Ronald Reagan's Washington would be a source of antitrust obstacles);
and NBC's broadcasting license would have to be transferred from
RCA to GE. Everyone from the business experts to the comedians had
an opinion of the merger. Tom Peters, coauthor of *In Search of Excellence*, observed: "My real deep sadness is that a company that was
once as vital as General Electric can't find internal areas to invest in."
Johnny Carson, host of NBC's "Tonight Show," joked: "It's a break for
me. The last person who hosted a GE show did very well"—referring
to Ronald Reagan's hosting of "GE Theater" in the 50s.[9]

Jokes aside, Jack Welch was buoyant about the new company's
prospects. He was confident that the merger would buttress General

Electric's drive into the service and technology fields—and would diminish its dependence on manufacturing businesses. After the merger GE expected to obtain 80 percent of its earnings from service and technology businesses. That helped to fulfill one of Welch's original goals from the early 80s.

The fit seemed ideal. GE and RCA seemed natural partners in defense contracting: General Electric had been building aircraft engines and guidance systems for ICBMs; RCA had made electronic equipment for the Navy's missile-launching cruisers. The synergy achieved by the merger would make the merged firm a stronger competitor for "Star Wars" contracts. That RCA's two largest businesses (Broadcasting and Defense) were largely free from foreign competition appealed enormously to Welch. NBC offered other dividends: It required little investment and generated much cash. "The merger," commented Welch, "gives GE the 'staying power' to compete abroad against government-subsidized and -protected companies."[10]

Foreign competition, especially from the Japanese and Koreans in consumer electronics, continued to threaten companies like General Electric and RCA. "Maybe," offered Welch, "two American manufacturers together can beat the competition." More than anything else, the merger made General Electric a global company. "We will have the technological capabilities, financial resources, and global scope," declared Welch, "to be able to compete successfully with anyone, anywhere, in every market we serve."[11]

Other synergies were expected from the two companies' Consumer Electronics businesses. Both businesses sold television sets and radios: The sales of RCA's business, $4.8 billion, were far larger than the sales of GE's business, $1 billion.

The reaction at NBC was mixed. Although the broadcasting industry had viewed GE as an outsider, GE had in fact owned eight radio stations, three television stations, and a cable television system. But by 1983 it had sold off most of those properties. NBC News executives and correspondents worried that General Electric might meddle with the way the news was presented; that their cherished independence might be compromised. Determined to ease their discomfort, Welch promised that "the traditional independence of NBC News' operation will be maintained."[12]

Entertainment accounted for 30 percent of RCA's sales of $10.1 billion and for 40 percent of its 1984 net profit of $246.4 million.

NBC was on the verge of its first victory in the prime-time ratings race. The hits just kept coming: "Golden Girls." "Alf." "Matlock." "L.A. Law." "Amen." The blockbuster of course was "The Cosby Show," which at times enjoyed a 50 share—one out of every two American homes tuned in. Winning the ratings race was Grant Tinker's grand moment. Welch thought Tinker and his crowd the greatest. "They're our type of people. They know how to be number one, and we know how to give people who know how to be number one money."[13] At first blush Tinker appeared pleased with the new owners. "They are good managers at General Electric, and good managers usually subscribe to the theory that if it ain't broke, don't fix it, and NBC ain't broke."[14]

Despite all the nice words a fear lingered that the competitors of this huge industrial firm called General Electric would stop advertising on the network. It was also feared that, as a major defense contractor, GE would want to censor NBC's coverage of defense news. The thrust of all this worry was that General Electric might use its newly acquired position as a media giant to influence all kinds of decisions, some major, some minor, that affected the company.

As the final date for the merger approached, Welch exuded optimism. In the spring of 1986 he spoke to General Electric share owners in Kansas City, Missouri: "We believe we have arranged a merger between two well-managed companies with businesses that, in the main, complement each other very well. Our defense businesses should be able to develop synergies that will benefit the nation as well as the company. The services and technology assets go together very well. Even in the Consumer Electronics business, in which we both face a very difficult market, we see possibilities for synergy. The television network, NBC, is a particularly attractive property, number one in an exciting services industry.

"The RCA acquisition fits into an overall strategic rationale that dictates that, for a company to be strong internationally, it must be strong at home. General Electric, as the nation's largest exporter five of the last six years, has clearly demonstrated its ability to win in world markets. But its competitiveness is chronically affected both at home and abroad by the strength of the U.S. currency and by political, monetary, and policy changes on the part of other companies and their governments.

"RCA, with its strong array of domestic businesses—Defense, Service, and the NBC network—will provide General Electric with a strong domestic earnings base to fuel many of our businesses that must win in the global marketplace."

When the merger took place, Welch, who became chairman of NBC, arranged that the new business would report directly to him "because when you make an acquisition in a very sensitive area, you want to be as close to the top as you can. Only so you can provide a cover for it to acclimate, for it to get on to the culture reasonably well."[15] The only other businesses that reported directly to Welch were Medical Systems and Major Appliances. The other GE businesses reported to the two vice chairmen.

One Aerospace business was created, with John Rittenhouse, then in charge of GE's Aerospace business, heading the combined business. The two Communications Services businesses were brought together under an RCA man, Gene Murphy.

Deciding what to do with the David Sarnoff Research Center in Princeton, New Jersey, considered a great RCA treasure, pitted Jack Welch against the protectors of RCA's great tradition. In Welch's view GE did not need two research and development centers, especially since its own Schenectady operation focused on the high-tech fields that were crucial to GE's strategy and the Sarnoff center concentrated on consumer electronics, a diminishing interest of GE. Eager to find a buyer for Sarnoff, Welch put out feelers to major research centers but drew a blank. He did not want to close the Sarnoff center though that appeared an increasing possibility. Public sentiment swelled against this move, partly because jobs were at stake, partly because it was believed that the center still had much to contribute to American know-how. Bowing to that sentiment, Welch decided in February 1987 to donate the Sarnoff center to SRI International, formerly the Stanford Research Institute. He also promised $250 million over the next five years for the funding of research there.

For years the three great television networks in America had functioned without interference from the people with the sharp pencils. The networks were glamorous, they were profitable, and they were seemingly immune to any bottom-line pressures. They commanded huge audiences and in fact possessed a near monopoly on television viewing around the nation. So, if you worked for NBC, or CBS, or ABC, you automatically deserved a big salary and lots of perks. Television news people were paid far more than print journalists, not because anyone had ever regarded them as better newsmen, but because they were television personalities. The same held true for the people who worked behind the scenes in television. They were highly paid even though they never appeared on camera. Since no one bothered to keep salaries in check, working for a network paid off handsomely.

The network executives even had a cute rationale for spending all of this money. By throwing around the cash, they were able to produce more programs, to air more news, and to acquire more sophisticated equipment. Bigger and better. Sophisticated was better. If you wanted the best possible network, the logic went, you had to spend lots of money. No one questioned whether this was an efficient way to run a network.

Then along came Jack Welch in the mid-80s: All he wanted from NBC was what he wanted from his Aircraft Engines business or his Lighting business. To be profitable, to be careful with expenditures— in short, to be productive. To fit into the General Electric culture. Welch looked at NBC's profits and asked this simple question: How was it that the network that had the highest ratings also had the lowest profits?

Welch could not understand how NBC could justify all those high costs: "The revenue stream in NBC is all Hollywood. It has nothing to do with the cost centers in New York. We had difficulties with the people in New York who were stuck in the 'network' glamour but had nothing to do with generating earnings. Those people with chauffeurs and all this stuff, who were network executives, presidents, executive vice presidents, were doing nothing." (Welch's voice rose to a pitch of irony.) "They didn't do revenue. They didn't do scheduling. They could have been in Motors. They were lucky where the parachute dropped some of them. They were paid $400,000 to $500,000 to do jobs that people in other businesses were paid $120,000 to do. Don't get me wrong. The creative talent in Hollywood and in NBC Productions is key to making that work. But why should the finance person there make $500,000 and the finance person [in another business make far less]?"[16]

Very quickly Welch sensed that NBC was a talent-driven business and that no greater talent existed at the network than Grant Tinker.

Welch was determined to keep Tinker at NBC. He understood how crucial Tinker had been to NBC's success in earlier years: Tinker had taken NBC from a bad third to a very good number one in the ratings. However, he wanted to leave NBC. He thought it was time to try some producing on his own. He had been commuting from California to New York every week and was tired of it. Thinking that the commute was a big part of Tinker's gripes, Welch offered to let him stay in California and remain head of NBC. "Grant," Welch told him, "you can be the chairman of this outfit. You never have to come East. All the people will come to you. Please stay with us." Tinker said no. He did not seem particularly fearful that Welch would cramp his style. He just wanted to move on.

With Tinker going, Welch did what he could to keep the other major talent at NBC—Brandon Tartikoff. Tartikoff was president of NBC Entertainment and along with Tinker, had lured important television producers away from other networks. He had held on to them with assurances that NBC wanted only quality programming and that slow-starting series would get a fair chance. The strategy had paid off wonderfully. The only trouble was that Tartikoff now wanted to make movies. Others were wooing him. GE offered him a way to stay on: He could remain at NBC and produce movies. Tartikoff agreed. In June 1986 he signed a three-year contract with NBC. The network, under his guidance, would produce as many as five motion pictures a year.

Welch had to replace Grant Tinker. The new person had to be someone with whom he could work. Someone who understood what Jack Welch's General Electric was all about; who was ready to take on and tame the network's prima donnas and high spenders. Welch needed to tame the lions, but he did not think that anyone inside the cage could do the job. NBC executives urged him to look within. Grant Tinker was one of them. He was concerned that, after winning the ratings race for the first time in the 1985–86 season, NBC would falter if an outsider took over. No, said Welch. The new boss would have to move fast. Only one of GE's own could do that. He was adamant.

The man Welch had in mind was Robert Wright, his associate from the days at Plastics. Wright, at 43, was a lawyer who loved business. A deal maker who had courage and patience. He had bagged the investment banking house of Kidder, Peabody for GE that summer of 1986. He was CEO of GE Capital, which in 1985 had had profits of $500 million—the fastest-growing business at GE. Above all, Wright was steeped in General Electric and an obvious admirer of Jack Welch. In short, his credentials were impeccable. Welch did not worry about whether Wright would get along with the people at NBC. He would give Wright a mandate to remove the irrelevant costs from the business, and that would be enough.

The two had talked in December 1985, at the time of the merger announcement. Welch let out that he was thinking of making Wright the new boss at NBC.

"It's not really what I want to do," Wright replied.

Welch appeared to understand Wright's reluctance. "I'm not asking you to do anything. I'm just asking you to be prepared to consider it." He asked Wright to chat with people at NBC and consider the proposal seriously "unless it just turns out to be a terrible idea." The NBC brass tried to convince Wright that it was indeed a terrible idea. They urged him to reject Welch's offer, but on August 26 Welch selected Wright as the new president of NBC. It struck some at GE that the selection reflected the company's great bench strength. "Most companies would not chance moving the head of their most profitable and dynamic business out the door on short notice to do something else," Larry Bossidy, a former GE vice chairman, told a news conference that September 2. "The fact that we did is testimony to the depth of talent at GE Financial Services."[17]

CHAPTER   NINE
◇

"I'm Not a Weasel"

To appreciate the anxiety at NBC over Bob Wright's arrival in the fall of 1986 one need only recall how proud NBC veterans then were of the high-quality programs being aired over the network. In September 1986 NBC won 34 Emmy awards, the most it had ever won. More important, it was enjoying record-breaking profits that were 54 percent ahead of its profits in 1984. Wright spent his first days in the job calming nerves. "General Electric," he asserted lightly, "simply wants me to take the best and make it better."

And—cheaper.

It is intriguing to compare the early days of Jack Welch at General Electric with the early days of Bob Wright at NBC 5½ years later. Both men were handed authority at a time when virtually all of their subordinates believed that all was going well. Both Welch and Wright thought that the subordinates were mistaken. And that the future was perilous. To Welch the threat came from increasing foreign competition. To Wright it came from the growing number of television programming options. Twelve national programming services, including Home Box Office, Showtime, MTV, and Ted Turner's WTCB superstation, now existed. Astonishingly, 10 of the 12 were making more than ABC. The network audiences were shrinking: In 1976 92 percent of all American homes watched one of the three networks, but by 1984 that figure had dropped to 75 percent. (By 1991 the figure had plunged to 62 percent, and some nights it fell below the 50 percent mark.) That was why Wright kept telling NBC personnel, "You've got to be prepared for a lot worse days."

◇

NBC had become, in the wake of his appointment, a seething cauldron of anxieties and fears. Wright knew and seemed to understand this. "It's very difficult. If I was in the middle management of NBC, I'd say, 'My God, these people from GE are going to come in— look what they're doing at ABC and CBS—these people are going to come in and fire people and do all kinds of dangerous things here.' There's apprehension, and I can't necessarily release all that tension."[1]

He was not their favorite person. "Look, Bob," they said with as much politeness as they could muster, "please stop saying that. Just let us enjoy the situation as it is." Inevitably, NBC people compared Tinker, the man who produced some of television's best programs, with Wright, who, so it was believed, did not like television. (Wright's wife was even quoted as saying that Bob preferred television that was not "overly complex," that did not "require an emotional commitment," because he did not have time.)[2] Wright was deeply injured by the accusation that he did not like television. "It's so farfetched. I watch a tremendous amount of television. This was such a slap in the face. They finally get somebody in the company who watches this stuff, and here I get nailed."[3]

Wright may have denied at the outset that he was going to shake NBC up, but it was inevitable and could not be kept a secret. In early October 1986 he told a luncheon meeting with reporters as much. While NBC's ratings success had given the network some latitude, he argued, the issues of stalled income growth and viewership decline that plagued ABC and CBS would force NBC into a reassessment of how it conducted business.

The chemistry between Wright and NBC did not work well. Wright could not figure out the hang-ups of the NBC staff. After all, NBC had been run by another big company before GE! Wright liked to say that it was not as if GE had some Machiavellian plan to make NBC a black-and-white station, or to put only sports in prime time.

He made no apologies. NBC's large costs, he argued, were a vestige from the days when the networks commanded 90 percent of the viewing audience and the largest share of television advertising revenue. In those heady days, if an advertiser wanted to reach a national audience, no better way existed than the networks. So from 1976 to

1984 advertising revenues grew an incredible 324 percent. Wright understood that he had to cut costs. He could cut the cost of labor. That would be painful. But it could be done. But how could he cut the other large cost? That of programs produced by those expensive Hollywood producers. For Wright to take on that challenge—and lose—might impair the quality of NBC's television programming. Viewers would never forgive Wright or NBC if that happened. So Wright concentrated on cutting the cost of labor.

Clashes were inevitable. An insider noted: "One of the difficulties in the coming together of GE and NBC was that the GE guys, probably flowing from Welch's style, had a view of management by confrontation. I should say management by provocation. Welch loved to go into a meeting and throw out some outrageous proposition which stimulated almost a verbal boxing match. He tried to get people a little angry so they blurted out things they might not ordinarily have said in a more judicious setting. The GE people were up to this free-for-all. The NBC people were not. NBC was a paternalistic, indulgent organization, and Welch would sit down—bring these guys up to Fairfield to discuss budgets, confront them, ask them tough questions. They were unhinged by that. They didn't know what to do. They took it as a personal inquisition, as insulting."[4]

It was also inevitable that those clashes would become public, for Welch and Wright were dealing with people who understood what was news, people who knew all too well how hungry the *New York Times* was for leaks of internal dissension within NBC. Both men underestimated the lengths to which the NBC old-timers would go when confronted with the threat of cutbacks. The clashes began, not surprisingly, when Bob Wright asked each division to plan budget reductions of 5 percent. The primary resistance came from NBC executives, including the president of NBC News, Lawrence K. Grossman. NBC News had enjoyed a string of fat years when its annual budget grew to $277 million. That budget, which had been "only" $207.3 million in 1983, had mushroomed to $282.5 million in 1984 and was around that level when GE took over. Advertising on NBC's news programs was supposed to cover the news budget but never equaled the news division's expenses, reaching no more than $250 million a year in the mid-80s (half of that from the "NBC Nightly News"). Grossman made it clear to Wright that he could not afford to cut $15 million. Wright was not impressed. Nor were others at GE. The feeling in Fairfield was best summed up by Dennis Dammerman, senior vice president for finance: "Nobody ever said we were going to get rich off news, and we never tried to get rich off news. The question always was: Do we have to get so poor?"[5]

In Wright's and Welch's eyes NBC News was the bad guy in the cost department. While it produced only 10 percent of the network's revenues, its $277 million budget in 1986 was 16 percent of the network's costs. In that year NBC News lost $80 million. Estimates were that the losses would rise to between $120 million and $130 million later in the 80s. It all stymied Jack Welch: He knew that Ted Turner over at CNN was putting on 24 hours a day of news for only $100 million and was making a profit of $50–60 million. His own NBC had been airing only three hours of news a day, spending around $275 million, and losing almost $100 million. How could that be?

It was a fight over costs, but ultimately the conflict was, in Wright's view, a personality difference with Larry Grossman, head of NBC News since 1984. To Wright he was not "a bad sort, but he was just so ill-suited. The poor guy was trapped. He wasn't that popular with the news people. And he wasn't popular with the business people. He was sort of a man without a country. He found himself caught in a situation where he wasn't really happy with the economic performance, but he was really trying to do a lot to curry favor with the news people. They hadn't accepted him either. I think he felt it was his worst nightmare when I arrived, because now he was going to be forced to get on the business bandwagon, and here he hadn't gotten the news approval yet. He tried to dodge the business bandwagon. I said, 'You can't do that, Larry.' He made it hard for himself. He made it hard for me. It became a very difficult situation."[6]

NBC had trouble accepting the hand that Jack Welch dealt them. In the past the relationship between the people at NBC and at RCA had been free and easy. "Grant Tinker," observed one NBC insider, "would come once a month or so to RCA and in his marvelously elegant style would just say, 'This is what's going on.' There were no questions. He disdained any budgetary issues. He would bring the budget guy [Don Carswell] with him, and he would occasionally address an issue. It was all very gentlemanly and clubby. It was a completely different environment when Welch came along. As for Larry Grossman, he never got called in when RCA was running NBC. Tinker and Carswell handled everything. Division people like Grossman never presented anything. Tinker did it."

NBC News executives admitted to Wright and Welch that they had no real budget plan. These executives had never been expected to present one to the big brass. That had been handled by others. Of course the executives did not like the losses. They made clear that they planned to deal with them—sometime in the far-off future. It was no wonder that Larry Grossman got on Jack Welch's nerves. Grossman tried to suggest to Welch that because NBC News was a public trust, it should not have to face the bottom-line pressures that were faced by other GE business units.

Welch exploded. As the chief executive officer of General Electric, Welch asserted, he too had a public trust, and it was a million times more important than that of NBC News. Because his public trust concerned refrigerators that could explode, airplanes that could crash. His customers put their lives, pretty high stakes, in Jack Welch's hands. Larry Grossman ought to consider Welch's situation when he talked of the network being a public trust. Welch went apoplectic when Grossman, after being asked to trim the budget by 5 percent in 1987, weighed in with a request for a 4 percent hike above the 1986 budget. Grossman got Welch's message. At a fateful meeting with Welch on November 16, 1986, Grossman agreed to maintain his 1987 budget at the 1986 level, which was in fact a drop of about 5 percent with inflation factored in.

It was not only the news staffers who winced at Bob Wright's belt-tightening. The entertainment team thought General Electric was being contrary: The folks in Fairfield applauded all that programming success, and then Wright, behind the scenes, stuck the knife in deeper by demanding budget cuts and insisting on layoffs. "Don't worry," the veterans kept saying, "we'll take care of the losses. It will get fixed." None of that washed with Bob Wright. "It's going to get fixed now," he barked. "We're not going to wait until some undetermined time, no matter how well intentioned you are."

Of course the programming success of the veterans pleased him, but he cautioned them that "if you have any more success like this, we're going to be out of business." Resentment built up. NBC employees noted that Grant Tinker never seemed overly stressed about cost. It wasn't a concern of his. Wright shot back at them: "Well, it's a concern of mine. You can't have a $130 million loss, because if the entertainment thing ever tanks, this company will tank with it."

Wright would win the battle. He was the boss. He had the full backing of Jack Welch. But would he win the war? Would he figure out how to win over the hearts of those who stayed behind? Would the profits that he would coax out of the business be worth the heartache and frustration that he would cause throughout the rank and file? These were questions that he did not dare to ask himself at the time of the worst cost-cutting. But by 1991 Bob Wright sounded ever-so-slightly remorseful. Not remorseful at having engaged in belt-tightening. But remorseful at having conducted the battle on his own. He regretted not bringing into NBC more clones of Jack Welch or of Bob Wright who could have strengthened GE's cost-cutting case against the veterans. He did not say this directly. But he gave the impression of a man who had carried the ball too much on his own: "The mistake I made was doing it all myself. I was the only person here with that point of view. I would have brought in outside people, people from another culture, anywhere, so that I wasn't constantly peeling the onion back. But I was still dealing with the same culture. I didn't bring in any GE people. I didn't bring in any nonmedia people in key positions. Jack and I were, if anything, overly sensitive to the issue that we would be tampering with NBC. Much too sensitive. We also had a number of RCA directors on the GE board—Thorn Bradshaw, Bill Smith, and General [David] Jones—and they were prominent people. Jack made a lot of promises about not changing NBC. You can't have a person at the top with a viewpoint that's different from the organization. It's very difficult. We struggled with that."[7]

Wright's assumption that putting GE people in key NBC positions would have alleviated some of the conflict is open to question. The bitterness of NBC executives toward GE might have been greater if they had been forced to endure an invasion of GE lieutenants. Wright seemed to be saying that the sniping from below made it lonely at the top. He simply wanted some company.

Bob Wright went ahead with his plans, and it seemed that all the veteran NBC executives could do was come up with nasty jokes followed by nervous laughter. In early November 1986 some of those executives started greeting each other with, "Have your suspenders on?" That was a reference to a three-page Wright memo sent on October 24 to top NBC managers in which the NBC president reminded everyone that he was looking for ways to trim costs. He warned against redundancy at the network by saying: "We will not operate this business with both belt and suspenders. This business is in a mature cycle, a cycle often characterized by inflexibility, reverence for the past, isolation from our realities. You must be intolerant of waste, bureaucracy, and those who do not carry their fair share of the load."[8] The memo, much to Bob Wright's chagrin, wound up on the front page of the *New York Times*.

Early that winter the cutbacks began. At first several hundred people lost their jobs. It seemed horribly unfair. Here was NBC at the top of the ratings heap for the first time in decades, and it was firing people. Wright shot back: "GE and Bob Wright will have failed if we wait until NBC stumbles and then try to fix it."[9] He did not wait. NBC's 8,000 employees were pared to 5,700 by the spring of 1991.

Indeed, Bob Wright won the early skirmishes. Whatever controversies arose in the first few years of his tenure, however much blood was spilled, if the bottom line was all that counted to Wright and Jack Welch, they should have been infinitely happy. In 1991 Wright crowed: "There's probably never been anything like it. There's no company in broadcasting that's ever enjoyed as much success as we enjoyed in the last five years."[10] In 1985 NBC had profits of $333 million. In 1986, the year Wright took over, its profits reached $350 million and its revenues were over $3 billion for the first time. NBC was first place in the ratings. The "Today" show was ranked first, and so was "NBC Nightly News" with Tom Brokaw. Wright and Welch had much to celebrate. The financial picture improved even more in the late 80s. NBC's profits reached $410 million in 1987, $500 million in 1988, $750 million in 1989, and $500 million in 1990. The cost-cutting had worked. Other NBC businesses, including cable and an NBC–Columbia Pictures home video venture, brought in cash. Most important, the seven NBC-owned television stations were profitable. In 1987 alone they earned $200 million, half of NBC's total earnings. From 1979 to 1987 their compound annual profit growth came to 20 percent, making them one of General Electric's best businesses.

Nowhere was the sense of independence and integrity felt more than at NBC. When it came to cost-cutting, Bob Wright could always argue, as he did, that NBC was not being singled out: The pinch was being felt across the entire network industry. And, of course, this was true. But when Wright sought to infringe on NBC's well-guarded sense of independence, he had a far more difficult challenge. It was unthinkable that the men and women of NBC would agree to an edict from General Electric or anyone else to involve themselves in politics. That was going too far.

Bob Wright did not agree. He looked at the network's financial prospects and decided that one of NBC's most serious problems was the heavy hand of the Federal Communications Commission. Since 1970 the FCC had barred the networks from owning their prime-time shows and thus reaping the profits from reruns when the shows were syndicated. "The Cosby Show," for example, earned $600 million when it was syndicated in 1986—more than the entire profit of GE's Broadcast Division. And none of these profits went to GE. Worldwide the sale of reruns generated $5.5 billion a year, and all of these profits went to the Hollywood studios that owned the shows. To Wright the issue was simple. The FCC had favored Hollywood because Hollywood had a strong lobby in Washington. Setting up its own PAC would, Wright thought, help NBC lobby the FCC to rescind the invidious regulations that had permitted Hollywood producers rather than the networks to reap profits from reruns.

To develop NBC's own strong political lobby, Wright turned to its employees. Would they help out? Would they join an NBC Political Action Committee? Surely they could not object. After all, the exercise was intended to bring more money into NBC's coffers. On November 6, 1986, Wright fired off another memo that landed in the papers. Seven paragraphs long, it was addressed to General Counsel Corydon B. Dunham and copies were sent to NBC's senior managers. "It is time for us to get off the dime on our political action plans," the memo began. Then: "Employees who earn their living and support their families from the profits of our business must recognize a need to invest some portion of their earnings to ensure that the company is well represented in Washington and that its important issues are clearly placed before Congress. Employees who elect not to participate in a giving program of this type should question their own dedication to the company and their expectations."[11] Bob Wright pulled no punches. He wanted the people at NBC to know how strongly he felt. He appeared to be hinting that those who did not sign up might lose their jobs.

Critics sailed into the proposal. Lester Bernstein, a former editor of *Newsweek* and a former NBC vice president, noted that the memo gave little or no weight to the long-standing principle that a major trustee of the public airwaves should not have a political ax to grind or even appear to have one.[12] NBC News officials said that they would refuse to join the PAC. Wright acceded to their refusal. He still, however, wanted others at NBC to participate.

Wright was as naive with the PAC memo as he had been with the suspenders memo. If he ever entertained thoughts of keeping the PAC proposal a family matter at NBC, he was sorely mistaken. Wright and his colleagues in Fairfield were dismayed by the media's interest in the issue. Why was the press looking so closely at General Electric? Had not NBC been run by another large corporation before this? Moreover, NBC represented no more than 7 percent of General Electric's earnings. Why all the fuss? What stirred the media so? Wright and all of the others at General Electric had been lulled during the 80s into believing that waves could be made in the company without causing a major public uproar. After all, even when Jack Welch's downsizing cost thousands of GE employees their jobs, the newspaper stories on the downsizing were often buried in the back pages.

Wright defended his memo: "I think it's fair for me to say people should be active in the political process. When I hear people say that they don't care one way or the other who's elected, or who's in office, I guess I don't have a lot of tolerance for that. I don't care who you support, but you should do something."[13]

This was a public admission from Bob Wright that he had little sensitivity to what NBC was all about. Here he was telling NBC employees that they had to get involved in politics when for years network news people had sought to insulate themselves from politics. Wright thought that by exempting NBC News from the edict, he was in fact showing sensitivity. What he overlooked was the fact that not only NBC News personnel wanted their independence. So did the rest of the network's personnel. Wright failed to understand the stand taken by NBC's employees: "This is their bread and butter," he told his aides. "This is how they're sending their kids to college. Why the hell don't they sign on?" Eventually Wright dropped the PAC idea, not because he thought it a bad idea but because it had become too public an issue.

No potential source of conflict was more sensitive than the question of whether General Electric would intervene in the coverage of daily news events by NBC News. The man at the top, Jack Welch, continued to contend that General Electric had adopted and observed a hands-off policy: "You couldn't find anyone who said we meddled in NBC. That's just not our game. Just like we don't meddle in appliance colors or appliance new product development. There's nothing they could do that would have us interfere, because I believe they're going to do the best they can do truthfully."[14]

In reality, however, senior NBC officials understood that Jack Welch expected them to protect General Electric from negative news coverage. Frequently it was not necessary for Jack Welch or Robert Wright to interfere directly, and for that reason both men had no trouble asserting forcefully that GE stayed out of the hair of NBC News. The truth was subtler. Sometimes the decision to cover or not cover a story dealing with General Electric was made at a fairly low level—by an editor at NBC News. Sometimes that editor decided on his own to protect the company by not covering a GE-related story. He never gave a reason, so no one ever found out why he acted as he did. Perhaps he feared the wrath of Jack Welch or felt a loyalty to his bosses. Or, most likely, perhaps he decided that spiking a GE story would avoid the near-certain wrangle with his superiors that would follow its airing.

No matter how much NBC News personnel wanted to avoid the issue, it never went away. Indeed, the PAC proposal raised fresh concerns among NBC News staff about this question. After the PAC idea and the Grossman budget-cutting exercise the News Division sought to be scrupulous about the way it covered GE: It wanted to be perceived as being fair, as not undercovering or overcovering the company. When GE announced in November 1989 that it had acquired Hungary's Tungsram, the largest single investment at that time by a Western company in Eastern Europe, the story appeared on the front page of the *New York Times* above the fold. ABC and CBS filed reports, as did *The Wall Street Journal*. Not NBC. The Tungsram acquisition was tossed around at an editorial meeting of NBC News. Subconsciously, editors may have wanted to demonstrate the independence of NBC News by standing clear of the story.

When the issue of possible GE interference in NBC was broached to Robert Wright, the NBC president, and Michael Gartner, the NBC News president, their reactions were strange. Both men, agreeing with Jack Welch, argued that General Electric did not interfere in news coverage. Yet examples then volunteered by both men left the clear impression that GE had intervened on occasion. When Wright was asked if the news reports of GE's interference were true, he reacted angrily—and with coarse language: "It's all horseshit. Absolute horseshit. Everything comes from me. I am *totally* informed on what goes on in that area. And it is just absolute horseshit. Jack has shown enormous restraint when you get down to it."[15]

But then, when Wright sought to illustrate his point, an ambivalence emerged: Wright acknowledged that he would defend any advertiser with a legitimate complaint about NBC News coverage of the advertiser's company or industry. If one of them came to him ("and they have to go through a lot of hoops to get to me") with such a beef, "I don't have any hesitancy in asking for an explanation of that. I think doing that is extremely proper, and I have no qualms about that." He added: "We take people's concerns about what's said about them on the air seriously." Wright doubted that he had acted in such matters more than six times since he became NBC president. Yet he had intervened.

Wright remembered the times when NBC News executives felt a need to let him know that General Electric was part of a news report. "I've had numerous cases where Michael Gartner or Larry Grossman before him kept coming to me about pieces that were being done that could reflect very negatively on GE. They come and tell me as sort of a 'you should know. We'd rather tell you than you find out on the air. We don't want you embarrassed by being someplace and having you say you never knew what the hell was going on. That we're doing a piece about Aircraft Engines or something like that, and it could reflect very negatively on the company.' And I'll say: 'What I ask you to do is make sure that it's fair and defendable.' " Wright noted that such warnings had come only six times in his years as NBC president.

Once, while engaged in a documentary on defense spending, NBC News brought advance warning to Wright. What did he tell them? "You don't actually have to tell them [to be fair] in point of fact. There is too much embarrassment to be had in the News Division before it even gets to my level, because if they intentionally underreport or intentionally overreport, then in the end they look like jerks. They really hate to deal with the GE issue because it has to be dealt with so carefully, because it will be looked at by peers in the press. It's hard to get that perfect [balance], and they're going to look like they lean one way or the other."[16]

One case of alleged GE interference became a public issue in July 1988. ABC reported that GE had been sued for allegedly building leaky nuclear power plants. NBC News president Larry Grossman was asked why NBC had not run a story on the suit. Defending his news staff, Grossman told a news conference that NBC had not missed the story. In fact it was involved in a major probe. "You can bet that we go after major GE stories, positive and negative, as hard if not even somewhat harder than we would about anybody else's stories." Grossman's comment elicited displeasure within the ranks of NBC News: Fear arose that if the story did not get on the air, NBC News would be assailed for caving in to General Electric pressure. In his book *Three Blind Mice* Ken Auletta wrote that Jack Welch phoned Grossman and complained that it was unfair for NBC News to pursue GE "somewhat harder" than it would any other company.[17] Auletta quoted Welch as saying that he did not recall phoning Grossman on this matter.

Michael Gartner succeeded Larry Grossman as NBC News president in July 1988. He also insisted that General Electric did not involve itself in the day-to-day operations of NBC News. "Everyone at GE," asserted Gartner, "is very interested in NBC and in NBC News. Everyone has opinions on stars, just as the man in the street does. But I've never seen a case of interference at all."[18]

Gartner then illustrated GE's nonintervention policy. Three years earlier, when Jack Welch learned that Gartner was sending a weekly newsletter to his staff each Friday, he asked Gartner whether he could be put on the mailing list "if I promise not to comment on it." Welch had been getting the newsletter for three years and had kept his word. In a second example Gartner showed that the brass at General Electric knew how to protect the company from NBC News. Gartner recalled: "We're always hitting GE's customers pretty heavy. A couple of weeks

America's most prolific inventor: Thomas Edison with his "Edison Effect" lamps.

Courtesy of the Hall of History, Schenectady, New York

Trying to prove he's no weasel: Robert Wright, president of NBC.
Courtesy of NBC

David Letterman's frequent barbs at GE upset some of the network brass.
© *1986, Ron Galella, Ltd.*

ago we had a big piece on French industrial espionage on "Expose" [the NBC News newsmagazine]. It involved Air France as a sort of unwitting accomplice in this French industrial espionage. Two weeks later, which was just the other day, I was at one of these GE meetings and at dinner I was sitting next to the vice chairman of GE. We were talking about this and that. He said, 'Did you know,' in a very interesting way, 'one of my houseguests recently was the chairman of Air France?' I kind of smiled. And he said, 'They're one of our biggest engine customers.' And I kind of smiled. And he said, 'I don't think he's as close a friend of mine as he was a few weeks ago.' That was it. Just cocktail kind of conversation."[19]

No other head of a General Electric business faced the dilemma of Robert Wright. Let us say, for example, that a junior manager informs the head of Aircraft Engines that a few employees have decided to leak a story to the media that a GE aircraft engine is inferior to that of a competitor. "This is going to affect GE negatively," the junior manager says, "and I have decided to let you know in advance so that you're not embarrassed by what these fellows do." If the CEO faced Bob Wright's dilemma, he would nod his head politely, thank the junior manager for the advance warning, and go about his business.

But at Aircraft Engines—or Lighting, or Financial Services, or any of the other GE businesses—such a reaction would be unthinkable. The CEO in any of these businesses would try to stop the leak and would probably fire the culprits. At NBC News, in contrast, "culprits" giving Bob Wright advance notice that they will drop a bomb on General Electric are praised for their independent spirit.

NBC's unique culture made Bob Wright's dilemma inevitable. No matter how hard Jack Welch and Wright tried, they could not turn NBC's news employees into GE automatons, eager to toe the company line. By prudent management Welch could keep the milk flowing from the NBC cash cow. But GE seemed to want NBC's affection as well. Jack Welch would never get that.

The "war" between General Electric and NBC, for that is what it seemed to be at times, was conducted on odd battlefields. It took place not only within the offices of NBC News—but on the nation's television screens as well! On one such battlefield the "enemy" was a pair of comedians whose enormous popularity appeared to immunize them totally. The two were David Letterman and Johnny Carson.

It became fashionable—indeed nearly obligatory—for Letterman and Carson to bite the hand that fed them. David Letterman jested about General Electric as if Jack Welch and his crowd had absolutely nothing to do with NBC. When NBC News planned to shine its spotlight on General Electric, senior NBC executives notified Bob Wright in advance. Letterman and Carson dropped explosives on GE over national television without warning. On one program Letterman said that the former head of GE's Small Appliance Division would "push for a miniseries about the development of the toaster oven." A character obviously meant to be Wright turned up on the Letterman show encouraging viewers to burn more light bulbs. Letterman routinely referred to Wright and his bosses as "those weasels from GE." When Carson could not get a set of plastic teeth to chatter on the "Tonight Show," he joked, "NBC probably cut out the chatter," obviously referring to GE's eagerness to cut out expenditures of all kinds.

For all their efforts to portray GE in nefarious terms, the truth is that Letterman and Carson could not bait Bob Wright or the corporate team in Fairfield into a fight. "All I ask," said Bob Wright matter-of-factly, "is that it's funny. And by and large it's very funny."[20]

Bob Wright brushed off Letterman's barbs as a tactic to negotiate better terms in his next contract. "I guess I'm pretty used to it, so I don't pay a lot of attention to [the GE jokes]. In some respects it's a way to negotiate. David's cachet is irreverence. I think he feels that makes him credible as an irreverent comedian. He's nobody's house-boy. I get a little more concerned about Johnny because that's not his normal approach. That's what [Letterman] is. If he is not irreverent, he is not David. GE is a company you love to hate as a comedian. It's like the government or the postal service."

When Wright and Letterman met from time to time at receptions, Wright did not want to show that he was affected, so he avoided the subject. Letterman seemed unsociable, according to Wright, as if he were uncomfortable associating with the GE brass. He undoubtedly was.

While Wright would never order Letterman to stop the GE jokes, he did acknowledge worrying about the comedian's effect on the other GE employees. Wright could take the ribbing, and yet "it troubles me when I sense that a lot of the GE people are upset. I don't mean the management. The lower-level people. One of the attractions of an NBC is that it gives the 300,000 people who work at GE a sense of participating in a different world. If they sense that the world is coming back and biting them, that's disappointing to me."[21]

On Letterman's digs Jack Welch noted: "Letterman is a successful guy. Shooting at the establishment is a successful virtue in most of popular America. Why would I want to try and injure [that]? I mean I'm not a weasel. I don't have any anxiety over that. I think our people in general take it with a lot of laughs. Willard Scott's been funny about us [on the "Today" show]. I think GE people kind of like it."

GE employees often asked one another if they had heard what Letterman had said about GE the night before. Sometimes videotapes were brought in for those who missed the comments. The tapes elicited laughter, not bitterness, according to GE executives.

Welch and Letterman had met infrequently. Once Letterman did an on-air piece showing up at GE headquarters with a fruit basket for the board of directors. A short time later, Welch returned the favor by appearing at a reception with a bouquet of flowers for Letterman. Letterman did not react. "He doesn't seem to have a sense of humor," Welch said.[22]

Welch could take the jokes, but he could not tolerate NBC's cavalier approach to excising fat and waste. In late March 1987 at a closed session in Florida he blasted NBC executives for being rooted in the past. If they did not change, he warned, "I'll guarantee you there's somebody out there who will want to do it."[23]

Welch sought to put NBC into a GE perspective. He was proud of what the network had accomplished, but NBC was only 1 player among 14 very big players. He tried to relieve the tension by joking about the PAC memo: He had not planned to attend the NBC meeting until he received "one of those warm notes" from Bob Wright saying that "employees who elect not to participate in this program should question their own dedication to the company."

Turning serious, he told the 100 assembled NBC executives that managers in other GE-owned businesses who had resisted the GE culture had been "sent home." They could not face the change in the world, "and nowhere do I feel it as deeply as in this room."

Welch wanted NBC to adopt a strict business discipline. (Ironically, of the three networks, only NBC was expected to show a profit for that year.) No one in the audience appreciated what he said next: NBC had some good people, but it also had some "turkeys." General Electric wanted to give the good people a chance "to chase and search for those who are hiding under the umbrella" and get rid of them.[24] One NBC executive fumed: "We didn't need that speech to know that the world is changing."

The executives reacted, not with surprise, but with dismay. "Chilling," commented one executive about the Welch speech. "Unbelievable," said another, who added: "It underscored that NBC is nothing but another product line to General Electric."[25]

Labor relations soon deteriorated. The issue was job security: NBC wanted the right to hire free-lancers to do work that had been done by full-timers. On June 29 one third of NBC's work force went on strike: 2,000 technicians, producers, writers, and editors in six cities. One result: The "Today" show was plagued with technical foulups, sloppy camera work, and sound lapses. At one point coanchor Bryant Gumbel was inaudible. The strike ended 110 days later, on October 24, with the union winning few concessions.

Meanwhile, the institution that had been known as the Radio Corporation of America was disappearing. After the merger GE sold off most of what was left of RCA. What remained were the NBC television network, five NBC-owned television stations, and the Defense Electronics Division. Even the RCA name was removed from 30 Rockefeller Plaza at Rockefeller Center in New York. It became the General Electric Building. By the summer of 1987 GE had cut the number of RCA employees from 87,577 to 35,900 through downsizing.

One of the hardest blows for RCA fans to absorb was the loss of the radio network. Ironically, the National Broadcasting Company, which became the largest of the early radio networks, had been founded in 1926 by the Radio Corporation of America, Westinghouse, and General Electric. For many years it carried "Amos 'n' Andy," the program listened to most widely in America, as well as "Fibber McGee and Molly." Its stars included Jack Benny, George Burns, and Gracie

Allen. It distributed programming to more than 700 stations around the country. In time, however, it was undermined by the advent of television.

In the summer of 1987 the NBC radio network was sold to Westwood One for $50 million. Not included in the sale were the eight NBC-owned radio stations. Westwood One, a Los Angeles firm, was best known for the radio programs it produced for youth-oriented music stations. It also owned the Mutual Broadcasting System, which distributed popular news and talk shows. The sale came as a shock to NBC employees, for the radio station had been an RCA treasure. Nearly as distressing, the sales terms allowed Westwood to use the network's name. In other words, Welch had sold the name NBC News to another firm. As a result of the transaction the NBC television staff now believed that General Electric might be tempted to sell its other "treasure"—the television network.

In July 1988 Michael Gartner replaced Larry Grossman as president of NBC News. Gartner's appointment was a major turning point in GE's stormy relations with NBC News. In Welch's view Grossman represented all that had been problematic at the network: Although the news end of the business had not been profitable, Grossman had acted with self-importance and condescension, jealously guarding his fiefdom at 30 Rockefeller Plaza. It was time for a change.

Bob Wright recommended Michael Gartner for the job. Gartner had all the right credentials. He had management experience, and he had run a large newspaper. At the age of 15 he began his career in journalism at the *Des Moines Register.* He was the page one editor at *The Wall Street Journal,* for which he worked 14 years. In 1974 he became the executive editor of the *Des Moines Register.* When Gannett bought the newspaper in 1986, Gartner was left independently wealthy.

Perhaps the most important difference between Grossman and Gartner lay in their attitude toward GE's bottom-line policies. Grossman always had trouble with them; Gartner was in fine harmony with them. Gartner noted: "In this era NBC couldn't have a better owner than General Electric. They demand accountability and strong management. They instantly provide resources if you have a good plan or a strong proposal, and they never interfere in the process. I've been here three years. Nobody from GE has ever tried to put something on the air or keep something off the air. In times of cutbacks they financed without a raised eyebrow coverage of the war, which out of pocket was $25 million and probably cost them another $35 million in lost revenue. When I came up with an idea to launch an all-news channel for my affiliates, it was approved within days."[26]

NBC News, meanwhile, was becoming leaner. Gartner described the news operation of the early 90s: "We rely more and more on [the affiliates] to cover routine news. They rely more and more on us for what we do best, which is the exclusive, investigatory, unique, big story. We no longer have what the chief financial officer of NBC who was here 30 years used to laughingly refer to as the network-quality hurricane. We go to the quickest and best source to get the news on the air. If there's a big storm in Topeka, five years ago we would have flown in someone from Atlanta to cover it. Now we just call the Wichita or Topeka affiliate. They're there. They know the area better. They're fine guys. They have good crews. That's not necessarily a function of GE. That's how we think we ought to operate.

"We've eliminated bureaucracy. We haven't eliminated many journalists. Overseas in the last three years we've probably eliminated 80 jobs. Only one was a correspondent; two were producers. In the rich years, the late 70s and early 80s, the networks (and others) developed these massive bureaucracies. I've eliminated nine vice president jobs. In news alone we had vice presidents reporting to vice presidents. It was unbelievable."[27]

During Gartner's brief tenure NBC News did better financially. According to NBC budget documents, the NBC News budget was down to $325 million (including $30 million in overhead expenses) in 1988, Gartner's first year in the post. It was down to $286 million in 1989, to $277 million in 1990, and the estimate for 1991 was $255 million. Gartner told me: "The trend is down. There's no question we've been cutting back and cutting down. Part of that [downward trend] is offset by the fact that NBC News has more programming on the air than at any time in history. We have 25½ hours a week."

Most important to Welch and Wright, NBC News was keeping its losses under control. Wright estimated that the NBC News loss would be only $50 million in 1991 and went on to say that while this seemed like a lot, NBC News had done a "marvelous job on the cost side."

As NBC moved into the 90s, the business was getting tougher and tougher. Profits began to skid as advertisers turned away from the networks and toward other ways of reaching consumers, including cable television and direct mail. Cable and other media continued to compete for viewers. Ironically, though NBC was the number one network throughout 1990, in that year its revenues fell 4.6 percent, to $3.2 billion, and its profits fell 21 percent, to $477 million.

NBC's profits in 1991 were estimated to be $300 million, down from the previous few years. The Persian Gulf war cost NBC $60 million in extra news costs and lost advertising revenue. Ratings fell too. Newspapers speculated that NBC was in play, and Wright acknowledged that he had listened to proposals about the network's future from investment banking firms. During the spring of 1991 former NBC executives rushed into print with complaints that GE had damaged the network irreparably. One former NBC executive was quoted as saying: "All the people who care are gone. People either still there or who just left, in Burbank or New York, say it's not the same company."[28]

NBC finished the 1990–91 television season in first place, its sixth straight triumph, in the closest ratings race in almost three decades. But for the first time NBC was no longer the top choice of advertisers with products for men and women aged 18 to 49. ABC was.[29]

As NBC's fortunes sank, second thoughts arose over whether Jack Welch had acted wisely in buying RCA. As Larry Bossidy, former vice chairman of GE and now head of Allied Signal, put it: "I don't know whether the Kidder, Peabodys and the NBCs of the world are the kind of companies we ought to [run], because the cultures are so different. The expectations are so different. The theory that you can run any business is strained."[30]

Although NBC seemed to occupy a disproportionate amount of Welch's time in 1991, he claimed to have spent no more time on the network than he did on appliances or medical technologies.

Was NBC clearly the most cantankerous of his 13 businesses? Welch would only admit that NBC was "the most exciting, the most intriguing, the fattest in terms of its overhead structure, the most set in its ways, unwilling to change."

What about the reports that General Electric planned to sell NBC if it could get a good price? At first Welch refused to answer. Then, after pausing a moment, he said that it was still uncertain whether organizations in the national media were going to earn their revenue back, whether advertising had dried up for good. "We don't know whether this is a fundamental structural change or this is an advertising downturn."[31]

By the summer of 1991 Bob Wright was sitting pretty. Even if NBC had a bad year and even if GE decided to dump the network, Wright would come out ahead. He had put NBC on a bottom-line basis, however controversial. If he managed to help GE sell NBC and realize a large gain on it, he would have done his job.

The general view was that NBC would not become profitable unless it could get the financial syndication rules changed. In April 1991 the FCC eased those rules a bit: It allowed the networks to produce up to 40 percent of their prime-time programming and to compete in the foreign syndication market. But it still prevented them from competing for domestic syndication of first-run entertainment shows. The days of high profits from NBC seemed over. If Welch could get a high enough price for the network, he might go for it.

In October 1991 Bob Wright was still pushing for change at NBC. "If anything, we move too slowly, all three of us. We at NBC got accused of moving too fast. I'll criticize myself that we've moved too slowly. That the marketplace has changed so dramatically and we aren't well enough positioned to deal with it as we should. We are very much in danger of being eradicated, and I still after five years here have not been able to convince people enough that that's a fact. We are suffering essentially the same fate as the big three automotives. We can be a big participant [in broadcasting], but we will be an unprofitable big participant. We can either try to structure ourselves as a business going forward which will be a much more modest business than we have been; or we can remain enormously visible, probably at a very unacceptable level of profitability."[32]

For all the trouble that NBC was causing Jack Welch and GE in the early 90s, Welch did not seem eager to sell it. No wonder. Its cash-generating capability may have diminished, but the glitz and the tinsel were still there. Welch might have found it easier to sell NBC if it made some arcane electrical product. But NBC meant Carson and

Letterman, Brokaw and Gumbel, "L.A. Law" and "Cosby." Who could fault Jack Welch if he got a high from rubbing shoulders with the stars, from dropping their names here and there? Though rumors persisted that the sale of NBC was all but inevitable, selling it would deprive Jack Welch of the chance to own the stars. If he were offered a high enough price, he might indeed sell the network; but no doubt the sale would sadden him.

CHAPTER TEN

"Just a Boy with Knickers and a Lollipop"

For Jack Welch, tradition was always irrelevant. He had been called a maverick in his earlier days. He was different from the managers of the great enterprises in America dating back to World War II. They had known how to manage well. But Welch thought that was not enough. For a manager had to lead as well. He preferred not to use the term *manager*. He preferred *business leader*.

Welch's ideal manager was his first boss at General Electric, Daniel Fox, the "father of Lexan." "Dan was the world's greatest manager. He was shy. He never had a bad word for anybody, certainly couldn't fire anyone, and was bored with the paperwork that went with management; but he was as aggressive and confident in the lab as he was unassuming and diffident outside it. His great personal talent was in the hiring and professional cultivation of scientists. Scores of us proudly call ourselves graduates of 'Fox U.' "[1] Clearly, what appealed to Welch above all else was Fox's ability to lead and choose others who would lead as well.

Welch seemed to hate the past, with its irrelevant habits and attitudes. General Electric was now in the hands of a man who did not want to be chained to the company's traditions and was insensitive to its history. Welch did not want the company to live on its laurels. For him, the past was over. "You can't do anything about it. Right or wrong, good or bad. You learn from it, but I mean it can't do much for me. I'm a person who does live in tomorrow, though, and tries like hell to get out of yesterday."[2]

What had been right for the company in the past was not automatically right for it now. Welch knew that what would make or break his career was not whether he paid enough attention to tradition but whether he could shape the company and the people who worked for it in new ways. He thought that molding people was as important as molding the company. In the old days at General Electric, managers worked with what they were given, with what they had.

The old way at the company was to "memo" a problem to death, to conduct meetings on a problem until the problem went away or was overwhelmed by another problem. Welch's way was to treat the company as an arena of competition in the same way that a hockey rink or golf course was. He played to win in sports. He did the same in business.

Welch's sense of competitiveness pervaded everything he did, not just business. "Discussions are competitive," declared Jim Baughman, the director of GE's Management Development Institute at Crotonville, "golf is competitive, choosing the right restaurant is competitive."[3] To be with Welch was to enter a contest. Just entering it, however, was not enough. To get his attention it helped to be competitive, clever as well, but most of all frank, brutally frank. He hated pomposity, phoniness, sophistry. "He dislikes anything that isn't totally honest," stated GE board member Walter Wriston. "He's a brutally honest person."[4] To display a lack of intelligence in encounters with Welch was to commit the sin of not wanting to give maximum effort to the game, of not wanting to be competitive. "Jack likes people with whom he doesn't have to finish the sentence," said Paul Van Orden, former executive vice president. "People who know what's going on and catch the obvious. One of his favorite words is 'right'. You say about three sentences, and [he'll say], 'Right, I got it. Now what do you want to do about it?' "[5]

It seemed only fitting. The man who had dedicated himself to the mission of creating the most competitive enterprise on earth had to be competitive himself. To carry out that mission he had to be tough-minded as well. Author Alvin Toffler must have had Jack Welch in mind when he wrote: "The task of restructuring companies and whole industries to survive in the supersymbolic economy is not a job for nit-picking, face-saving, bean-counting bureaucrats. It is, in fact, a job for individualists, radicals, gut-fighters, even eccentrics—business commandos, as it were, ready to storm any beach to seize power."[6]

An apt description, Jack Welch as business commando.

Indeed, Welch's style was combative. "You can't say hello to Jack without it being confrontational," said Ralph D. Ketchum, the former head of GE's Lighting business. "If you don't want to step up to Jack toe-to-toe, belly-to-belly and argue your point, he doesn't have any use for you. He's very smart, so he has an opinion about everything."[7] John M. Trani, senior vice president for Medical Systems, observed, "The Welch theory is those who do, get, and those who don't, go." And those who don't may sometimes be rewarded with bluntness. Leonard Vickers, a former marketing vice president, recalled reviewing an advertising agency presentation with Welch. "I was using my indirect English to tell the agency it wasn't on target," Vickers said. "Jack just picked up the storyboard, threw it on the floor, and said, 'See? We don't like it! It doesn't work!' "[8] In short, he did not like to waste time, his or someone else's. He had, in the words of Crotonville's Jim Baughman, "much more of a collegial style than at a lot of places. You still know who's the boss, but he's genuinely open to everybody. Anathema to him is somebody who's in the room who never says anything. If they don't have anything to say, they shouldn't be in the meeting. Or if they're in the meeting, he'll go out of his way to find out why they're in the meeting. In the system he inherited, there would be lots of people in the room, kind of a supporting cast. In his system the smaller the table, the better. Everybody's at the table to play. It's not a spectator sport."[9]

But Welch was informal. When a GE executive went in to see Reg Jones, he was expected to have thought through the answer to every question that Jones would raise. Jones wanted to get involved in issues only after they had been thoroughly staffed and tightly packaged. Because Welch wanted to put his imprint on issues at an early stage, an executive could say, "I don't know. I hadn't thought of that." Welch hammered away at staffers, searching relentlessly for detail. Part of that was his hunger for information. Michael Gartner, president of NBC News, noticed that hunger at once. "He'd be a great newsman because he's insatiably curious."[10] For Welch, one way to avoid falling back on old habits was to make sure that General Electric was always open to change. He had unleashed a revolution at GE. But it would do the company no good to move from old patterns to the Welch way—and then freeze in another inflexible pattern. Welch wanted agendas to be constantly reexamined and, if necessary, rewritten. Even his own precepts could be discarded if shown to be wrong. He wanted managers to occasionally come in to work and act as if they were brand new on the job—and to think hard about what could be changed for the better. Paul Van Orden called that "a remarkable strength, because I think the toughest thing is for a successful businessman to act as though he's new on the job." Van Orden recalled a time in 1987 when Welch came upon the manager of one of GE's major businesses. Welch told the manager that the business had been doing well but that he felt it could do much better. The manager had no idea of what Welch wanted.

"Well, help me with that," he pleaded to Welch. "Look at my earnings. Look at my return on investment. All the things I'm doing, all the people I've taken on. What the hell do you want me to do?"

"I don't know," Welch told him in all honesty. "I just know your business could be doing better. What I'd like you to do is take a month off and just go away. Come back and act as if you were just assigned to the business and you hadn't been running it for four years. And you just want to come in brand new, hold all the reviews, and start slicing everything in a different way."

The manager still did not get the point. He still did not understand that Welch simply wanted him to rewrite his agenda. A year later he was dismissed.

Welch had to figure out how to shake the management system at GE out of its lethargy. Until he took over, GE's planning system had been centered on "The blue books," the name executives had given to a system of annual, formal series of presentations that dealt with year-to-year planning. A noble effort, but, Welch believed, one that gave managers too little time to run their businesses. So he got rid of these fixed sessions and instituted operating plans that could be changed without resort to formal meetings.

He also encouraged people to speak out, to take risks. The only way to encourage such daring, he believed, was to reward failure—not just success. "We have to get people to trust that they can take a swing and (for the right reason) not succeed. In big corporations the tendency is not to reward the good try."[11] So when a $20 million project was killed because the market changed, Welch promoted the manager and gave him a bonus. The 70-member project team received VCRs, courtesy of General Electric.

All of this was designed to kick the habit of conformity. Getting a bunch of yes-men to say yes a hundred times a day to the CEO was not difficult. Welch wanted his associates to stick their necks out, to say what was on their minds. That was what he meant when he preached putting "reality" into discussions at GE. Frank Doyle, senior vice president for external and industrial relations, recalled a managers' meeting at Boca Raton in January 1988. At the meeting Welch and Doyle argued at length over whether GE should keep wage bargaining with the unions in all its businesses together or should split the bargaining up. "The audience asked questions. He and I went back and forth. The temperature went up. He was being directly challenging. He took the view: Why don't we consider breaking this up? He thought in this way we could get wages that would be better adjusted to the industry norms and to the competition. We'd pay our Appliance people more like Whirlpool paid theirs and our Motors people more like Emerson paid theirs. It was a legitimate, thoughtful debate. I took the opposite view that on balance we were better served by having centralized labor negotiations. He and I proceeded to have a fairly open discussion which got quite heated and quite aggressive on both parts."

Finally, Ed Hood, GE's vice chairman, thought it had gone far enough. He said to Doyle, "Frank, it could be you're not listening."

Doyle answered, "Ed, that's one of the two possibilities."

Enormous laughter erupted. Some people went up to Doyle and told him ominously that he would pay for his insolence: "You're not going to survive this morning." Doyle knew better, knew that Welch would not be upset by the public display of their differences.

And in fact just before the cocktail party that evening Welch came up to Doyle and asked, "Have you been getting a lot of feedback?"

"Yeah."

"Why? We do that all the time."

Doyle nodded and laughed. "Yeah, but not normally in front of 500 people."

"The hell with them," said Welch dismissively. "They should know that goes on."

Somebody then said to Doyle, "Enormous credit to you, Frank."

Doyle retorted, "You don't understand. He's the guy who can stop it tomorrow, if he wants."[12]

Such incidents showed Welch to be sensitive, understanding, willing to tolerate other opinions. Yet he was known as a tough guy.

Unfortunately for Welch, just as he was at the peak of his downsizing effort, *Fortune* magazine reported the results of a survey in which it had asked who America's toughest bosses were. The *Fortune* article on the survey appeared in August 1984. Guess who came out on top? Some CEOs might have been flattered by the "compliment," but not Welch. He took the *Fortune* piece personally—very personally.

In its survey *Fortune* asked a wide variety of people ranging from management consultants to investment bankers, from corporate chairmen to psychiatrists, who they thought the toughest bosses in America were. The magazine indicated that it was looking, not for ogres, but for bosses who were demanding yet fair.

Fortune listed its "10 toughest bosses" in alphabetical order, which ironically made it look as if Welch were 10th, not 1st. Among the others listed were Fred Ackerman, chairman, Superior Oil Company; Martin Davis, chief executive, Gulf & Western Industries, Inc.; Andrew Grove, president, Intel Corporation; Richard Rosenthal, chairman, Citizens Utilities Company; Joel Smilow, a senior executive with Beatrice; and Richard Snyder, president, Simon & Schuster, Inc. Welch received the most votes, more than twice as many as were received by Smilow and Rosenthal, who tied for second place.

The text drew a portrait of Welch that was not altogether sympathetic: "Extraordinarily bright, penetrating in his questions, and determined to get results, Welch has carved out quite a reputation for abrasiveness since going to work for GE in 1960. According to former employees, Welch conducts meetings so aggressively that people tremble. He attacks almost physically with his intellect—criticizing, demanding, ridiculing, humiliating. 'Jack comes on you like a herd of elephants,' says a GE employee. 'If you have a contradictory idea, you have to be willing to take the guff to put it forward.' "

Fortune then offered a bunch of anonymous quotes from anonymous "others," apparently former associates: "He has a high IQ, very abrasive, doesn't want 'I think' answers. . . . I've never met a man with so many creative business ideas. . . . I've never felt that anybody was tapping my brain so well. . . . He's a high-strung instrument. . . . Misses the opportunity to get input from people who don't have the skill or courage to play him like a violin. . . . Too determined to get a notch on his six-gun. . . . Working for him is like a war. A lot of people get shot up; the survivors go on to the next battle."

Fortune offered Welch's rebuttal: "Fair, fair, fair. That's what we're trying to do with this company. Our company expunges that sort of macho behavior. I have to be perceived as demanding. There are six companies going after every order out there. . . . There is an atmosphere of rigor at GE but not of fear." Others defended Welch's methods and drive as necessary to rehabilitate GE. Reuben Gutoff, one of Welch's former bosses, said, "His attitude is, 'Look, you've got to know what you're talking about when you're talking to the boss.' There's nothing wrong with that." Gutoff maintained that large organizations tended to slow down, like an obese person. He credited Welch with bringing to GE the passion and dedication that characterized the best Silicon Valley start-ups.

The Fortune portrayal of Welch created an image he detested. He protested: "I don't think anyone would like being in an article with the overtones of the Fortune piece. I hope I am decisive, tough-minded, and all the other positive adjectives [Fortune] used; someone who sets high standards, who is demanding, who wants General Electric to be the most competitive sustaining enterprise in American business. But I don't want anyone in GE to think that toughness for toughness' sake, that macho or mean behavior, has any place in this company. We are desperately trying to increase candid, open dialogue. And anything— an article in a national publication, a hearsay story—anything that discourages that candor is a disservice to our company and what we're trying to do."[13]

Seven years after the appearance of the Fortune article Welch was still enraged by the "toughest boss" label. "The basic headlines," he told me, "were a killer." He hated being called "the toughest boss in America." "I took it as a personal offense. I really hated it." His voice was sharp and angry. "I didn't think it was the right portrayal. It hurt me. I thought we were ahead of our time. I would like to think that tough-minded is totally different than bullying. I'd like to believe that if they went back and asked all those who worked for me in the days of growing from 1960 to 1977, they couldn't have gotten a vote. I haven't changed. A lot of things I'm doing now, I did in 60, in 61."[14]

In the ensuing years Welch drew praise from the business community. A *Fortune* survey of 206 CEOs of Fortune 500 and Service 500 companies published in October 1988 cited Welch as the third most effective leader in American business (the first was Don Petersen of Ford; the second, Lee Iacocca of Chrysler). On various occasions respected organizations named him CEO of the Year. Still, the "toughest boss" designation lingered painfully in his mind.

General Electric was more sensitive about the role of women in its workplace than about most other issues. It was no wonder. No one in corporate life wanted to appear to be downgrading women. Thanks to the feminist movement, GE was increasingly being judged on whether women were given the same chance as men to advance through its ranks. When GE officials learned that a disgruntled ex-employee had complained bitterly to me that putting women into senior positions was not a top priority for Jack Welch, these officials protested, louder and with greater feeling than on any other issue I had discussed with them.

How high a priority was it for Welch to help women succeed in GE's workplace? His speeches were not memorable for appeals to place more women in senior roles. On the one occasion, at Crotonville, that I heard Welch touch on an issue close to women's hearts—creating on-site child-care facilities—he expressed adamant opposition to the idea. A woman in the audience asked Welch whether GE would consider building such facilities. Displaying more emotion than on most other occasions, Welch argued that he did not want GE to become a baby-sitter for its employees' children.

Had women inside GE been a more forceful lobby, or had others outside GE made more of a fuss about the subject, Welch might have been forced to respond more affirmatively: He might have felt compelled to make sure that a plentiful number of women occupied senior roles at GE. But the plain truth is that few inside or outside the company seemed to care. No militant lobby waged a feminist battle inside GE, and the media did not focus on the plight of women in the workplace too often.

GE officials insisted that the company was better at addressing this issue than most other American companies that remained male-oriented. But the company gives out no figures on the proportion of men to women in its work force, so it's impossible to determine how well GE is doing on the woman issue.

The few feminists with knowledge of GE willing to speak on the record insisted that the time had come when women should be given the chance to prove themselves as senior managers. Loud and sometimes strident, they blamed Jack Welch and noted that women had become an increasingly important force in the American workplace. That companies had stopped portraying women in unattractive "bimbo" roles in their advertising. That women were every bit as capable of managing large businesses as men.

To buttress their case, the feminists noted that until the end of 1987 Joyce Hergenhan, vice president for public relations, was the only woman officer at GE. And before she was chosen, in 1982, GE had no women officers. By early 1992 it had five women officers. GE called that "progress." The feminists laughed—or rather, cried.

The feminists were equally discomforted when they looked at other parts of GE's top echelons. They noted that of GE's 13 corporate staff officers, three are women: Pamela Daley, vice president and senior counsel for transactions; Joyce Hergenhan, vice president for public relations, and Susan M. Walter, vice president for state government relations.

They noted too that of the 113 officers who run the GE businesses, two are women. Teresa M. LeGrand is the president of GE Capital Fleet Services, one of GE's most successful businesses; it had revenues of $750 million in 1991. And Hellene S. Runtagh is president of one of GE's 13 businesses, GE Information Services, which in 1991 had revenues of $650 million.

And they pointed out that of the 16 directors on the GE board, two are women: Barbra Scott Preiskel, former senior vice president of the Motion Picture Association of America, and Gertrude G. Michelson, senior vice president for external affairs of R. H. Macy & Co., Inc. Preiskel has been on the board since 1982; Michelson, since 1976. GE has never had more than two women board members.

GE contends that no other company has so many women running key businesses. Moreover, Teresa M. LeGrand told the author on May 15, 1992, "I have never felt there was an antiwoman strategy at GE." LeGrand is held up as one of the great success stories for women at GE. She joined GE in 1974 and held management posts in Lighting and Corporate Trading Operations. She became vice president of the Corporate Audit Staff in 1989 and president of GE Capital Fleet Services in 1991. GE Capital Fleet Services, the top fleet finance and services company in North America, has 1,500 employees; it leases and manages more than 500,000 vehicles.

Defenders of GE insist that the situation with regard to women is improving. "Historically," noted Joyce Hergenhan, "GE has been a company of engineers and financial people. Historically, very few women went into either of these fields. This has changed significantly during the past 15 years. More women are going into these fields. So we have a huge number of very talented women moving up through the pipeline. We've had a new woman officer for each of the last four years."

Joyce Hergenhan also pointed out that very few women are running businesses as large as those run by Hellene Runtagh and Teresa LeGrand. [15]

Nancy Dodd McCann has been critical of GE's efforts to move women into senior positions. A human resources manager for GE for 16 years before she left in 1988, she is now an author and a business consultant on mergers and acquisitions. Though appreciative of Jack Welch and GE, McCann contended that Welch, competitive and combative, had created an environment unpalatable to women. The most prominent example, said McCann, was NBC's decision to replace "Today" show co-anchor Jane Pauley with Deborah Norville. "Deborah was more combative. Jane was warm and pleasant. Out she went. And Deborah was in. Jane Pauley helped people to feel good, not confrontational."

Added McCann: "If you read the (1990) annual report, people weren't mentioned, only money and ideas. Welch talks about tearing down boundaries, but he doesn't talk about recognizing people. He produces a very combative culture. That is not a culture that a lot of women feel comfortable in. It is a culture that is attacking rather than synergistic. I don't see any focus on people at all. That's a real problem for a lot of women. They are not going to choose to stay in a company that is not people-oriented. Jack Welch's style is not people-oriented. Never once did I hear someone say, 'Your bonus depends on growing people.' "

GE took exception to McCann's description of the annual report. "Once we got past the required business information," said Joyce Hergenhan, "the entire letters in the 1990 and 1991 annual reports are about people. Work-Out is about people. Empowerment is about people. Boundarylessness is about people."

McCann dismissed GE's argument that the paucity of women in technical professions was the reason so few women had been given managerial leadership positions. Too many GE managers, she noted, did not have technical degrees for that argument to hold up. Rather, she contended, "There isn't a fight to get women in those positions. I don't see women in the bowels of the organization coming out, and that bothers me a lot."

McCann's displeasure with GE was not angry or emotional. She was not, she insisted, "negative on GE. I'm high on GE, and I'm high on Welch." She called Welch "a man of vision" and "probably the world's greatest competitor." She had, she added, no ax to grind. "I just see that this area [women] is getting lost, and I'm personally concerned about it."[16]

The 1991 annual report, contended the critics, illustrated how women had been treated at GE. The report showed women in traditionally female roles: a woman with her daughter buying light bulbs at a supermarket; a woman med tech operating a CT-Scanner, a nurse-like task; a woman sitting with paper and pen in hand, looking like a secretary. It showed men in action roles: as electronic technicians fixing equipment and as corporate officers. The critics did not believe that GE had purposely used the annual report to suggest that women were still confined to traditional roles. But, they noted, no one was reviewing the report beforehand to eliminate such antiwomen messages.

What can one say about GE's record with respect to women in its workplace?

First, in the last five years an effort has been made to bring more women into senior roles in the company.

Second, until the proportion between men and women at those senior levels is more in balance, there will be feminist voices who will object. Even the women who have those senior roles acknowledge that General Electric is not quite the ideal. "Everyone agrees that we could do more," says Teresa LeGrand.

Thriving on competition and tension, Jack Welch was not content to conduct his affairs on a small playing field. He did not find business particularly difficult, and he constantly told associates that it was not complex. He was once asked how it could be "simple" to run a $50 billion enterprise. Were not management layers, extensive review systems, and formal procedures needed? No, said Welch. "People always overestimate how complex business is. This isn't rocket science; we've chosen one of the world's more simple professions. Most global businesses have three or four critical competitors, and you know who they are. And there aren't that many things you can do with a business. It's not as if you're choosing among 2,000 options. I operate on a very simple belief about business. If there are six of us in a room and we all get the same facts, in most cases the six of us will reach roughly the same conclusion. The problem is, we don't get the same information. We each get different pieces. Business isn't complicated. The complications arise when people are cut off from information they need."[17]

It amused Welch to find others calling business "complicated." All one needed for any business plan, he liked to say, was to ask five questions. Not any five questions. But five specific questions. He ridiculed employees who insisted that they had to invest 90 hours a week in their work because it was so difficult. Welch retorted that he did not work 90 hours a week and that anyone who did either did not know how to delegate work or was doing tasks he did not need to do.

Because he regarded business as essentially a knowable science, Welch was not put off by dealing with large enterprises. In fact, the bigger the better. He enjoyed presiding over General Electric because it was the most complex, the most diverse American company. Paul Van Orden, who worked closely with Welch in Fairfield for years, recalled that Welch once expressed distaste for the idea of running a single-product company, even a large one. "Who would want to run IBM?" Welch asked. Van Orden sensed that General Electric's very complexity made Welch rise to the challenge. "To him GE is the most complicated game in town. What can be more complicated than customers, and competition, and the environmental situation, and research and development, bringing this whole thing together in a way that wins?"[18] Still, it seemed unbelievable that one man could run 13 major businesses. How did Welch keep up with each of them? "There are a series of mechanisms," he explained, "that allow you to keep in touch. I travel around the world often, so I'm smelling what people are thinking. I'm at Crotonville. I get feedback sheets. I have CEC [Corporate Executive Council] meetings where GE's business leaders come in for two days and talk about the businesses. None of us runs the businesses. I'm never going to run them. I don't run them at all. If I tried to run them, I'd go crazy. I can smell when someone running [a business] isn't doing it right."

The real answer, Welch suggested, was that "business is simple. Business is very simple. People who try to make it complex get themselves all wound around."[19]

Welch said that a *Fortune* reporter once came back from a visit to GE facilities and said to him in awe, "Do you know what the hell you've got out there?" His meaning: Do you know how complex your businesses are? Welch replied, "Look, I'm feeling very nice. Look out the window. It's a beautiful day in Fairfield. Why tell me how complicated it is? Why do we want to know about it?" Welch said simply: "It works."

In retrospect Welch's performance during the 80s was so spectacular that some thought he possessed a magic formula. His record was far from perfect. He got off to an unspectacular start, and true achievement only came a few years after he took over as CEO. Setbacks occurred, but they appeared trivial in comparison with the accomplishments. Accordingly, those who had called him "Neutron Jack" and "the toughest boss in America" were no longer the dominant voices at the start of the 90s. Those who judged Jack Welch after his first decade as CEO thought him close to a business genius. "The level of leadership is unprecedented," remarked Leonard Schlesinger, associate professor of business administration at the Harvard Business School. "Welch is always out in front of the organization. There is a continuous sketching of visions of what the organization is capable of becoming and pushing to make it real. He's willing to take bolder steps. He spends more time thinking about people and organization than other business leaders. He's willing to invest time in the Pit [Crotonville's cavernous lecture hall] to get real data about what's going on."[20]

Some have suggested that the ideas of management theorist Peter Drucker offer a window into Jack Welch's mind. Welch, it is said, is a prototype of the manager of the future that Drucker envisaged. An article by Drucker in the January–February 1988 issue of the *Harvard*

Business Review showed the connection between Drucker and Welch nicely. In that article, entitled "The Coming of the New Organization," Drucker asserted that 20th-century management theory was entering its third phase.

The first phase began at the turn of the century, when the industrial barons who owned and ran large companies were replaced by professional management. The second phase started in the 20s, when Du Pont's Pierre Du Pont and General Motors' Alfred P. Sloan structured their companies as command-and-control organizations in which huge corporate staffs and staff planning processes were put into place to oversee decentralized enterprises. GE perfected this phase with its intricate planning and control system of the 60s and 70s.

Now, wrote Drucker, "we are entering a third period of change: the shift from the command-and-control organization, the organization of departments and divisions, to the information-based organization, the organization of knowledge specialists," in which information flows as efficiently as possible throughout and to the top of the company.

Industrial organizations in this third phase will resemble a symphony orchestra, Drucker wrote, with many professionals and experts guided by a conductor. "We can perceive, though perhaps only dimly, what this organization will look like. We can identify some of its main characteristics and requirements. We can point to central problems of values, structure, and behavior. But the job of actually building this information-based organization is still ahead of us—it is the managerial challenge of the future."

In some extraordinary ways Jack Welch's GE seemed to be the prototype of this third-phase organization. It was Welch who championed the dismantling of GE's command-and-control systems, the abandonment of "departments and divisions" that he called "delayering." It was Welch too who wanted to create an organization in which the people at the top could easily communicate with everyone in the organization. Drucker's information-based organization peopled with knowledge specialists resembles the model that Welch had in mind: What Drucker called an "information-based organization" was for Welch an organization that transmitted information accurately and quickly up and down its rungs. Within that organization were managers whose self-confidence, authority, and knowledge enabled them to make their own decisions. They bore some resemblance, therefore, to Drucker's knowledge specialists.

Building the kind of corporation that Peter Drucker envisioned was a full-time job for Jack Welch. It meant devoting every ounce of his energy and gray matter to the task of overseeing the company. Given this single-mindedness, almost nothing outside General Electric seemed very important to Welch. Certainly not the accolades that automatically came to a person bearing his responsibilities. Certainly not the bright, burning klieg lights of television that would have shone on his countenance every day of the week had this been his wish. Certainly not the hobnobbing with the greats and the near greats (Welch would say "the not-so-greats") in Washington.

The man was simply not a Lee Iacocca, his face all over those Chrysler television ads; or a Donald Trump, his name emblazoned on skyscrapers and gambling casinos; or a CEO whose photo frequently appeared in the *New York Times* because he mingled with Manhattan society. He was not even a Reg Jones, taking on the role of spokesman for American business. Determined as he was to sink his teeth into GE, Jack Welch allowed nothing—not a request from Ted Koppel, not a chance to appear on "Donahue," not even a White House invitation!—to interfere with the task at hand.

The White House invitation came in June 1991. Welch had been asked to attend a state dinner for Britain's Queen Elizabeth, but at the time of the dinner he was scheduled to speak to a group of GE Aircraft Engine employees in Cincinnati. He wanted to say no to the White House invitation. Associates told him, "You don't do that. You don't turn down an invitation to the White House. The people in Cincinnati will understand." Welch persisted: "They invited me to Cincinnati, and I said I was coming." Only after Larry Bossidy agreed to fill in for him in Cincinnati did Welch reluctantly agree to attend the state dinner.

Welch's low-key profile did not seem in keeping with his "toughest boss" image. It did not seem to jibe with Welch's image as a man who was the very epitome of certitude on a host of business issues. Nevertheless the fact is that Jack Welch did not enjoy stepping out of his role as just another businessman and into celebrity. In March 1984, when consumer advocate Ralph Nader told Welch that he wanted to include him in a book, Welch demurred, saying that he was too new in the job. When a persistent Nader phoned back a few months later, he was greeted with a mixture of rapid pleading and a "lemme outta here" tone. "I don't need this," Welch argued. "I'm just a boy with knickers and a lollipop. I don't want to be part of a book. I'm just a grungy, lousy manager. You can have access to the company on any other basis. I don't want a high profile. I'm just a grunt. I'm just a man in a room."[21]

In time, as General Electric's accomplishments in the 80s attracted increasing interest, Welch received a growing number of invitations to make public appearances. He said no to nearly all of them. He rarely granted newspaper interviews. Despite Welch's avoidance of personal publicity his photo appeared a number of times on the covers of *Fortune* and *Business Week*. When it did, Welch was gripped by a pang of guilt because he was "stealing the thunder," as it were, from the other GE employees.

Swamped with speaking invitations, Welch had no desire to wag a finger from a pulpit every other day. He accepted only one speech invitation out of a thousand. He turned down almost all requests to accept an honorary degree. (Though he did accept honorary degrees from the two schools he attended as well as the University of Connecticut—because GE is based in Connecticut and Welch is a resident of that state.) Unlike most CEOs, Welch also rejected all invitations to join the boards of other firms. He served as chairman of the Business Council for a two-year term beginning in October 1990, but even that post was in keeping with his low profile. The council, composed of 100 CEOs from America's largest companies, met three times a year to discuss public policy issues, but it took no public positions on those issues and it did not engage in lobbying.

It was hard to penetrate into Jack Welch's private domain. Welch had made such a point of wanting to avoid publicity that it became nearly impossible for him to change his stance. When *Three Blind Mice*, Ken Auletta's book on the television networks, appeared in the fall of 1991, Phil Donahue approached Joyce Hergenhan, the GE vice president for public relations, and asked if Welch would appear with Auletta. Without consulting Welch, Hergenhan fired back a no. She knew her boss. Or so it seemed. Soon thereafter Welch said to an audience at Crotonville: "I had a chance to go on 'Donahue'. Joyce wouldn't let me go. It would have been great fun."

Fun—and significant. For it would have been one of the infrequent times that Jack Welch appeared before any audience outside the business community. Welch was well known to the American business community and was frequently called "the best chief executive in America." He enjoyed appearing before business groups, though he restricted even such appearances to no more than one a year. He repeatedly turned down the chance to be chosen as *Chief Executive* magazine's Chief Executive of the Year because the editor insisted that Welch promise in advance to collect the award at a dinner—and be interviewed by the magazine!

Welch used some forums not merely to communicate but to learn. To find out what America's next generation of businesspeople were thinking, perhaps to mold them a bit, he appeared before students of the most important business schools—Harvard, Columbia, the Wharton School. Among his favorite devices for explaining his business philosophy were the letters to the share owners that he spent hours preparing for GE's annual reports. Not surprisingly, financial analysts read GE's annual report first.

Why the reticence? Joyce Hergenhan thought that Welch was basically shy. "He'd be very happy if no one ever wrote about Jack Welch. He would like every article to be just about GE and about the guys who run the businesses. He feels that it's the guys who are running these $6 billion and $7 billion businesses that should get the attention. That's bothered him as much as anything in the last 10 years: the fact that the media keeps focusing on him. We have an Aircraft business. Here you have Brian Rowe who is the head of it. The media is always doing stories about guys who head freestanding $8 billion businesses. That's a big business. But when they come to GE, they want Welch and not Brian."[22]

In keeping with his view that anyone who had to work 90 hours a week was doing something wrong, Welch enjoyed his leisure. Larry Bossidy, former GE vice chairman and a close friend of Welch's, called him "an engaging conversationalist. He's well aware of what goes on in the world outside of business. His whole day isn't spent talking about business."

Welch enjoys his privacy. Not just to get away from GE, but, Bossidy believed, to reflect. "He's a man obsessed with growth, personal growth. If you came back and interviewed him a year from today, he won't be the same guy he was today." While Welch reflects, he absorbs himself in all kinds of reading material. He reads several newspapers a day. At one stage he enjoyed popular novels, but more recently he has preferred memoirs. "He looks for things in those books," said Bossidy, "that give him some guidance or reassurance."[23]

Welch does his best to keep his private life well guarded. He has succeeded thus far in keeping the names of his four children out of print. Articles on Welch note only that he has four grown children. Family photos of Welch rarely show up in newspapers or magazines. One such photo, which appeared in *Fortune*, showed him as a youngster with his mother.

Welch was not always shy or aloof from the high and mighty. A former GE executive heard the following tale about Welch's dealings with Henry Kissinger from Kissinger himself.

A GE appliance belonging to Kissinger's wife, Nancy, once broke down. To get it fixed, Henry called Reg Jones, who was then the CEO.

"Why, of course, Henry. We'll have someone sent around right away."

The machine was fixed. Nancy was happy. So was Henry.

The next time a GE appliance went on the blink, Henry again turned to the man in charge at GE. It was now the fall of 1981. The man in charge was Jack Welch.

The former secretary of state thought he would try the same straightforward approach that he had used with Israel's Golda Meir, Syria's Hafez el-Assad, and China's Chao En-lai.

"Would you mind helping Nancy with her little problem, Jack?" asked Kissinger, turning on the charm as if East-West relations were at stake.

It was hard for Jack Welch to contain himself. He did not even try. "Henry," he began, "I'm going to do this for you this one time. But that's all—because I don't want you to think that I'm some kind of fucking service manager."

It would be incorrect to think of Jack Welch as a manager in the normal sense of the word. Welch is more of a supermanager, overseeing 13 businesses all at once. "My job," he said by way of summing up the task of running a $60 billion enterprise, "is to put the best people on the biggest opportunities and the best allocation of dollars in the right places. That's about it. Transfer ideas and allocate resources and get out of the way."[24] But because Welch was so successful at managing, his views on what it takes to be a good manager were listened to attentively.

This was somewhat paradoxical—for Welch believed that a good manager is someone who all but gives up managing! "It's sometimes dangerous to call somebody a manager." For the term *manager*, said Welch, had come to mean someone who "controls rather than facilitates, complicates rather than simplifies, acts more like a governor than an accelerator."[25]

Welch liked to distinguish between leaders and managers. "Leaders—and you take anyone from Roosevelt to Churchill to Reagan—inspire people with clear visions of how things can be done better. Some managers, on the other hand, muddle things with pointless complexity and detail. They equate [managing] with sophistication, with sounding smarter than anyone else. They inspire no one. I dislike the traits that have come to be associated with 'managing'—controlling, stifling people, keeping them in the dark, wasting their time on trivia and reports. Breathing down their necks. You can't manage self-confidence into people. You have to get out of their way and let it grow in them by allowing them to win, and then rewarding them when they do. The word *manager* has too often come to be synonymous with control—cold, uncaring, buttoned-down, passionless. I never associate passion with the word *manager*, and I've never seen a leader without it."[26]

Welch fired an early shot on the subject of management in a speech he gave 18 months after becoming chief executive officer at GE. At Fairfield University on October 14, 1982, he recalled that in the high-growth period of the 50s and 60s "there was a real need for caretakers. But in the 80s, where growth is anything but a given, we're going to need the entrepreneurs, the leaders, who won't be handed growth opportunities but who will make growth happen."

In a period of slower growth the best kind of businessman, said Welch, was the one "with the courage to take command, to run with it." That meant instilling greater self-confidence in General Electric's employees. "We're trying to give people who run our businesses a keen sense of ownership, so they will run them as entrepreneurs rather than as caretakers."

Welch pointed with admiration to Steven Jobs, who in six years had taken his Apple Computer Company from his parents' garage to within sight of the Fortune 500. "We are now seeing . . . almost reverential feelings developing toward entrepreneurs in our largest corporations—toward those eager to dream and willing to dare." Those people, he argued, were a crucial part of the country's competitive strength.

In an interview Welch gave to GE's house organ, *Monogram*, in the fall of 1987, he elaborated on what it took to be a good manager. "Clearly, a manager will have to be much more comfortable being open. The idea of the manager knowing a little bit more than his or her subordinates is over. The manager who does that—thinking it's a sign of strength—is a weak, yesterday's manager. The manager—and maybe I like the word *leader* better—who is able to get everybody to share information, to really communicate until they all know the same thing and thus share a common vision, is tomorrow's manager— just like this is tomorrow's company. The idea of the foreman, the manager, knowing a few more facts and then using those facts to become 'the boss'—that's 1950s, 1960s stuff. Today, tomorrow, it's everybody sharing the same information at every level—from the top to the bottom. And, hopefully, top to the bottom is fewer and fewer layers every single day.

"The mind-set of yesterday's manager was to accept compromise and keep things neat, which tended to breed complacency. Tomorrow's leaders, on the other hand, raise issues, debate them, resolve them. They aren't afraid to go against today's current because they know their constituency is tomorrow. They rally people around a vision of what a business can become. They rely less on controls than on trust. Managers and officers need to do better at one-on-one communicating with individuals—about their jobs and aspirations. Compensation, performance appraisals, and career tracks are critical issues."

Early in his GE stewardship Welch talked a great deal about ownership. It was crucial, he felt, that the people who ran GE's businesses think of themselves as the owners of those businesses. "Ownership and entrepreneurship are expressions of both attitude and action. It doesn't matter whether you are running a business or are an individual contributor; ownership means having the freedom to take advantage of an opportunity, to move quickly before being told what to do. When people take ownership at any level in the organization, the freedom to act brings with it the responsibility to manage the impact of their actions—on corporate earnings, on corporate reputation, on quality, and the long-term health of the company. I hope ownership creates an environment where self-initiation is expected; where individuals are willing to bring up ideas, to challenge the status quo."[27]

Welch understood early in the 80s that General Electric faced both an external and an internal challenge. Externally, it faced a world economy in which stronger global competitors were going after an economic pie that was growing more slowly. When Welch became CEO, GE's main competitor was a single domestic one—Westinghouse. That, however, was swiftly changing. A whole new set of overseas enterprises had burst on the scene, intensifying the competitive threat.

The only way to cope with the external challenge was to improve the company. That was the internal challenge. "We had to find a way to combine the power, resources, and reach of a big company with the hunger, the agility, the spirit, and the fire of a small one." Small companies had obvious advantages, and Welch enumerated them this way: "For one, they communicate better. Without the din and prattle of bureaucracy, people listen as well as talk; and since there are fewer of them, they generally know and understand each other. Second, small companies move faster. They know the penalties for hesitation in the marketplace. Third, in small companies, with fewer layers and less camouflage, the leaders show up very clearly on the screen. Their performance and its impact are clear to everyone.

"And, finally, small companies waste less. They spend less time in endless reviews and approvals and politics and paper drills. They have fewer people; therefore they only do the important things. Their people are free to direct their energy and attention toward the marketplace rather than fighting bureaucracy."[28]

Always, Welch argued that the key to business success was empowerment of the individual, whether he or she was a middle-level manager or a fellow on the floor. "We can say without hesitation that almost every single good thing that has happened within this company over the past few years can be traced to the liberation of some individual, some team, or some business."[29]

And the only way these could be liberated was to rid GE of its excess fat. Accordingly, layers of management had to be peeled away. "Delayering" was what Welch called the process of slicing away the management levels. Some said that getting rid of these levels reduced GE's needed command and control and harmed the company. Welch disagreed.

"I couldn't wipe out the command-and-control system that's inherent in this company financially. We attempted to eliminate the command portion while keeping the subtleties of the control. Big corporations are filled with people in bureaucracy who want to cover things—cover the bases, say they did everything a little bit. Well, now we have people out there all by themselves, there they are, accountable—for their successes and their failures. But it gives them a chance to flourish. Now you see some wilt. That's the sad part of the job. Some who looked good in the big bureaucracy looked silly when you left them alone." Perhaps because no one knew what they were doing. Welch noted: "They looked OK. They had support. They presented themselves well, came in with charts, didn't look anywhere near as bad as they looked all by themselves."[30]

To get rid of the command portion Welch embarked on a methodical campaign to dismantle the layers of bureaucracy that had grown up in the 60s and 70s. He had a dual purpose: to turn the strategic planning function over to the businesses and to remove the obstacles that prevented direct contact among the businesses and between the businesses and the CEO's office. The subtleties of control would remain, but it would be far easier for everyone to communicate with everyone else.

When Welch took over as CEO in April 1981, he found that three layers of bureaucracies were sandwiched between him and the businesses. Business leaders reported to six group executives, who in turn reported to six sector executives, of whom three reported to Vice Chairman John Burlingame and three to Vice Chairman Edward Hood. The only people who reported directly to Welch were Burlingame, Hood, the general counsel, and the chief financial officer.

In the next few years the raison d'être of the group executive layer—riding herd on GE's 350 business units—disappeared with Welch's rationalization of GE's businesses. Since the rationalized businesses were fewer in number than the business units and were capable of handling the command-and-control functions assigned to the group executives, Welch felt free to jettison the group executive bureaucracy as a first step in the delayering of General Electric. Business leaders now reported to the six sector executives.

Welch planned to slice away even more bureaucratic layers, but he chose to act cautiously at first. At the end of 1984, when John Burlingame retired and Larry Bossidy, executive vice president and sector executive for Services and Materials, moved up to vice chairman, Welch made a fateful decision. He chose not fill Bossidy's slot as sector executive. The Services and Materials Sector was disbanded, and all of its businesses—Plastics, Financial Services, and Information Services being the three most prominent—reported directly to Bossidy as vice chairman.

At the end of 1985, after a few other sector executives had retired, Welch abolished the entire sector executive layer. The leaders of all save two of the businesses then reported directly to Hood and Bossidy, the two vice chairmen. Medical Systems and Major Appliances, which had reported to Welch when he was a group and sector executive, reported to him directly. In June 1986, with the completion of the GE–RCA merger, Welch acquired two more "direct reports": NBC and Consumer Electronics. With the sale of Consumer Electronics in 1987 he was down to three direct reports.

At the end of 1990 Major Appliances began reporting directly to Bossidy and Medical Systems began reporting directly to Hood. So Welch had only NBC as a direct report for the first six months of 1991. To Welch, that was far too few. He discounted the traditional business theory that a business leader should have no more than six or seven direct reports. The right number, he believed, was closer to 10 or 15, for this would force the business leader to avoid the minutiae and focus on the major business issues. When the chance arose to implement that notion in the early summer of 1991, due to Bossidy's departure from GE, Welch ordered all 13 businesses to report simultaneously to him and to Vice Chairman Edward Hood.

All of this delayering reduced the number of headquarters employees in Fairfield from 1,700 in 1981 to only 1,000 by 1987. By 1992 the number had dropped to 400. That placed new responsibility on the people who remained. Because they were far fewer, they no longer could do everything that they had been doing. For Welch, that was a positive development. "They have to set priorities. The less important tasks have to be left undone. Trying to do the same number of tasks with fewer people would be the antithesis of what we set out to achieve: a faster, more focused, more purposeful company. As we became leaner, we found ourselves communicating better, with fewer interpreters and fewer filters. We found that with fewer layers we had wider spans of management. We weren't managing better. We were managing less, and that was better."[31]

There it was—the nub of Jack Welch's business philosophy: Managing Less Is Managing Better.

A good manager was one who did less supervising, who delegated further down into the company, who let the businesses under him or her develop plans that made sense for their marketplaces. A good manager was one who allowed the people under him or her to decide how and when and where to spend large sums of money on their plant and equipment. A good manager took it as a given that the people under him or her—the lower-level managers, the foremen, the employees themselves—had a better grasp than he did of what the reality of a business was, of how the marketplace was shaping up. A good manager expressed a vision and then had the good sense to let the people who worked for him or her try to implement it on their own. (Part of that vision concerned getting the most possible out of employees, not holding back, encouraging them to take risks. In the early days Welch had made his name by marketing products with brand-new features that bested the competition—such leapfrogging was part and parcel of what he called the "quantum leap." The good manager searched for such a quantum leap, whether it was marketing a superior product or acquiring a business that boosted market share dramatically.)

Though Jack Welch's good manager "managed" less, great responsibility was placed on his shoulders. Welch suggested that the right number of people reporting to a senior manager at General Electric was, not 5 to 8, as had been the practice, but more like 15. Paul Van Orden: "That way you don't overmanage. You go in, you see the highlights, you see what's important for you to be working on. You don't get in there and overmanage. Jack would say, 'I'd go nuts if I had too few reports.' Welch believed that the senior manager's job was to deal with complexity."[32] The more responsibility a manager had, said Welch, the better decisions he would make. "I think people take more responsibility for their action when they're the last signature. If you're just 1 of 20 signatures on a decision to buy a new thing, and you're the 17th signature, and it's got to go to three more bosses, I think your signature means less than if you're the final decider."[33]

Welch liked to point to the experience of Appliance Park in Louisville, Kentucky, to illustrate what empowerment could do. For years the product had moved down the assembly line whether or not a worker was finished doing his job. Welch had that system changed. The employee was given the responsibility of deciding when to move the product from his station to the next. Welch noted: "People on the assembly line suddenly found two levers in front of them. One lever stopped the line. The other sent a part on its way only after an individual was satisfied that it was perfect. The line workers suddenly became the final authority on the quality of their work. The cynics scoffed when this system was proposed, predicting chaos or production at a snail's place. What happened? Quality increased enormously and the line ran faster and smoother than ever."[34]

Welch believed that his most important task was to find good people and to move them along when he did. Take the example of John Rice. What happened proved a shocker to Rice. In October 1991 Rice was the general manager for materials at Appliance Park. Seven years earlier, as a corporate auditor, he had just concluded an audit in Louisville and had liked Richard Burke, the head of manufacturing there. Back in Schenectady the week before Labor Day, Rice was sitting at the same lunch table as Jack Welch. Rice wanted to switch from finance to operations, and the company had encouraged cross-functional moves. He thought GE had merely paid lip service to such moves, and he told Welch so. "I was frustrated because I didn't see any way to make that happen."

Having lunch with the boss was a good way. Welch said little about the problem of career paths. Suddenly he took a table card and wrote on it furiously. The following Tuesday Rice got a call from Burke. A month later Rice began working in Louisville.

What Rice could not have known was that Welch did not simply impose John Rice on Dick Burke. Welch's phone call went like this:

"You know John Rice?"

"Yeah," replied Burke. "Good kid. He did a nice audit. Good style."

"Will you hire him?

"No."

"Why?"

"Well, I've got some paperwork on one of my guys, and if you'll sign it so that the guy can get to his rightful level, I'll hire John."

Welch screamed, "You bastard!" Then he calmed down. "OK, tell all those relations guys, get the paper to me, I'll sign it. It'll be over and you hire him."

Well, Jack Welch wanted candor in the organization and Dick Burke gave him some of his own medicine. (Perhaps out of embarrassment, Burke waited a year before telling Rice that story.)

Every time Welch saw Burke, he said, "Goddamn it, haven't you promoted Rice yet? He's a bright, upcoming star, and we've got to move him along."

Ironically, language and communication played a large role in Jack Welch's achievements. The man who became the Great Communicator around GE had to overcome the burden of a speech handicap. It was no coincidence that his heroes were Franklin Roosevelt and Winston Churchill, both renowned orators. No one had to tell Welch that eloquence was a gift given to very few, that a great leader had to be able to address a crowd convincingly. Though he retained a trace of the childhood stutter, he was determined not to let it deter him. He was at ease before audiences. Within seconds he had their attention. And he spoke clearly, articulately, often with a sense of humor, always with self-confidence.

Welch wanted GE's other senior executives to communicate with their employees. "He understands," said Frank Doyle, senior vice president for external and industrial relations, "that communication is a much more complex process than just having a communications department. He expects all of us to be out talking to management groups, to employee groups. You don't spend as much time at your desk doing the routine work of management in this company as you would elsewhere. I can be away from Fairfield visiting a plant, talking to employees, anytime I want, and there's no criticism. It's approved behavior."[35]

Jack Welch knew the value of choosing just the right word or phrase. Other CEOs innocently believed that to reshape their businesses, they needed only to offer one in-depth speech laying out their visions. To his credit, Welch understood it would take many speeches, much prodding, to get a corporation the size of GE to change. It bothered him when the media adopted its own language in portraying his actions at GE. He talked of "paring" businesses to describe his restructuring of GE. He preferred the term *leader* to the term *manager*, *individual contributor* to *staff person*, *rightsizing* to *downsizing*. The media, however, talked only of his *downsizing* and *reducing* and *cutting*. Words that sounded negative, nasty.

The word that gave him trouble at the outset was *ownership*. No matter how much he talked about it, the employees in the trenches had a hard time understanding what he meant. They took him literally and became confused. "You say 'ownership,' but we don't own this place," they told him. So Welch adopted new language. He talked about empowerment, about the need to liberate human energy and initiative. "We asked, 'Are you freer to do more things? Is your job more exciting, more challenging, than it was a year ago, two years ago?' That's more understandable than 'Do you feel ownership?' We're trying to say, 'Take charge of your actions.'"[36] Was *empowerment* only a synonym for *ownership*, or had he changed his business philosophy as well? No, Welch insisted: "*Ownership*, for example, and *empowerment* are the same words. Reality—that's critical. I haven't changed candor. Speed. I used *agile* [earlier]. But I meant speed. *Speed* is a word that dominates our thinking today. I used agile to mean faster. I used to say we want to have all the power and might of a big company and the speed and agility of a small [one]—I said that in 81. I feel that way today."[37]

Welch was merely suggesting that a good manager was Jack Welch: the man who had articulated a vision in the early 80s and then had made certain that the vision was implemented throughout General Electric.

CHAPTER ELEVEN

◇

"The Harvard of Corporate America"

All of Welch's management ideas come together in the Management Development Institute at Crotonville, New York. *Fortune* magazine called it "the Harvard of Corporate America," and indeed the place known as Crotonville looks like a college campus. General Electric bought the property in the 1950s: It was originally a farm, then became an artist's colony. To the people at General Electric Crotonville is far more than a location on a map. It is the company in a nutshell, a boot camp at which GE executives take part in a continuous debate about the nature of the corporation, of good management, of the changing business environment. General Electric was the first major company to create its own management development center, and from that center the highly respected management style of GE, dating back to the 50s, circulated through the nation's business schools and American business in general.

Crotonville opened its doors early in 1956. It was Ralph Cordiner's brainchild. Cordiner realized that decentralization would not work unless he made his managers much smarter. So he created a place to teach the skills that his managers would require. In a deeper sense Crotonville was created as a command and general staff school to disseminate the virtues of decentralization. Its operations had a military flavor. All senior General Electric executives were sent there for several months of courses. No one went home during the courses. (Borch and Jones, Cordiner's first two successors, used Crotonville as an indoctrination center, to spread the notion of strategic planning.)

◇

The original textbooks that were written for the Crotonville seminars became legendary in the business world. The founding "professors" of Crotonville wrote eight volumes on professional management, known simply as "the blue books." By one means or another many American business schools obtained copies of those Blue Books, which then formed the basis of their curricula. Reg Jones was a member of Crotonville's first class, which began on January 2, 1956. He recalled: "We felt like guinea pigs. The company was trying to feel its way into the field of management development and education. We had the opportunity to spend a lot of time with some very thoughtful people within General Electric and outside. Peter Drucker was one of our very early instructors in those days. One of the most interesting things about the course was that while we were given a great deal of information to absorb, we also had some time for reflection. This you never got to do when you were in the press of the business situation."[1]

The ruler over Crotonville these days is a large-framed, white-bearded hulk of a fellow named Jim Baughman. He has spent a good deal of time in both the business and academic worlds. Baughman came to General Electric full-time in September 1980, at the end of the Jones years, though he had served as a consultant to GE since 1965. He gave up a Harvard Business School professorship to head Crotonville. He ran the shah of Iran's management studies center in the late 70s and had to flee for his life in 1979. If another vortex of the revolution besides Jack Welch existed at General Electric, that vortex was Jim Baughman.

When Welch became CEO, he could have shut Crotonville down. He could have deemed it too costly, he could have accused it of serving the irrelevancies of the past. Instead, he saw in Crotonville the same potential for transmitting the CEO's message that his predecessors had seen. "You know," Welch told Baughman soon after becoming CEO, "I really want to use Crotonville and the Crotonville process to have a cultural revolution in this company. Are you up to that?" Baughman, being the kind of fellow who loved change and excitement and challenge, had no trouble nodding yes.[2]

Poring through the 154-page curriculum and gazing at the various courses offered, one might think that Crotonville is just another business school. It offers courses in The New Manager, The Experienced Manager, Advanced Financial Management, Advanced Information Technology Management, Advanced Marketing Management, Applied Creative Thinking, and Interpersonal Communications. How-ever, it is not just another business school, but rather the place where the Welch philosophy percolates through the GE layers. It is where senior executives, among them Jack Welch, learn what is going on in the company. Welch remembered one of the sager lessons that Walter Wriston imparted to him on his first day as CEO: "Jack," the former Citicorp chairman advised, "remember one thing, you're always going to be the last one to know the critical things that need to be done in your organization. Everyone else already knows."[3]

Crotonville, Jim Baughman likes to say, is not restricted to a single location. It is truly a process. Managers are engaging in Crotonville-driven exercises around the world. Baughman again: "It's like a force field in the company. We've tried to use that force field, so to speak. Sometimes it's a platform, sometimes a listening post, some-times a debating mechanism, sometimes a pulpit, sometimes a crying towel. It's been everything. That process gives all the members of the CEO—not just Jack— a way on any given day to track the company. Because on any given day we have 150 people here from all over the company, in all stages of development, with all points of view. At any given time we have on campus three programs from three different stages of the game. For advanced people, people in the middle, and people just starting out. You can't tell a VP from a foreman. You can put your feet up on the desk, shoot pool in the basement, play Ping-Pong. If you want to listen, it's a great place to listen. If you want to talk, it's a great place to talk.

"Everything's designed to reinforce the ice-breaking of people who haven't met each other as well as to fuse them into a working team. The number one thing we're trying to achieve is to create and nourish a high-performing team. That's what leadership is. It isn't someone on a horse commanding the troops. It's the ability to succeed through other people's success, to create a vision, to have a high-performing team around that vision. The high-performing team is the key orga-nizational ingredient in GE today."

Welch used Crotonville to get across some of the central themes of his business philosophy. Baughman explained that "Crotonville plays a major role in the globalization process and in importing, as well as disseminating internally, the best technical and business know-how that we can find anywhere. The third aspect is leadership. You could be very globally sophisticated, you could be very skillful in terms of technical or managerial practices, but if you say 'Follow me,' will anybody do that?" Baughman said that leadership was the hardest to teach.

The Crotonville atmosphere and regimen are reminiscent of a summer camp. The fitness center opens at 6 A.M. Breakfast, at 7 A.M., is followed by classes from 8 A.M. to 5 P.M. Evenings are free except for homework. Though participants in the Crotonville program can leave the sprawling campus if they wish, Baughman noted that "they're on the job when they're here. It's not summer camp."[4] Still, the participants can engage in a wide range of sports—from baseball to basketball, volleyball to tennis, racquetball to golf—in their leisure time. Each guest room has closed circuit television. Machines in the corridors carry the stock quotations of the day.

All of Crotonville's purposes come together in the Pit, a large lecture hall whose elevated seats force the lecturer to look up at the audience. Hence the lecturer feels as if he were at the bottom of a pit. In some strange way the name and the surroundings encourage give-and-take. It is in the Pit that GE executives speak their mind, argue, dissent, take on Jack Welch and other senior GE executives. Welch visits Crotonville every 10 days or so to lecture and answer questions. He missed a scheduled visit only once—when his helicopter was fogged in.

Outsiders—that is non-GE people—have not been permitted to attend Crotonville classes on the ground that the participants, knowing that their views might be publicized outside the company, would be less candid if outsiders were present. An exception was made for the author. Welch travels by helicopter from Fairfield to Crotonville. The view from the helicopter that fall day in 1991 was of the New England landscape awash in a sea of orange and red. Welch noticed the colors too and at times just stared out at them, as if this were his first helicopter ride. He hardly seemed to notice that he was in the air. He never buckled up, though the pilot switched on the seat belt sign with a ring. Welch had been in the Far East a month earlier and planned to lead off his talk with thoughts on that visit. Looking up from his graphs, he admitted that he had been up until 1:30 A.M. watching the Clarence Thomas–Anita Hill hearings. "I couldn't get away from it. I'm a junkie."

Upon landing at Crotonville at 4 P.M., we were met by a driver and a car, though the building where we were headed was only a hundred yards away. Welch said, "Let's walk, it's a beautiful day." Leaving the car and driver behind, we traipsed unescorted to the administration building. At the front door stood a large figure with a white, bushy beard—Jim Baughman.

Welch grabbed a soft drink from a makeshift bar in the lobby, placed his coat on a rack, and then stormed into a nearby classroom to meet executives from two recent General Electric acquisitions in the Lighting business. These "students" were from Tungsram, a Hungarian firm, and THORN, a British firm. They were in the United States for meetings with GE managers from the Cleveland headquarters of the Lighting business. Welch was to open their meetings. He went to the center of the room. Thirty people sat around several horseshoe-shaped tables. The Hungarians wore headsets through which they could hear a simultaneous translation. Welch began speaking.

He was a charmer. He had a way of winning over his audience with a few humorous remarks, some innocuous, some outrageous. Noting that this was everyone's first get-together, he said in all seriousness, "You barely know enough to yell at each other." He was most enthusiastic about Tungsram. He congratulated the executives present: "This is the fastest product transfer I've seen in the business. This is the fastest product introduction I've seen in a long time."

After his 15-minute opening pep talk Welch fielded a few questions. The first came from a THORN executive.

"How does a large company like GE plan for succession?"

An odd opening question that Welch thought was premature.

"You throwing me out already?" he deadpanned, getting a big laugh. "I'm healthy. Do I look that bad?" By now he had the audience in stitches. Rather than answer the question directly, Welch gave brief descriptions of recent CEOs of General Electric. Ralph Cordiner was "introverted"; the company enjoyed "great growth" during his era. Fred Borch had started lots of businesses: "A lot went well. A lot went sideways." Welch called Reg Jones "the little accountant who fixed the balance sheet." Finally, he got around to the present, when "they hired a crazy Irishman." Again the self-deprecating humor, and it worked beautifully. All he said about himself was that he had done a few things in the past 10 years. He had come to listen, not to praise Jack Welch.

Well, what about succession? Welch ducked it, saying: "We're the only company that still exists from the original Dow Jones 30. One of our strengths is that we are always adapting. The worst thing in succession is to pick oneself. We've been lucky. Our 13 businesses are all Fortune 500 businesses, and some are Fortune 50 businesses."

Someone else asked a question. Instead of replying, Welch interrogated the audience. He was the CEO and he wanted their opinions. How refreshing. He needed the give-and-take. It relaxed everyone and encouraged what he was after, as much candor as possible. Sometimes it worked too well. In what seemed like gentle ribbing of his Hungarian guests, Welch launched into a tirade against lighting fixtures: "I hate fixtures. It's a terrible business." It was unclear whether he was serious. Most of the audience laughed, but some seemed to think he meant what he had said. A Hungarian fellow from Tungsram condemned Welch in broken English. After all, while GE did not sell lighting fixtures in the United States, only light bulbs, its European facilities did sell them. The Hungarian had taken Welch at his word. "I'm not happy you hate fixtures, because I sell fixtures."

It was 4:32 P.M. Welch moved on to the Pit. The audience comprised the same group plus some new people. A banner overhead and behind Welch proclaimed, "Winning in the 90s. GE People . . . Finding a Better Way . . . Every Day."

Welch said that he planned to go over four charts that he had used at a GE officers' meeting to describe his recent Far East trip. Although he went to the Far East every year, this time he had sensed more than ever its potential for General Electric. He directed some Tungsram people who arrived late to vacant seats. Again the self-deprecating humor: "I feel like an usher in a theater." Welch took a black-and-white graph and inserted it into the slide projector. At the back a translation of Welch's speech was whispered to the Hungarians.

He began with an anecdote, recounting a meeting he had had with a former Toshiba boss in Japan, who said: "Jack, when are you going to learn? You've been coming here for 20 years. This is our market, not yours." Welch ran through an analysis of the Asian markets with ease, talking about their good points and their bad points.

Taiwan: "They're all fast, smart entrepreneurs, tons of money. We have to be selective in our alliances."

Korea: "I have yet to find a winner in an alliance in Korea."

Welch's slight stutter was noticeable every so often. He fought it all the time. Speaking rapidly, once in a while he lost out to the stutter, which caught him like an unwelcome friend. He quickly overcame the problem.

Welch said that the growth rate in Asia was going to be substantial and talked about how GE had to adjust its human resources to deal with that change. "All the people are in the wrong place. District managers in Atlanta, Dallas. They'll get an order by 1993 if they're lucky. We need resources transferred. We need thousands of people there in Asia."

The speech was beginning to sound like a pep talk. Jack Welch as football coach. GE had advantages over others, a 10-year advantage in high-tech businesses. He asked the audience where it thought the "big hit"—the best foreign market—would be between 1991 and 1993. He mentioned Mexico, Iran, China. Coach Welch talking: "Let's see if we can do [in one of those countries] what GE has done in Europe in the past few years."

During question time certain questions recurred: child care, defense spending, GE's relations with employees, and NBC. Today the first question was no surprise since the Thomas-Hill hearings had concluded the night before. It dealt with GE and sexual harassment. A woman asked Welch if GE was planning to refine its policies toward sexual harassment in light of the Hill-Thomas controversy. The question did not seem to rattle him. He replied as if he had spent the whole weekend explaining to friends that General Electric had a superb record on the subject. "We have a good program," he told the questioner. "Videotape training. Our policy is clear." (He never said what GE's policy was, but the company was clearly against sexual harassment in the workplace.) "We'll put more emphasis if we see there is a problem. Before Friday [when the hearings started], we weren't hearing that it was a big issue [at GE]. I think we have a pretty enlightened crowd. I may have my head in the sand. I don't think it's an issue. But I wouldn't want to bet my life on it." That got a laugh.

A typical Welch response. When the entire nation was in hot debate over the delicate question of how to deal with sexual harassment at work, the head of one of America's great corporations was looking the issue right in the eye before a GE audience, sounding sober at times, playful at others. No one in the audience thought he was trivializing the subject. No one seemed to think that he had his head in the sand. The man exuded credibility.

Questions followed about GE and various world markets.

On Russia: "I think Russia is a place where you don't have to be first. They have no idea of what an economy is. And therefore you have a very difficult problem. I was taken in by Gorbachev. I saw Yeltsin. He gave me a sales pitch. He said, 'Do in Russia what you did in Hungary.' "

On Latin America: "People say, 'Why aren't you in Brazil?' Because Mexico is a lot better. You have to make your bets."

Someone asked the inevitable question: How was General Electric doing? "We make mistakes," Welch opened. "You have to go to bat a lot. We get a hit about three fourths of the time, I hope. But we're wrong a lot. You've got to be able to say 'I'm wrong' and be comfortable with it. It's something we've all got to handle. You don't take a 110-year-old bureaucracy and change it that fast. But we'll get there. You'll never believe how fast things are going."

Someone asked about the "changing culture" at GE. Welch interrupted: "I like to call it 'evolving.' " Welch talked about the four types of people at GE: "The first is the person who has our values and makes the numbers. We like him a lot. [Laughter.] The second has our values, is trying, but misses his numbers. We give him a second chance. The third has no culture and no numbers. He's out. It's easy. The fourth is the brutal one. No values, but he makes the numbers. That's the one all of us sort of cringe about. We're wrestling with it. We don't know how to handle it. How we deal with this one is where we fail most. We don't have the answer. We have had some success."

Someone from GE's Aircraft Engine business in Lynn, Massachusetts, said he knew people of this last type. "Instead of playing to win, they play not to lose. I don't know the answer."

Welch said neither did he. "I wish I did. Wouldn't it be good if I did? Maybe if you talk abut it, we'll make a lot of progress. I don't know how to fix it." Welch was saying something very simple: All managers were supposed to "make the numbers," but those who did not would still be looked upon sympathetically. All managers were, however, expected to support and take part in the new Welch culture at GE. The shirkers would not be treated kindly.

Back to the Pit. A question about General Electric's stock. A year ago it had been 50. Today (October 14, 1991) it was 67. Last month it had been 72. How the stock was doing, Welch argued, depended on what time frame you used to measure it.

A question about NBC. Did GE plan to sell the network? Not surprisingly, Welch said, "No comment." The NBC question led to one about Johnny Carson and David Letterman. How could Welch let them knock GE over the air? Might that not turn off potential GE customers? Welch adopted an I-can-take-what-they're-throwing-at-me attitude. He was not going to be bothered by them. "It's in good humor. I don't take what they say seriously. I've never heard anybody say they wouldn't buy a GE light because of a joke on Johnny Carson. It's a form of advertising."

A question on the effect of a lowered defense budget on GE. How would the company stand it? Welch showed no distress at this prospect. He knew that his cavalier attitude would not sit well with the folks in Aerospace or Aircraft Engines. His main thought: Reducing the defense budget would free up money for education and for reducing the deficit. (Someone whispered, "Preferably the latter.") "I know the Aircraft Engine people want to stone me. But it's good for the country and for the company. Does this cause anyone problems?" No one said it did.

Then came the inevitable question about child care. A woman said that GE should organize child-care facilities in the workplace. No other question seemed to agitate Welch more. He barked that GE was not going to get involved in this arena. "We'll pay a fair wage, but we won't get into the child-care business. We ought to get better child care elsewhere." The most heated debate of the session then occurred.

A man in the audience shouted out, "Here at Crotonville you provide a service. What's the difference?"

Welch: "No. I am not [providing a service here]. This isn't a hotel service. Crotonville is about integrated diversity. That's why people here don't go to 20 different hotel rooms at night. That is why they stay here, to meet one another, to chew over problems of their businesses."

The female questioner persisted: "Child care is similar."

"No, it's not," shot back Welch. "What you do with your family is your business. If you can't do it, it's your problem. It's not my problem."

"But working is very hard on women."

"I don't want to be sued. I have enough problems. I don't want to manage your children. When your child grows up to be a robber, I don't want to be held responsible. [*Slight laughter.*] I don't want GE in the business of managing children or being on premises."

Then a question about Iran and whether GE had an opportunity for doing business on a large-scale there. This was October 1991, and the hostage issue had still not been fully resolved. Welch replied: "Until the hostage issue is solved, Iran's not going to be a good market for us. It's a question mark. It's a huge opportunity. I don't know enough about Iran. What I know you can put in a thimble."

Welch ended his time in the Pit that day with some uplifting words, weaving into his remarks what might have been taken as an insult to the Hungarians in the audience. Welch, however, remained master. No one got upset. "This is the most exciting company in the world. We can differ [as on child care]. You tell me what you think. I have to explain my position. That's all right. That's healthy. You people have a chance to reshape and redefine one of the largest companies in the world. Even Hungarians have to get excited after 40 years. It's hard to turn a Hungarian on."

Welch was given huge applause. Then came a reception. The reactions to Welch varied. A fellow from Major Appliances in Louisville said that he had been surprised at how soft and easygoing Welch had seemed. Not at all like the Neutron Jack he had read about. The meeting had apparently energized Welch. When we choppered back to Fairfield, the contented look on his face seemed to say that he had picked up some valuable information and would use it at the first opportunity. He had made sure that he was not the last person at GE to find out what was going on in the company. Today he had been the first.

CHAPTER TWELVE

◇

"The 'C' Word"

As the second half of the 80s began, the jury was still out on Jack Welch and General Electric.

With good reason. He had delayered and downsized, invested in factories and rationalized them, bought and sold businesses. And he had called it all "a revolution," hoping that everyone would have the patience required for results to emerge. Wall Street was a wee bit breathless and incredulous. Thousands of employees had been laid off or fallen under new ownership. Nearly 200 businesses had been sold and another 70 bought. Welch insisted that GE had to streamline to be competitive, that in time his efforts would bear fruit.

Still, concern existed. The GE balance sheet did not appear to reflect a successful revolution. The company's sales had risen $737 million between 1981 and 1984 and another $1.3 billion in 1985. Its earnings had risen at an annual average of $200 million between 1981 and 1985 but by only $56 million in 1985.

To most other companies Jack Welch's "problems" would have been most welcome. Few companies had sales or earnings as large as GE's. Welch, however, did not measure GE against the herd because Wall Street did not measure GE against the herd. Wall Street had special rules for companies like General Electric. The standards were tougher. No mercy was shown.

Wall Street had one set of standards for single-product businesses, and another for companies that clustered a host of businesses. Single-product businesses "only" had to show good results on the bottom line. The companies that operated like General Electric had

◇

187

to show more than that. They had to show that their totals were greater than the sum of their parts, that the people in corporate could exploit the synergies of their businesses, could allocate resources so that these businesses were better off under one huge umbrella than as stand-alones.

Welch's buying and selling of businesses troubled Wall Street the most. Though Welch insisted that the purchase of such giants as Employers Reinsurance and RCA made strategic sense for General Electric, the Street unsympathetically accused him of acting without rhyme or reason. It even mentioned the "C" word, the epithet that rankled Jack Welch almost as much as being called "Neutron Jack" or "the toughest boss in America."

"Just another conglomerate," the analysts began saying dismissively of General Electric.

They were increasingly fearful that Welch's frantic race to transform GE would lead him to gobble up some acquisition that would prove a financial disaster, seriously affecting GE's balance sheet. The Street wanted to believe that Welch knew what he was doing. It wanted to give him more time. But the analysts wanted to see a rosier balance sheet. They wanted Welch to say that it would be all right. Calming Wall Street became one of Jack Welch's major challenges in the second half of the 80s. He refused to give up on his revolution.

In 1986 General Electric began to possess the aura of genuine success. That was the year in which Jack Welch sensed that his luck was changing. The crippling recession of the early 80s had ended. So too had the myopic view of the politicians in Washington.

Welch had held his peace during the early 80s, but now that the sun was starting to shine, he chose to be candid, to point an accusing finger at the culprits in Washington. "Midwinter for me and for all those whose livelihood depends on how well we compete in the international marketplace dragged on for four long years," he said, arguing that Ronald Reagan's ascendancy to the presidency in 1981 had been a cause of GE's slow growth between 1981 and 1985. The high dollar during those years, for which Reagan had to bear responsibility, had hurt General Electric's exporting prospects. The president's laissez-faire approach to the value of the dollar, which allowed that value to be determined by the free market, had offered no hope. Shifting gears in September 1985, however, Reagan did take steps to lower the value of the dollar. By early 1986 Welch could declare, "I see daylight ahead."

Washington was taking other steps to improve the position of American business vis-à-vis foreign competition: Commerce Secretary Malcolm Baldrige and the Justice Department were giving greater weight to global competitive factors in their reviews of mergers. And Ronald Reagan was increasingly prepared to use the Export-Import Bank to help American firms compete against foreign counterparts whose efforts were subsidized by their governments. Most important, the president now appeared to understand that the playing field for American business had become global. "That one big thought," noted Jack Welch, "represents the reality that can get us back on the road to world competitiveness."

Indeed, the sun was shining in Fairfield. Sales in 1986 were $36.725 billion, a whopping 26 percent increase over sales in the previous year. And earnings grew 9 percent, to $2.492 billion. It was a red-letter year for GE in a number of ways. The RCA merger was sewn up in June. Kidder, Peabody, a veteran investment banking firm on Wall Street, was purchased. GE's globalization policy was strengthened by an increased use of alliances with overseas firms: Of these alliances, 12 were either started or expanded in 1986, helping GE to generate more product lines, open new markets, and become more competitive with existing products. GE's factory automation business formed an alliance with the Japanese firm Fanuc, Ltd.; Medical Systems increased its investment in a Japanese joint venture with Yokogawa Medical Systems; and Aircraft Engines continued a long-term alliance with SNECMA of France.

The previous six years of the Welch revolution now showed impressive results: GE's earnings had risen 10 percent a year compounded since 1980 (40 percent faster than the GNP during that time). GE's stock, whose price per share reached $44 in 1986, had risen 19 percent a year compounded, compared to 11 percent for the S&P 500. In 1981 GE was the 10th-largest company in market value; five years later it was the 3rd largest.

The merits of Welch's strategies were now revealed. Welch had gambled heavily—risking $11.6 billion in investments. The gamble had been aimed at eight GE businesses—Aerospace, Aircraft Engines,

Factory Automation, Financial Services, Major Appliances, Medical Systems, NBC, and Plastics. By 1986 these businesses accounted for 73 percent of GE's earnings. General Electric had moved far afield of its original core businesses in electrical manufacturing. Now 70 percent of its key business earnings were in technology and services (a 20 percent hike since Welch took over). The contribution of the service segment to key business earnings had jumped from 20 percent in 1981 to 29 percent in 1986. This did not mean that the core manufacturing businesses had become stagnant. Their earnings had grown 30 percent since 1981. An obviously pleased Welch reported to share owners in the 1986 annual report: "Looking at GE's three groups of key businesses at the end of 1986, we believe we have accomplished much of what we set out to do in 1981—developing one of the most competitive and winning sets of businesses in the world by the end of the decade."

It had seemed like such a natural step to take. Other American corporations had acquired Wall Street investment banks earlier in the 80s. These alliances made great sense. First, for Wall Street firms that were eager to get their hands on capital. And second, for corporations that had billions of dollars in capital. These marriages seemed to have been arranged in heaven. The investment bank received the financial aid it needed in order to compete on a global basis. The corporate parents happily raked in new profits.

Jack Welch also went to the altar. He had no way of knowing that the bride had a skeleton in her closet.

When General Electric bought 80 percent of Kidder, Peabody for $600 million in the summer of 1986, the purchase seemed, at first blush, a brilliant idea. By taking over Kidder, General Electric added financial muscle to the investment banking firm. For Kidder, falling into the arms of GE Capital, the largest diversified finance company in America, seemed like a dream come true.

Though not a bank (it did not accept deposits, for example), GE Capital was considered the best bank in the country. It certainly seemed like a bank in some respects. It began in 1932 as GE Credit, lending money to GE customers who wanted to purchase major appliances, such as refrigerators, but were strapped for cash because of the Depression. GE Credit continued to finance installment buying for such products until the mid-60s, by which time banks and independent financing companies were performing this function, thus making it unnecessary for GE Credit to remain in business.

Employees at GE Credit balked, however, at the idea of going out of business. They argued successfully that their experience in financing products enabled them to offer financing for a wide range of products. In the 60s and 70s GE Credit offered this broader variety of financial services, eventually becoming one of GE's most profitable enterprises.

Had GE Capital been a bank, its $22 billion in assets would have ranked it among the nation's 20 largest. Few banks came close to matching its 21.6 percent return on equity. The fact that Kidder also had a return on equity of more than 20 percent appealed to GE Capital. Making the GE Capital-Kidder link even more natural was the advantage that the link gave GE Capital over its commercial bank competitors: They were barred from many areas of investment banking by federal law. Kidder, an investment bank, was not.

Though Kidder had been losing market share in securities underwriting and other important businesses, it had always shunned selling out to outsiders. Meanwhile, rivals less reluctant to shed their independence had benefited from doing so. Salomon Brothers had only $331 million in capital in 1981; four years later, its ownership having passed to Phibro Corporation, it had $2.3 billion. Kidder's capital in 1985 was only $363 million, making it only the 15th-largest investment bank on the Street. Ralph DeNunzio, Kidder's CEO, grudgingly acknowledged that lack of capital had cost Kidder chances to do business. That had to change. He decided that it was in Kidder's best interest to become part of a strong corporation with expertise in financial services. Hence the sale to General Electric. The final deciding factor was the defection, in February 1986, of star investment banker Martin Siegel to Drexel Burnham Lambert.

Hoping that a revitalized Kidder could become a serious competitor of the first-tier investment banks, GE paid three times the book value for the investment house. A strange decision, considering that only two of Kidder's businesses—mergers and futures and fixed-income trading—had been profitable. Nonetheless, Wall Street reacted warmly to the deal, dubbing Jack Welch's company "Generous Electric." Initially GE pumped a modest $130 million in capital into

Kidder. Sensing that it would be difficult and perhaps unnecessary to
impose the GE culture on Kidder, GE promised to adopt a hands-off
strategy. Kidder's employees were individualists—some at GE later
called them "prima donnas"—who already possessed the entrepreneurial spirit that Welch was trying to incorporate into other segments
of GE. At first all went well. In 1986 Kidder turned in record profits
of $81 million. The Welch selection process appeared to be working.

Then the roof fell in. Martin Siegel, the boy wonder who had
almost single-handedly given Kidder a reputation as a first-class mergers and acquisitions firm before jumping ship to Drexel Burnham
Lambert, pleaded guilty in New York Federal Court to insider trading
charges in early 1987.[1] Though Welch had no reason to feel responsible or culpable, the downfall of Marty Siegel proved one of the
most devastating moments in Welch's decade as chairman of General
Electric.

One minute Welch was on top of the world, having gained a foot-
hold on Wall Street. Soon afterward he was forced to spend time and
energy explaining that General Electric had not known about the
Marty Siegel affair and had been an innocent bystander in the whole
mess. Welch was infuriated by the refusal of some people to accept the
fact that General Electric had been unaware of Siegel's guilt. "There's
no way I could have known." When GE called a news conference to
announce the Kidder purchase, journalists asked in surprise, "How
can you buy this company? Siegel's gone to Drexel Burnham. He was
the star. You've lost the asset." Welch was annoyed when the same
people turned around and said: "You didn't know Siegel was cheating?
How stupid can you be?"[2]

Although GE had adopted a hands-off attitude toward Kidder,
with the investment banking house in crisis it could no longer stay
aloof. It had to try to restore some semblance of Kidder's vanishing
reputation and to keep Kidder intact. The courtship had been fun, but
the honeymoon was a disaster. All Jack Welch could do was to try and
pick up the pieces.

GE moved fast. Larry Bossidy, GE vice chairman and the chief
executive of GE Financial Services, put a GE deputy counsel with
criminal experience in charge of day-to-day dealings with the crisis. A
team of GE auditors began checking into Kidder, Peabody to see how
deeply the scandal had permeated the firm. One financial analyst believed that GE had tried to negotiate a deal with the SEC as fast as

possible in order to prepare for a quick sale of Kidder. That may have been true, but would anyone out there have been interested in buying damaged goods?

GE had a more pressing problem to worry about. It had to keep Kidder from going under. The danger was genuine. Clients that trusted Kidder might bolt in a flash because of new developments in the Siegel scandal. The way to keep the firm intact, to keep Kidder's clients and employees from scurrying away, was to avoid an indictment against the investment banking house itself. GE pursued the no-indictment strategy with relentless energy. It argued that the charges against Marty Siegel dealt with events that had occurred before the acquisition. It also pointed out to the Securities and Exchange Commission that an indictment against Kidder and Kidder's inevitable subsequent collapse would put 7,000 innocent employees out on the street. Bossidy urged U.S. attorney Rudolph Giuliani not to prosecute Kidder. In return, he promised that Kidder's senior management, including Ralph DeNunzio, would be dismissed and that Kidder would abandon arbitrage, the financial practice that had become associated with the insider trading scandals. Finally, Bossidy assured Giuliani that Kidder would work out a proper settlement with the SEC.

The GE strategy paid off. Bossidy's approach, said Giuliani, was a "breath of fresh air" compared with what he had heard from other enterprises involved in the scandal. Living up to its word, GE fired De-Nunzio and two other senior managers. Though he possessed no investment banking experience, a liability that in time proved costly, Silas Cathcart, former chairman of Illinois Tool Workers and a member of GE's board of directors, was named Kidder, Peabody's new chairman. After General Electric's own probe uncovered "substantial weaknesses" in Kidder's managerial and financial controls, GE moved its own people into senior management posts. Soon thereafter the SEC announced that it was settling with Kidder for $25.3 million. Happily for GE, Giuliani announced that Kidder would not be prosecuted. Larry Bossidy savored the small triumph. Although Kidder's survival seemed less in doubt, whether it would thrive remained an open question.

Especially after the next blow occurred. In October 1987 the stock market crashed. Kidder's reputation nose-dived. Silas Cathcart had to cut 1,500 employees from the rolls by the end of 1987. He was forced to approve meager bonuses. Employees balked, and some decided to quit, taking clients along. Jack Welch was furious. No one automatically deserved a bonus. "Our rules are: 'You deliver, we deliver.' "[3] Kidder's earnings sank dramatically: It recorded a $28 million loss for 1987, due in part to onetime charges of $67 million to cover the SEC settlement in the Siegel affair and layoff costs.

It was hard to find a positive note in the Kidder fiasco. Welch tried, however. With a masterful euphemism, Welch wrote to shareholders in the 1987 annual report that the investment banking firm had experienced "some difficulties" that year. He mentioned the Siegel scandal and the market crash as if they had been minor blips and then offered these upbeat words: "Kidder is taking the decisive steps needed to weather turbulent times, and it remains an important part of our Financial Service business."

Welch vowed to prevent any more Marty Siegels from surfacing at Kidder. "Although the alleged wrongdoing happened long before we bought them, we're putting in new policies and management so that, going forward, it shouldn't happen again. But all the practices and all the paper in the world will never stop one or two individuals from going outside the corral. Our job—everybody's job—is to talk integrity, preach integrity, and, in every instance, live integrity."[4] In mid-1988 Welch was honest enough to admit that if he had it to do all over again, he would not buy Kidder, "knowing Marty Siegel was a cheat."[5] That fall he told Kidder employees much the same thing.

GE turned in another solid performance in 1987. Nearly all of its key businesses increased their market share. Its earnings, now nearly $3 billion ($2.915 billion), were 17 percent higher than its earnings in 1986. Its sales were superb too, topping $40 billion for the first time ($40.515 billion), and 12 percent higher than its sales in 1986.

Despite the naysayers and doubters on Wall Street, Jack Welch was on the prowl again in the summer of 1987. He was searching for a way to strengthen GE's Medical Systems business. He focused on the French-owned Thomson conglomerate, whose businesses included Medical Diagnostics and Consumer Electronics. Welch sounded out Thomson's boss, Alain Gomez. Though Medical Diagnostics had never been a big winner for the $6 billion Thomson, acquiring it would automatically erase GE's weak position in Europe: Its market share would leap from 6 percent to 20 percent. (GE already had a strong position in the American market and a good one in Japan.)

Listening to Welch's proposal, Gomez made a startling counteroffer: Why not make a trade? Your Consumer Electronics business for our Medical Diagnostics business plus $800 million in cash. Welch could not believe his luck and decided quickly. "We didn't need to go back to headquarters for a strategic analysis and a bunch of reports. Conceptually, it took us about 30 minutes to decide that the deal made sense." A two-hour meeting with Thomson executives followed. Within five days the two parties signed a letter of intent.[6]

For General Electric, it was, as Welch said, "the chance of a lifetime." The opportunity to dump one of the businesses Welch liked least, Consumer Electronics, and pick up a potential jewel for GE's crown. It was as if a football team had traded an aging, second-string player for a young, record-breaking one. "Jack couldn't believe it," said a senior GE executive. "He thought he'd died and gone to heaven."

And so the deal was struck. GE announced that it was selling its $3.2 billion-a-year Consumer Electronics business to Thomson. In exchange GE acquired CGR, Thomson's Medical Systems business. Thomson acquired all of the audio and video products that carried the RCA and GE labels: televisions, radios, videocassette recorders, stereos, and tape recorders. Televisions were the most important line. The RCA brand was the top seller in America, with a 16 percent market share, and GE's televisions added another 3 or 4 percent.

Consumer Electronics was the sixth RCA business that GE had sold or closed. (The other five: RCA Records; Nacolah, a life insurance business; Coronet, a carpeting firm; the NBC Radio network; and RCA New Products.) Thomson acquired 31,000 employees, 17 factories, and the right to use the GE and RCA labels on everything from cordless telephones to videocassette recorders.

By taking over Thomson's Medical Systems business, GE took a giant stride in Europe and went from number two to number one in

Medical Systems worldwide. Until then GE's Medical Systems sales in Europe had been only $75 million a year, far less than the sales of Siemens or Philips. By purchasing CGR, which did $700 million a year in sales, GE automatically increased its annual Medical Systems sales in Europe to $800 million. By the summer of 1991 the sales of GE's European segment had grown to $1 billion a year.

Thomson was pleased to get GE's Consumer Electronics business. Gomez dreamed of making his $3 billion Consumer Electronics business, heretofore mostly in Europe, truly global. Thanks in part to the GE swap, Thomson became the top television maker in America and the third largest in the world.

For General Electric, the chance to dump its unprofitable $3 billion Consumer Electronics business was too good to pass up. With frequently small profit margins and the need to turn out new products requiring much investment every year, Consumer Electronics was, in the words of one GE executive, "a swamp, an absolute mess." Because of cheap labor costs, one country after another had managed to undercut American consumer electronics products. Welch had long believed that the Consumer Electronics business was a drag on his high-growth strategy. Yet events had forced him to hold on to it. He had always been turned off by consumer electronics because of its domination by the Japanese and its cutthroat price wars: Once in the early 80s, when prices dropped suddenly, GE's television makers lost a quick $50 million. In Welch's mind Consumer Electronics was the GE business that most deserved being on the auction block. Selling it, however, seemed less likely after GE acquired RCA's troubled $2.3 billion television and audio business as part of the 1986 merger.

The top brand name in American television sales, RCA had nonetheless been losing market share in the early 80s. Still, Welch took a gamble. Rather than discard the newly acquired RCA television plants and purchase sets in Japan, he lingered in consumer electronics even after the RCA merger. The gamble appeared to pay off. Within a year GE had become the world's largest seller of color televisions. With the rising exchange rate of the yen General Electric enjoyed a new advantage over Japanese firms. Therefore it terminated its sourcing agreements with its Japanese suppliers. And it gave responsibility for the annual production of 500,000 GE television sets to RCA's 1.7 million-square-foot Bloomington, Indiana, plant.

The GE-Thomson swap did not appeal to GE workers, who once again were being asked to switch owners. Shock mixed with rage swept through the Bloomington plant. GE had bought the plant from RCA only the year before, and now had sold it to Thomson. Workers kidded about having to wear tilted berets and to take lunch breaks with red wine. They ruefully called their new employers "the French connection." The jokes did little to comfort the 1,700 hourly workers who feared for their jobs.

"Most of us are real depressed," said Sierra-Sue Hill, who had worked in the plant since 1961. "GE told us they would make a go of the plant when they bought us from RCA. But we find out that we've been sold again." Employees said that they were willing to help their new boss, Thomson, take on the Japanese and East Asians. They had to confess, however, that knowing nothing about the French firm made them jittery. Unease about job security persisted. "I have a kid on the way, and this does not really help things," said one worker. "We have reason to be worried," said Jessie State, a 16-year veteran at the plant. "Cutting jobs, saving money, and competition is the whole ball of wax. And that is what it's like to be working in the 80s."[7]

To Welch's great discomfort and surprise, however, critics jumped all over the deal, just as they had when he sold Housewares in 1984. This time cynics insisted that Consumer Electronics, however little profit it generated, was a marvelous "image product" for GE, putting the company's name before the public, in effect offering free advertising. Wrapping themselves in the American flag, other doubters argued that manufacturing television sets was a patriotic duty. How could General Electric turn over the consumer electronics field to foreigners? (After the swap the only American manufacturer of television sets and video equipment was Zenith, though consumers could still buy Thomson equipment carrying the RCA brand name.) J. P. Donlon, editor of *Chief Executive* magazine, explained: "People do think there is such a thing as growing and nurturing a business where you may not be number one or number two. If you're out of certain businesses, you're out for good, and GE, having gotten out of electronics, may have actually ceded that market without a fight. GE is probably the only American company that could have given the Japanese a run for their money. There is a school of thought that GE, perhaps like IBM, should have done more than look at its Consumer Electronics business in purely clinical [read "bottom-line"] terms. At least IBM, being the largest maker of chips, went into alliances with Intel and others to make certain that chip production stayed largely in the United States."[8]

Once GE executives might have been swayed by these arguments. Certain product lines had been sacrosanct—and consumer electronics was one of them. Selling those product lines was once as unlikely and unacceptable as scrapping the famous GE logo—or changing the company's name!

Welch thought that the critics made no sense. Why let history and tradition dictate a company's business decisions? Why treat the past as if it had valuable lessons for the present? All that should matter was the bottom line. The rest was of no interest to Welch. He knew that the combined GE–RCA television business had been a severe cash drain and that the business had been a miserable number three or four in the global market, with almost no prospect of becoming the market leader. He knew too that Thomson's Television business, which faced similar market share difficulties, would benefit enormously from acquiring GE's Consumer Electronics business. True, in 1986 the combined GE–RCA Consumer Electronics business had generated $3.5 billion in revenues and had manufactured nearly 25 percent of all American televisions. But the Television business had lost $125 million in the early 80s and had little chance of becoming first or second in the world market.

Welch could not understand why everyone did not see the situation as he did: "Here you've got a global Medical business where you're number one. You're weak in Europe against Siemens—your major competitor. You've got a chance to get out of Consumer Electronics where you're a weak number five. You're getting battered. The industry as a whole isn't making much money. You can trade your position in that weak business to get a winning business in a global Medical business. And we end up with these crazy articles. Selling America's birthright. Flag-waving. It was outrageous, the stuff we went through. . . . Ludicrous, absolutely ludicrous."[9]

The sale of the Consumer Electronics business unleashed fresh feelings among the media that GE was behaving in the willy-nilly fashion of conglomerates, buying and selling indiscriminately, despite protests to the contrary. If it was willing to sell a sacrosanct treasure like Consumer Electronics, what would it do next? Financial analysts had been taken aback by Welch's bold downsizing of RCA, as he sold off six of its enterprises in little more than a year and reduced the number of RCA employees from 87,577 to 35,900 through asset sales or layoffs. Some of GE's stars had lost their glitter: Kidder appeared to be floundering. So did Calma, the computer-aided design firm, once flaunted as a centerpiece for the factory of the future but now losing millions annually. Michael Porter of the Harvard Business School thought that the ferment at GE had produced little more than an updated version of a 1970s conglomerate. Thomas Peters, author of *In Search of Excellence*, sensed that GE, once "the most glorious technology company of the century, has become a hodgepodge." Nicholas Heymann, then of Drexel Burnham Lambert, asked: "Who can figure out how things fall to the bottom line in Financial Services or what GE pays in taxes? Nobody. People have a tendency to say, 'I can't understand it.' "

Could the Welch strategy be flawed? Not at all, parried Welch. "If we had never done Calma, we'd be better off, but if we had a policy of no acquisitions, we never would have touched Employers Reinsurance or RCA."[10]

Had not all of this deal making drained GE's resources? No, said Welch. The record showed that RCA, Kidder, and Employers Reinsurance—three of the most important GE acquisitions—had added to GE's earnings in the very first year. Well, then, did the buying and selling not taint GE's image, making it appear more and more like that unwelcome monster—the conglomerate? "We're not even close to being a conglomerate," insisted Welch. "A conglomerate is a group of businesses with no central theme. GE has a common set of values. We have Crotonville, where we teach leadership. We have a research lab that feeds all of our businesses. We have all the resources of a centralized company. Yet we've been able to go in and out of businesses for more than a century and stay ahead of changing times."[11]

To underline his contention that GE was no conglomerate, Welch noted that all sorts of synergies existed at GE. This "integrated diversity," as he called it, gave General Electric a value that made it no mere ITT or Textron. The CEOs of those companies, in Welch's view, served largely as a bank and taxing authority for the businesses of the companies, not as a spark for finding and exploiting synergies.

General Electric, ever since it diversified beyond its core of electrical manufacturing businesses and into such "nonelectrical" businesses as Aircraft Engines and Financial Services, had always made a conscious effort to move human, financial, and technical resources around the company. What Welch did was to make the process more visible, to engage in it more assertively. In the past GE would transfer a manager from Aircraft Engines to Lighting if an opening arose. Under Welch, teams from different businesses moved back and forth to help one another out of problems. That is precisely what was done when Major Appliances discovered a defect in the rotary compressor that went into its refrigerators. Personnel from Aircraft Engines and Power Generation, considered the finest rotary motion engineers in the world, were brought to Louisville to look into the problem.

During the late 80s and early 90s Welch sought to extract as much integrated diversity from GE as possible. One business that was caught by the "diversity" bug was GE Capital. Bob Lewis, the senior vice president and general manager of GE Capital's Transportation and Industrial Financing business, oversaw the financing of all sorts of equipment built by other GE businesses, including Commercial Aircraft Engines, Locomotives, and Power Generation. It had not always been that way. Among other GE businesses, GE Capital had been a much misunderstood, much ignored segment of the company. Because GE Capital was not a hardware business—not in the manufacturing end—other GE businesses had regarded it with suspicion. It was Welch's appeal for integrated diversity that suddenly made GE Capital look more appealing to other parts of the company. Bob Lewis observed that Welch, "in forcing that interaction among the various businesses, has changed the way GE Capital thinks about itself and the way it operates. While it certainly isn't perfect, we do an awful lot with other GE components. We learn from them. They are a tremendous resource for us in trying to understand an industry or a segment."[12]

One of the great sources of synergy at GE was the Research and Development Center in Schenectady. Jack Welch, chemical engineer and high-tech zealot, pounced on the center when he took over, urging its scientists to find more business applications for their products. The results were incredible. By 1986, 150 major applications had resulted from the 250 technology projects that GE had undertaken in the four preceding years. For American industry as a whole, an average of 1 out of 10 research projects produces an application! Not only were the applications up. So were the synergies. The imaging technology developed for Medical Systems turned into a highly efficient piece of equipment for inspecting jet engines in the Aircraft Engines business. Highly sophisticated machining and coating techniques designed for the Aircraft Engines business wound up in Power Generation as well.

All of this cross-pollination—this integrated diversity —helped General Electric to shed that nasty image of a conglomerate. James C. Corman, manager of the Advanced Projects Laboratory at the GE Research and Development Center, credited Welch's streamlining of the company into 13 businesses as having been a major aid to the R&D scientists in their dealings with the businesses. Synergies became easier, he said. By way of illustration he mentioned emission control work of his laboratory that had resulted in applications for GE products in three businesses—Power Generation, Aircraft Engines, and Transportation. "These are three very diverse businesses," said Corman, "but in the area of emissions control they're very synergistic. We have had very active technical interchanges between those businesses. This was driven into us by Welch. His perception was that the 90s were going to be driven by environmental concerns. It was very evident that there was going to be a major pressure on the Power Generation business to meet tighter and tighter emission standards. He perceived that technology was eventually going to find its way into Aircraft Engines and Transportation systems for diesel locomotives."[13]

While Welch worried about the judgment of Wall Street, General Electric rolled up another successful year in 1988. Earnings reached $3.386 billion (for the first time GE had quarterly earnings of over $1 billion). Revenues topped $50 billion ($50.089 billion). Return on equity was 19.4 percent, up almost a point. GE Financial Services, with nearly $75 billion in assets, had profits of $788 million, 43 percent higher than its profits the year before.

With $1 billion in earnings in 1988, GE Aircraft Engines had an excellent year. After having been treated like an orphan when it first entered the commercial jet engine field two decades earlier, this GE business was now a true champion. Nearly all of the jet airliners built at that time, including the long-range Boeing 707 and the shorter-haul McDonnell Douglas DC-9, were powered by Pratt & Whitney engines. Despite success in developing high-thrusting jet engines for the military, GE had ranked a distant third after Pratt & Whitney and Rolls-Royce in selling the more fuel-efficient engines needed for passenger planes. When a GE agent tried to sell a new aircraft engine to Donald Nyrop, then president of Northwest Airlines, Nyrop pointed to a ceiling fixture and wisecracked, "Whenever I want a light bulb, I'll pick GE's. For jet engines, I'll stick with Pratt & Whitney!"

In later years GE Aircraft Engines had surged ahead by refining its military designs into a line of passenger jet engines. In 1988 it captured 63 percent of the market. The $6 million GE CF6 engine, used in jumbo jets, evolved from a design developed in the late 60s for the Air Force's giant C-5A cargo plane. That engine was the first to use a high-bypass technique in which a fan, working like a turbocharger in an automobile, pushes large quantities of air past the combustion core, producing far greater thrust.

Other GE businesses also did well in 1988. Aerospace had $640 million in earnings; Materials, $733 million; and Power Systems, $503 million. GE Medical Systems, thanks to its growing magnetic resonance business, had a good year (GE does not provide exact figures on this business). The magnetic resonance business returned profits for the first time following a $300 million investment during the previous nine years. GE had more CT–scanners and more MR systems installed worldwide than any other manufacturer. In a speech to share owners on April 27, 1988, Welch was able to say: "No one in the world has a set of powerful businesses like ours. They've never been stronger." Indeed, most GE businesses had become global, fulfilling one of Jack Welch's goals at the start of the decade. Some key acquisitions, alliances, and joint ventures had raised revenues from international operations to $11 billion and produced earnings of $2 billion—a 50 percent increase of earnings from two years earlier.

The General Electric brand name had always stood for high-quality, state-of-the-art technology, the latest design, the top of the line. If you went into a store and bought a GE dishwasher or electric range, a GE dryer or refrigerator, you had every reason to believe that they would work—and operate flawlessly—for a long time to come. Consumers depended on General Electric. That was why GE sold so many of these large appliances. The factories could not ship them fast enough. It had been like that for years. And it had been like that right up to the moment that the defect was discovered in the design of GE's razzle-dazzle top-mount refrigerator early in 1988. (Top-mount refrigerators have the freezer above the refrigerator section.)

No one at GE had wanted to believe that the top-mount refrigerators were anything but perfect. How could they not be? This particular model, with its highly touted rotary compressor, had been tested and had passed with flying colors. All had been smooth sailing from the very first day that GE decided back in 1986 to build the new model. The Major Appliances people hoped to demonstrate that GE could produce a refrigerator Americans would buy, that the refrigerator division would not have to go the way of manufacturers that had lost out to foreign competition.

GE thought the new top-mount refrigerators, which sold for over $1,000 each, would wipe the enemy out. The huge GE compressor plant in Columbia, Tennessee, turned out one compressor every six seconds—more than 1 million in its first year of operation. (Essentially the "heart" of the refrigerator, a compressor is the pump that creates cold air; as important to a refrigerator as an engine is to a car, it is by far the most expensive refrigerator component.)

In its 1987 annual report, GE boasted that the top-mount refrigerators were the product of GE's recent $238 million investment in its refrigerator business. "Assembled in highly automated factories in Kentucky and featuring rotary compressors manufactured at a newly opened plant in Tennessee, the refrigerators have been completely redesigned to meet consumer expectations for high quality, large capacity, and convenience." That was the GE line.

Meanwhile, according to a GE executive, low-level indications of trouble had begun to surface as early as the fall of 1987. One general manager passed on his suspicions, but senior executives apparently refused to believe that the problem was serious. It was not until January 1988 that a number of GE people believed that a serious problem existed. *The Wall Street Journal* reported that some engineers had spotted the flaw before the compressors had gone into production. But their supervisors and managers did not listen because they were under so much pressure from above. One engineer was quoted as saying: "It would have taken a lot of courage to tell [Jack] Welch that we had slipped off schedule." If someone was listening, it had made no impact on production. Not until the real danger signals began.

Appliances spokesman Jim Allen asserted that by the time some of the danger signals got to the top, they were not viewed with alarm. "We were trying to be fast to market at a time when the organization couldn't be fast, and that's when the problem occurred. We had a real tight time schedule to get this compressor on the market very quickly. The information flow was slow, our attempt to get to market was fast, and they clashed."[14]

At one point some of the large compressors began to fail. It did not matter that only a small percentage of the entire line had gone on the blink. Once word got around that GE was on the verge of a fiasco, Roger W. Schipke, senior vice president of Major Appliances, set up a team of design engineers that worked for weeks, often through the night. It soon became apparent that while only some compressors had failed, others could fail too.

In time the difficulty was discovered: excess wear in the cylinder. A lubricating device had failed. To get a sense of how monumental this problem was, one only had to listen to Richard Burke, vice president of manufacturing for Louisville, describe it as "the third-biggest industrial disaster," after the Exxon Valdez oil spill and the poison gas disaster at Bhopal. That was a bit of hyperbole: Since nobody died it was clearly not the third biggest industrial disaster.

Gary Rogers, then senior vice president for GE Appliances, believed that a more open organization would have led to discovery much earlier. "If the people above had gotten unfiltered messages from the people turning wrenches and doing tests on the compressor, we probably could have avoided that." Agreeing with him was Richard Burke, who believed "with every bone in my body" that someone saw an anomaly and tried to get through the bureaucracy but was stifled.[15] Jack Welch disputed all of this: "Any explanation of failure has a thousand fathers. So now there was always somebody that knew something. There was no one in the low management and up that knew a thing. There just couldn't have been. They were having reviews. They went out there and checked it all."[16]

The flaw was incredibly costly—$500 million. It sent Major Appliances' profits for 1988 into a tailspin—a mere $61 million as compared with $490 million the year before and $399 million the year after.

A team comprising GE people from Corporate Research and Development, Aircraft Engines, and Major Appliances unraveled the mystery. Ironically, a great deal of work had been put into building the factory so that the compressor could be produced. But one senior GE executive acknowledged that not enough testing had been done on the compressor itself.

After the defect was discovered, GE executives had to make a painful decision. Should GE replace only the compressors that had broken down? Or should it replace every compressor in the public's hands? Replacing only the broken ones would be cheaper. Only a small percentage of the compressors were expected to fail. However, GE officials thought it wrong to be expedient. For one thing, redesigning the flawed equipment would take months. For another, GE's reputation would be damaged if nothing were done about the refrigerators that had been sold, any of which might develop problems. It was costly, but 700 technicians were hired and trained to replace the compressors in all of the 1.5 million refrigerators that had been sold to the public. Each visit made by the technicians, which lasted an hour or so, cost GE $300 at first and $200 later.

In the spring of 1988 Roger Schipke made a controversial decision: Louisville would purchase 4.5 million reciprocating compressors from Singapore, Japan, and Italy. Layoffs at Columbia followed. Buying the reciprocating compressors proved expensive. Turning to foreigners for a major refrigerator part seemed demeaning. Morale plunged. "People were walking around with a black cloud over their heads," Richard Burke said.

The 1988 annual report tried to put as good a face as possible on the problem. "There is no safety issue involved, and we are in the midst of an active campaign to replace every one of these compressors with minimum inconvenience to our customers. Our aim is to come out of this situation with our reputation for customer support and satisfaction not only intact but—if anything—enhanced. While the cost to the company will be substantial, we have set up reserves to cover the estimated cost of the fix—and we still had a record performance in 1988." (Welch was talking about GE as a whole, not Major Appliances specifically!)

The compressor episode was a great embarrassment for Welch and GE, as it should well have been. In the new era of openness and candor such things were not supposed to happen. Indeed, the virtue of openness and candor was that they would enable GE to uncover flaws early and thus to prevent just this kind of disaster. Welch and others did their best to divert attention from what had in fact been a major blow to his revolution. By constantly noting that GE's resources and its integrated diversity had permitted the company to deal with the issue comprehensively and quickly, GE sought to downplay the true significance of what had happened: A design flaw that GE executives later admitted should have been spotted at the outset had cost a major GE business hundreds of millions of dollars, not to mention vast, immeasurable amounts of prestige.

This had to be one of those times when Jack Welch felt the frustration of running a company the size of GE. He acted as if the episode had not gotten to him. But, clearly, it had.

The "Wall Street" problem persisted into 1988. While the Dow Jones Industrial Average had rebounded 22.7 percent since the October 19 market crash of 1987 and the S&P 500 index had climbed 21.4 percent, GE shares had risen only 0.9 percent since then, closing on August 3, 1988, at $42.25, only slightly above their 12-month low of $38.375. Analysts said that GE shares were 36 percent below the previous year's high partly because portfolio managers had found the company too complex. A perception had formed that GE was not focused, not steady. On August 4 a front-page article in *The Wall Street Journal* suggested that, despite all the admiration for Jack Welch, a minority view had arisen: "It pictures GE as a growing collection of disparate companies in which a domineering personality substitutes for business focus. That it has worked so far, critics say, is no shield against a day of reckoning."

To Jack Welch, Wall Street's reaction was incredible. He had taken a company with sales of $26.8 billion and earnings of $1.5 billion in 1980 and by 1986 had increased its sales to $36.7 billion and its earnings to $2.4 billion. The *Wall Street Journal* quoted him as saying: "Maybe we are dull, but we ought to get points for being consistent. In any three-month period you can pick a better investment. But I don't think you can beat [GE] over a sustained period of time."

When pressed to explain why GE's return on equity was only now approaching its 1979 high of 20.2 percent, Welch exploded, threatening to walk out on the interview. Then he calmed down and answered: "From peak to trough, it's a 10 percent change! If you were talking about a 30 percent drop, maybe you'd have a discussion."

Early in 1989 Welch penned his annual letter to shareholders for the 1988 annual report. If Wall Street still had trouble understanding his business strategies, he would make one more attempt at explaining them—and defending them. The record showed that anyone who had held GE shares since the early 80s had enjoyed an average 20 percent return compounded, which was significantly better than the 15 percent annual return for the Standard & Poor's 500. That, of course, was "yesterday's performance," Welch admitted. The riddle was why GE stock in 1988 had not kept pace with the company's performance. In 1985 GE stock fluctuated between 27¾ and 36⅞; in 1986, between 33¼ and 44⅜; in 1987, between 38¾ and 66⅜.

"We're not sure why this is the case, but it occurs to us that perhaps the pace and variety of our activity appear unfocused to those who view it from the outside. The general media and the financial press have, for the most part, been more than favorable in their appraisal of our performance, but as we've picked up the tempo, especially in 1988, we began hearing: GE is 'too difficult to understand' and 'portfolio managing.' We even heard ourselves described by the 'C' word—*conglomerate*—with its usual pejorative corollary: 'Who knows what they'll buy or sell next?'

"You get the idea.

"Perhaps a strategy that appears to us crystal clear and consistent—because we live by it—seems less so to some of our key constituencies in the media and financial community.

"This is more likely a failure of our communication efforts rather than one of understanding."

Welch then used the annual report to explain the premises that had guided GE since 1981: "There is no denying we are a diverse company. We are not a computer, or oil, or auto, or steel monolith. . . . We have businesses ranging from plastics to network broadcasting to the manufacture of jet engines to reinsurance. But the strategy, the management philosophy that drives the company, is the essence of simplicity."

That strategy was based on two premises: being first or second in each of GE's businesses and developing the sensitivity, leanness, simplicity, and agility of a small company.

Welch acknowledged, but with a sense of disbelief, that the inability to understand GE arose in part from the GE-Thomson swap: "Suddenly the manufacture of televisions became something quintessentially American, like baseball. Some felt we had betrayed our heritage in our compulsion to 'do deals.' We heard phrases like 'un-American,' 'giving up on manufacturing,' 'exporting jobs.' " Welch, however, insisted that this swap was one of the most important, logical, and universally beneficial moves made anywhere in the 1980s."

CHAPTER THIRTEEN

"Rattlers and Pythons"

It was no accident that by the fall of 1988 Jack Welch was ready to begin the second phase of his revolution.

The first phase, conducted during the early 80s, had brought sweeping change to General Electric.

By the end of the first phase 350 businesses had been transformed into 13. The core electrical manufacturing businesses were no longer the focus of the company. High-tech and service segments were. Plants had been closed. Buildings leveled. Existing factories had been made state-of-the-art. New plants had been built. Layers of management had been scattered to the wind. In some respects General Electric seemed a smaller organization. In others, a larger one. It had fewer employees (down 25 percent to 300,000) but larger revenues and earnings. Jack Welch called these years "the hardware phase."

For all its help to GE's bottom line, this hardware phase had left many of GE's employees disconcerted. Many of their reference points had been cut from under them. They worked in new plants, had new bosses, new jobs. Frequently the jobs they had hoped to attain through promotion no longer existed. New people, meanwhile, had come along to compete for the fewer promotions that remained. These changes in GE's culture were disorienting to the survivors of the hardware phase. In the place of drift they wanted new reference points.

This became a serious issue for Jack Welch. GE's work force, though far smaller, would be expected to become even more productive. Yet it still trembled from the earthquake of downsizing. Now that it was clear that GE employees no longer had the promise of a job for life, how could Welch guarantee that the surviving work force would feel impelled to work as hard as before? The bitterness was reflected in a letter that Mark Markovitz, a GE engineer in Schenectady, wrote to the editor of *Fortune* magazine: "Jack Welch berates GE managers and professionals who must work 90 hours a week to get their jobs done. I know many of them. I am also one of them. We are spending time on customer service, engineering, development, manufacturing, cost reduction, quality control, and troubleshooting problems because many of our colleagues were nuked by Welch. Is this bureaucratic work?"[1]

Because of downsizing, it would be difficult to convince employees that their work burdens had diminished. But some way had to be found to make them feel less like overworked cogs in a machine, more like "owners" of the business. Delegating authority to them was a first step.

Traditionally, the managers had had the responsibility for improving productivity. That would now become the task of the men and women on the factory floors. A new concept. "For 25 years," a middle-aged hourly worker in the Major Appliances business declared, "you've paid for my hands when you could have had my brain—for nothing." It would not be easy for GE to abandon its tight supervision and control over employees. Managers would find it bizarre to suddenly let workers on the floor make decisions, contribute ideas, organize their workdays. As GE managers liked to say, they had been used to workers who parked their brains at the factory gate each morning.

The managers liked the old way. Workers were kept in their place through "a whips and chains environment," acknowledged Jim Carter, general manager of manufacturing in the Power Generation business. The "whips and chains" sometimes led to diffidence, sometimes to strikes. Never to anything beyond simmering tension. "All you got," recalled Jim Carter, "was what you specified and nothing else. None of the heart or the inspiration of the person."[2] Rather than joining hands in a common effort to improve the business, management and labor looked at each through a prism of venom. "We spent 90 percent of our time on the floor figuring out how to screw the management," an employee told Jack Welch in the spring of 1991. "That was all right, because you guys spent 95 percent of your time figuring out how to screw us."

Even at their most benign, the relationships between managers and employees lacked camaraderie. Managers dictated, employees obeyed. "General Electric," said Wally Croote, an area machinist in the Power Generation business in Schenectady, "didn't want any reaction from the employees. I used to come to work and stand in front of a podium and wait for the foreman to tell me where to work. I never said anything. If I had a problem with what I was working on, I stopped and sometimes had to ask three or four managers before I was allowed to change my routine. I would never catch myself going to the manager if I had a complaint. I went to the union. It wouldn't have mattered if Moses were the foreman. I disliked whoever it was because he wore a certain tie or whatever. I came to work with a certain amount of anger. I left thinking, 'Thank God, the day is over.' "[3]

Could Jack Welch assuage that anger? Could he use the brainpower of the Wally Crootes of General Electric? Would a pleasant workday make the floor worker more productive? Welch came to believe that relying on the gray matter of the labor force to solve the day-to-day problems on the factory floor might be the way to fire up employees emerging from the mayhem and anguish of restructuring. By making employees feel that they had a stake in the company's future, he might inject a spirit of common purpose that would impress outsiders. He remained troubled by Wall Street's assessment of his business strategies as ineffectual in creating focus and coherence at GE. Blaming himself, he sensed that more had to be done than write articulate letters to share owners in the annual report.

Welch had a tinge of regret that he had waited seven years to empower the GE work force. His one consolation was that starting earlier would have been impracticable. GE was in too much ferment, too many stomachs were churning each morning as workers wondered whether their jobs were on the line. Thousands of employees were leaving the place, thousands more were joining the GE ranks. Amid such uncertainty and sweeping change employees would not have been receptive to a corporate plan to make them more productive and give them cheer. Welch sensed this: "Empowering and liberating and exhilarating a bloated bureaucracy in the beginning would have been impossible. It would have produced a mixed message because we were shocking them. I'm not sure you could have sold that and been credible."[4]

The turning point for Jack Welch was that day in September 1988 during a routine visit at Crotonville. Standing in the Pit. The audience, comprising a mixture of upper and lower levels of GE management, bombarded him with questions different from those asked in the past. Not about where he was taking the company or how GE would fare in the near future. But hard-hitting, specific queries about the businesses. A Power Generation employee started. Someone in Aerospace chimed in. As always, Welch was candid. If he knew the answer, he gave it. If he did not, he said simply, "I don't know. I hope you'll have the courage to ask that tough question of somebody who can do something about it when you go home."

One member of the audience summed up the frustration that some other members had also experienced: "When I'm here at Crotonville, I understand what you're saying. I have a chance to talk about it. I get it. But back home it's not like that. It's not happening that way. We don't have this kind of dialogue with our managers."

Crotonville's Jim Baughman accompanied Welch on the helicopter trip to Fairfield. Both men were annoyed at having heard the same questions asked over and over again in the Pit, questions, they felt, that should have been addressed back home in the businesses. Welch thought hard about why there was no dialogue within those businesses. The answer was that General Electric remained hierarchic. Senior management talked to junior management. Junior management talked to subjunior management. Subjunior management talked to the workers, who were expected, not to engage in dialogue with their superiors, but simply to work. Was it not time to end such chain-of-command rigidity? To harness the obvious energy and talent that existed among the people who has asked tough questions in the Pit that day?

Turning to Jim Baughman, Welch began: "Jim, we have got to capture what happens here at Crotonville and push it across the whole company. We have to create an atmosphere where people can speak up to somebody who can do something about their problems. The reason these people say these unpleasant, difficult things to me is that they don't have an address. The trouble is, I can't impact their lives. I hear what they say all right. But I go home. I get on the helicopter. I don't do something to fix their problems."

The two men talked for a long time. The outcome of their conversation was the second phase in Jack Welch's revolution. The first had dealt with buildings and businesses—the hardware. This one affected people, and so Welch called it "the software phase."

The hundreds of thousands of GE employees who were both frustrated and willing to share their ideas presented an opportunity. Why not exploit that? The question was how. Crotonville's seminars were not enough. Nor were the videotapes that business leaders sent around to employees or the once-a-year speeches they gave. The time had come for managers and workers to talk with one another, to explore ways of improving the day-to-day workings of the business. Just as Welch had left his desk to stand in the Pit, he wanted GE's business leaders to go eyeball-to-eyeball with employees.

Definite risks to senior management existed. General Electric had prided itself on knowing how the company should be run. It had written the book on management strategies for decades. Was it genuinely prepared to turn over the "managing" of the company from the qualified managers to the unqualified "soldiers"? What were managers for if not to—manage?

Welch was prepared to take the risk. He did not believe that managers had a monopoly on ideas. He was convinced that most of the creativity and innovation, which drove productivity, lay in the men and women closest to the actual work.

Employees had to be able to make suggestions to their bosses face-to-face. And to get a response—on the spot, if possible. The wall of hostility had to come down. Welch and Baughman thought that the New England town meeting, which provided local citizens with a forum for dialogue with city fathers, might be an applicable model.

General Electric was going to hold town meetings! In all of its businesses. They were to last three days. Attending would be a cross section of GE's personnel—senior and junior managers, salaried and hourly workers. Fifty or so at a time. To break the ice, to get the ball rolling, to "facilitate" the dialogue, outside consultants and academics with expertise in business organization would be present and would encourage the audience to speak out frankly.

The first speaker was the business leader, who described the particular business, its strengths and weaknesses and how it fitted into the overall General Electric strategy. Over the next two days members of the audience were asked to evaluate four aspects of their business: reports, meetings, measurements, and approvals. Which of these made sense? Which did not? What could be eliminated so that the business shot itself in the foot a little less?

The intention was to get people to talk about what Jim Baughman called "the low-hanging fruit," the easy issues that could be picked off without too much effort. These were the nonsense habits that, with no one questioning their worth, had accumulated over the years and slowed down productive work. As employees grew comfortable in confronting the boss, the level of candor was supposed to increase, allowing tougher issues to be kicked around. In general, said Jim Baughman, the aim of the town meeting was "to work on how we can get more speed, simplicity, and self-confidence into this operation."[5]

All of this needed a name. Welch and Baughman sought to convey the idea of getting the nonsense "worked out" of General Electric, of the "workout" people engaged in to make themselves lean and agile, and of the problems that needed to be "worked out."

They called the program "Work-Out."

Some mistakenly thought the name was meant to justify further downsizing. They feared that Work-Out meant "taking out" people. To such carping Welch and Baughman said, "Indulge us."

In time, both the plan to create internal dialogue at forums within the company and the effort to import ideas from the outside came to be known as Work-Out.

Welch assigned Jim Baughman to launch Work-Out. In October 1988 the director of Crotonville recruited 25 experts on cultural change and organizational effectiveness to put in 40 days of consulting. These were the "facilitators." They had a dual purpose: to introduce Work-Out to the businesses and to customize it to the needs of each business. That same month the concept was introduced to GE's 120 officers; then, in January 1989, to the senior 500 people. Work-Out began two months later, in March.

By late 1988 the Work-Out concept was broadened to include ways of improving productivity, not just from within the company, but from outside the company as well. GE people were to search for companies that had come up with ways of improving productivity, ask the companies to share their knowledge, and incorporate the improvements into GE's operations. (The arrangement was reciprocal: The other companies learned about GE practices in return.) This effort became known as the "Best Practices" segment of Work-Out. If a company like Honda had figured out how to reduce its product development cycle substantially, might its "secret" not be of advantage to Aircraft Engines, Power Generation, Major Appliances or some other GE business? To pursue the Best Practices effort, Welch had to convince GE personnel that it was necessary to break out of the "not invented here" mold. At first 200 companies were selected as possible targets for Best Practices research. The list was later narrowed to roughly two dozen. GE officials would not confirm which companies the list included. They did note that, while GE had been expected to look at only Japanese companies or only American companies, in fact it had sought out a mixture of Japanese, American, and European companies. Press reports have noted that among the companies GE targeted were Sanyo, Ford, Hewlett-Packard, Toshiba, AMP, Xerox, Chaparral Steel, and Honda.

The "town meetings" began in March 1989. The participants were asked to dress casually—chinos and T-shirts—to blur distinctions between managers and workers. At first the invisible walls between the two groups still loomed tall, inhibiting free-flowing conversation. Then, in one session after another, someone would screw up his courage—and talk. Ask a question. Raise a problem. To his surprise the manager listened, quietly, patiently. He seemed genuinely sympathetic, not at all disturbed that one of the privates was challenging a major. After the ice had been broken, someone else in the audience caught on and raised his hand. Again the manager listened—and responded. Soon hands were raised all around the room.

Not every experience went smoothly. Especially when senior managers seemed to have trouble explaining themselves. Fran Ahl, a spray painter in the Large Steam Turbine Generator facility in Schenectady and a member of Local 301's executive board, remembered the first time GE executives visited the union hall with the first proposals about Work-Out. "We were always leery when the company came forward with a proposal and wanted to sit down and talk about it, because in the last eight years we've gone through some awfully hard times here." However suspicious, the union board listened. Ahl noted how much difficulty the executives had in explaining what they planned to do. "If somebody can't tell me what he wants me to do, it's awfully hard to get involved. Employee empowerment was something we weren't familiar with."

Nonetheless, the Schenectady Work-Out effort began in the fall of 1990. Hourly workers were pulled out of shops. The first sessions did not go well. To the union members who attended, Work-Out seemed little more than a glorified opportunity for workers to squeal on one another: Someone had tattled on a person who read the newspaper when he should have been working. Someone else had accused an associate of "hiding behind his machine" all day. "From that day on," said Fran Ahl, "we took Work-Out to be a rat session. People did not want to get involved."[6] Was it possible to prevent the town meetings from degenerating into nothing more productive than pointing out who was lazy or who was calling the boss an idiot?

This was a major test of the program. In time, Fran Ahl and his union colleagues began to sense that management's purpose was to get rid of bad work habits, not to uncover laggards.

The facilitators wanted candor. So they laid down no formal rules.

At early Work-Out sessions in GE Supply the participants broke work issues into two categories. They called them "rattlers" and "pythons." Someone noted that rattlers made a good deal of noise and were immediately recognizable. It was therefore easy to find and shoot them. Pythons, however, made no noise and lay entwined in trees. Thus it was far more difficult to eradicate them. These categories appeared to neatly represent GE, which, like pythons entwined in trees, was often tied up in knots by its bureaucracy. The idea was to untie the knots by attacking a variety of problems, easy and hard. The easy problems that could be solved at once became rattlers. Pythons were the hard problems that needed more time and effort.

Jim Baughman recalled a rattler. It occurred at a factory where a young woman who put out a popular and well-received plant newspaper had encountered a key frustration that she had kept to herself. She waited for Work-Out to fire away at her boss.

"Look," she said after raising her hand at a town meeting of her business, "it takes me seven signatures every month to get my plant newspaper released. You all like the plant newspaper. It's never been criticized. It's won awards. Why does it take seven signatures?"

Her boss looked at her in amazement. "This is crazy. I didn't know that was the case."

"Well, that's the way it is," she replied.

"OK," the general manager said, "from now on, no more signatures."

The newspaper editor smiled.

A factory worker tossed out a rattler at a town meeting of another business.

"I've worked for GE for over 20 years, I have a perfect attendance record, I've won management awards. I love this company. It's put my kids through college. It's given me a good standard of living. But there's something stupid that I'd like to bring up."

The man's work, operating a valuable piece of equipment, required him to wear gloves. The gloves wore out several times a month. To acquire another pair he had to call in a relief operator or, if none was available, shut his machine down. He then had to walk to another building, go to the supply room, and fill out a form. Then he had to track down a supervisor of sufficient authority to countersign his request. Only after he returned the countersigned form to the supply room was he given a new pair of gloves. Frequently he lost as much as an hour of work.

"I think it's stupid."

"I think it's stupid too," said the general manager in front of the room. "Why do we do that?"

From the rear came the answer: "In 1973 we lost a box of gloves."

"Put the box of gloves on the floor, close to the people," the manager ordered. Another rattler shot.

At the Research and Development Center in Schenectady an employee attending a Work-Out session asked why managers were given special parking places. No one could think of a good reason. The managerial privilege was rescinded.

At a Work-Out session for the company's communications personnel, a secretary asked why she had to interrupt her own work to empty the out tray on her boss's desk. Why, on his trips outside his office, could he not drop the material on her desk? No one had a good answer, so a few steps of unproductive effort were scratched from the secretary's routine.

At a Work-Out session involving Power Generation personnel someone noted that the Purchasing Department chose welding equipment without consulting the welders who used it. As a result equipment inappropriate for certain tasks had sometimes been chosen.

Why not have welders join the purchasing team when it visited vendors to order equipment?

Without hesitation the manager said "Fine."

Changing such procedures—eliminating the seven signatures needed for the newspaper, removing parking privileges for managers, or even asking bosses to empty their own out trays—required little time or study to implement. These were examples of Jim Baughman's low-hanging fruit.

But as employees dealt with even the trivial, easy issues, Work-Out was giving them an increased sense of participation in their jobs and a good feeling about themselves.

Mary Byrum liked that feeling. She was a clerk in the payroll department in the Major Appliances business in Louisville when she attended a Work-Out session in May 1990. Most of those present were members of middle or upper management. At first, intimidated, she was reluctant to talk in front of her bosses. When she finally did speak up, she found that she was good at it. She grew comfortable talking to upper management. "Maybe I was born for this moment. I got so many compliments on my speaking that I thought: 'Golly, maybe I have a talent for it after all.' " Later she took a Dale Carnegie course in public speaking and went back to school.

She also made a specific contribution to productivity. In the course of the town meeting she mentioned the problem of surplus equipment gathering dust in many offices due to downsizing. It had been obvious to her that the equipment should be utilized, but no one had been prepared to make the decision. Byrum was selected to serve on a committee to examine what to do with the equipment. Suddenly she was helping to shape decisions. She enjoyed that. "Work-Out definitely impacted my life. It broke down all the barriers. I was impressed that the managers accepted my ideas." Within the first two months she and the committee had saved $65,000 by redeploying the equipment to other offices. And that would continue, Byrum said, "until we run out of equipment or"—and she laughed heartily at this thought—"until we quit downsizing." By the fall of 1991 Mary Byrum had become a consumer service representative.[7]

At one stage Welch and Baughman realized that GE might be able to get productivity improvement ideas, not just from the company's Mary Byrums, but from customers as well. At first glance it seemed preposterous that customers would be willing to advise GE on how to improve productivity. But some were.

At one session in 1990, officials of a hospital that was a customer of the Medical Systems business objected to the time it took GE to deliver a certain piece of relatively inexpensive equipment. GE discovered that nearly half of the delivery time was devoted to checking the hospital's credit. For a multimillion-dollar item, that caution would have been justified, but not for this item. GE dropped the credit check at once.

A python appeared at a Power Generation Work-Out. Attending the session were personnel in turbine manufacturing, sales, and field service. One gripe came from field service engineers who questioned why they had to write 500-page reports. The reports detailed the work to be performed and forecast which turbine parts might need to be replaced the next time an outage occurred. Knowing that no one looked at the reports, the field service engineers often turned them in as much as six months late, if at all. This problem required some time to resolve. New equipment had to be purchased. Eventually the lengthy reports were scrapped and in their place field personnel, using laptop computers, prepared briefer, more up-to-date reports that were turned in immediately—and were read! The new procedure enabled the power generation business to forecast and produce the parts customers would need.

Rattler or python, easy or hard, the problems that cropped up at Work-Out sessions led not only to productivity improvements but to changes in the way GE employees felt about themselves and about one another. In a number of cases management-labor relations thawed. New feelings of self-esteem and pride in work welled up in factory floor laborers. Managers came under new pressures but responded well. Forced to stand in front of their employees at town meetings, they had to be on their toes, to look afresh at their business strategies.

Work-Out took on its own dynamic. "We lost control," admitted Rodger Bricknell, general manager for continuous improvement at the Power Generation business in Schenectady. "And that's what we wanted to do. A year ago people would call me up and ask permission to hold a Work-Out session on some problem. Now I get phone calls from Fairfield congratulating me on this great Work-Out that I didn't even know was going on."[8]

An unexpected dividend surfaced during Work-Out sessions. Out of the candor came a fresh reality: Managers and employees now had more or less equal access to information about the business. That had not been the case before. Often employees kept problems to themselves; middle-level managers were often afraid to report difficulties to superiors; managers were often kept in the dark. This new enlightenment and information sharing made Work-Out enormously appealing to Jack Welch. "If we get the same data, and we're all within [a similar] IQ band, we will come out the same door." Emerging from "the same door" was a key to success in business, according to Welch.[9]

Jack Welch became Work-Out's most ardent devotee. Visiting a GE plastics plant in Holland in June 1991, he spoke with 30 senior managers, one of whom declared: "Jack, you've been coming here for 20 years. You bought this land. You started this plant. I want you to know something. It's not as much fun as it was 10 years ago."

Welch pulled a rabbit out of his hat.

"Let me tell you what I'm going to do about your comment. It's 3 o'clock now. At 3:30 I'm getting on a plane, going back to Paris for dinner tonight, and I'm not going to think about this plant for a year, probably until I come back again. So I'm the last guy in the world who's going to solve this problem.

"But since you're a leader of this business and you were here 10 years ago, why don't you get 30 others who have been in this plant for the last 10 years and why don't you have a Work-Out for three days?

"List on the left-hand side of the page all the things that made it great fun 10 years ago, and on the right all the things that are inhibiting that fun today. And why don't you guys fix it so this place becomes fun again?"

As Welch parted, he said: "The test will be whether you do it or not."

To prevent Work-Out from adding to GE's bureaucratic headaches, Welch ordered that none of the town meetings be documented. It seemed an odd decision. After all, valuable ideas emerged and someone ought to be taking notes. Welch was adamant. Some recoiled. After one town meeting in Lighting the general manager insisted that a follow-up report be put in writing. The audience erupted. Heeding Welch's dictate, one employee yelled, "No, don't do that.

You're just going to end up with more bureaucracy." The report was never filed. Welch also urged GE managers to resist adding up how many Work-Out sessions they had arranged. "Don't ever tell me you had 41 Work-Outs. I don't want to know." If the program were working, Welch said, it would show up in the only measurement that counted: increased productivity. Still, businessmen rated success and failure in quantitative terms. Some managers could not help boasting of how many Work-Outs they had under their belts.

In the early summer of 1991 Work-Out was just over two years old. Welch was immensely pleased with its results thus far. "If we are going to win world economies, we've got to take the energy and the passion of an irreverent, American melting-pot work force where we have Catholics, Italians, blacks, whites, Hispanics, whatever, and unleash them. If you have a culture that is numbing and boxing them in, you play to all the weaknesses. The Japanese can have this numbing culture with their uniformity and homogeneity, and it's their strength. If we tried to do that, we'd just box in a group that doesn't want to be boxed in." Letting employees speak their minds, Work-Out was the perfect antidote to bureaucracy. It released tensions and frustrations. It forced people to come up with better ideas for doing their work. Most important, it kept workers from "taking a punch in the wall at night."[10]

A few months later, in the fall of 1991, when Welch spoke in the Pit at Crotonville, he was just as exuberant about the program, a mixture of a football coach at halftime and a preacher at the pulpit. "What employees like about Work-Out so far is the right [to bitch], but they don't like the responsibility of taking it through the system and fixing the problem. Normally you'd be empowered here [in Crotonville]. But if you were only one person taking back the message to your business, your boss would say, 'Take what you heard and shove it.' [Laughter.] With Work-Out there's a group that's involved. The group has to get together and fix the problem. I'll be on the helicopter by 6 P.M. and be out of here. You've got to take the responsibility. [He banged his fist on a desk.] To take the ball. We've got to yell at leaders. I'm here to empower you, but if you're chicken, afraid, it's not going to work. If you sit and gripe, it won't work. If you take it on, it will be the most exciting place in the world."[11]

How long would it take for Work-Out to be used throughout the company? Welch guessed a decade. Workers were far more inclined than managers to embrace the program. The chairman found that out firsthand when a GE technician showed up at his house to install an appliance.

"The guys at my level understand what you're talking about," the technician told Welch. "We'll be free to enjoy our work more, not just do more work. And we can do more work on our own."

Welch broke into a smile.

He should have waited. "Do you know how our supervisors interpret the program?" the technician asked.

"They tell us: 'You hear what Jack Welch is saying? You guys better start busting your butts.' "

As the business community and the media became cheerleaders, Welch realized that no matter how long it took, he was on the right track. Some predicted that the Work-Out concept would become a major feature of the American workplace in the 90s. GE was frequently asked for information about Work-Out; even the secretary of commerce called to inquire. The *Washington Post* enthusiastically described Work-Out as perhaps Welch's most unusual effort to remake the company, "because it strikes right at the heart of GE's corporate culture and represents a significant rethinking in the way companies are managed."[12]

After a while it was not clear whether Work-Out belonged to Jack Welch or to the businesses: A variety of nuances crept into the ways that managers and employees incorporated the program. Welch was thrilled. "Thank God," he said. "All of it is just an idea. The businesses have got to put it in practice."[13]

Power Generation discarded the designation Work-Out. The management in Schenectady had bowed to a union complaint that Work-Out signified job reductions. "It was what you guys did during the 80s," said one union man. "You took work out of this place. We've had enough of that program." So at Power Generation Work-Out was called "High Involvement." Welch did not object.

When the Work-Out program was transmuted, as in Schenectady, Welch took that as a sign of affection for it. At Power Generation managers and employees decided to shift from the town meeting approach to one that was less "event-oriented" and more enduring. Toward that end they created High Involvement work teams comprised of 15 to 20 factory floor workers who took on the responsibility of running their segments of the business, distancing themselves as far as possible from managers. By the fall of 1991 these teams had become an increasingly visible part of the GE workplace.

High Involvement teams played a vital role in reshaping the Major Appliances business in Louisville. That business had been reeling since the rotary compressor disaster in 1988. "Morale," in the colorful phrase of Bob Colman, manager of human resources for GE Appliances, "was dogmeat."[14] Gary Rogers took over as head of Major Appliances in the spring of 1990 and brought a breath of fresh air to it. Rogers was intent upon implementing Jack Welch's policy of openness. He thought that the old bureaucracy was good for controlling things but bad for making fast decisions.

Fast decisions, said Rogers, were vital because the industry remained so competitive. The industry's growth was expected to be only 2 percent into the mid-90s. The industry was changing, with fewer independent appliance dealers and more megadealers. "You have a huge retail share battle. Everybody's out there trying to sell every appliance they can. If you take your eye off the ball or you don't pick up a trend somewhere, you can get hammered in a matter of days. So you've got to be fast enough to pick up a change and react to it so you don't get killed."

Rogers candidly offered an example. In 1991, despite slow sales in appliances, GE had not cut its prices. Its competitors, however, had reduced their prices and taken some market share away from GE. "We've been fighting to get it back ever since. And we are. But had we picked it up sooner and reacted to it faster, we'd be better off today than we are."[15]

To achieve that speed Louisville pressed on with Work-Out and Rogers encouraged his associates to take an interest in it. Hence Richard Burke, vice president of manufacturing, sought an explanation of the program early in 1989. He heard that the silicone products facility in Waterford, New York, had started the program. He flew there and took Norm Mitchell, the union head, with him.

"We watched this Work-Out, and it was like magic," remembered Burke. "It was unbelievable." The two men attended a session and sat fascinated as facilitators got employees in the audience to put their ideas on a blackboard and to reduce them to a few key ideas. Later in the day the employees presented the key ideas to management. "We watched this whole thing, and lights were going on and bells were going off for both of us. We came back to Louisville and said, 'OK, how the hell are we going to get this thing started?' "

Town meetings took place, but Rogers quickly realized their limitations. For workers to feel empowered, they had to experience empowerment at all times during work, not simply during some meeting. It was vital to move, as Bob Colman noted, "from the more unnatural places and acts [at town meetings] to more natural acts and places." Colman merely meant that as a vehicle for solving minute-by-minute problems, the town meeting was less natural and practical than the factory floor.

Veteran union men harbored deep suspicions about the factory floor teams. They had bitter memories of how similar efforts had been tried in the 60s to deflate the power of the unions. They also sensed that the unions would hold less sway over the workers once the workers felt that management was not only listening to them but also giving them the authority to make decisions. Who needed a union if the workers no longer required protection? Once the High Involvement teams were in place, what would happen to the notion, so important to the unions, that each employee knew precisely what the dimensions of his job were? Now team members were expected to help one another out, in effect to blur the distinctions between job functions. What was more, newly empowered employees carried out a brand-new job function: thinking! Should they not be paid for the "extra work"? For all these reasons, the unions were suspicious at first, but in time they came around.

Rogers and Burke began with a steering committee. Then Work-Out committees were placed in each plant to come up with topics for steering committee approval. By the fall of 1991 each plant committee was evolving into a new organization comprising a plant manager, an operations manager, and some self-supervised teams. Richard Burke was plainly excited by all of this. "It would bring tears to your eyes" to see the teams in action, he said.

Thanks to the new system, Burke said, goals were met. "We were supposed to hit 1,440 refrigerator units a shift, two shifts a day, 2,800 a day in March 1989. These were 14- and 16-cubic-foot, no-frost refrigerators, midsize, sold under GE, Hotpoint, Sears, and RCA labels. The 16-cubic-foot one cost $499. We hit the objective on March 12. We met every cost objective, every quality objective, and we got a wonderful refrigerator. And we can't make enough of them. I just love it." By 1991 the plant was producing 747,000 units a year; and, Burke said, it could have sold 900,000 if it had been able to make that many.

Burke was ecstatic about the Work-Out program. "It uncovers all kinds of crazy stuff we were doing in this business. It's a remarkable tool. You can use it anywhere."[16]

Work-Out had trickled down to the GE's dishwasher facility, with its 1,300 employees and its 18 acres of manufacturing floor space. One million dishwashers moved out every year. The place was noisy as the parts clanked along the assembly line. The men and women on the line seemed cheerful, though their jobs appeared repetitive. Television screens—called in GE language "quality monitors"—hung at different spots and reported on the five most frequent defects each hour and each shift.

High Involvement teams routinely held meetings to deal with what the quality monitors were kicking out. Reviewing the three most frequent defects, the teams tried to correct them right away. "Quality was good before," said Carl Liebert, plant manager for the dishwasher production operation, "but with the start of Work-Out it really became a rallying point for the production worker."[17]

At the Power Generation business too, Work-Out was changing the GE work force. The program, whose overall aim was to make the employees more productive, could not have come at a better time. Of late the business had come under increasing pressure to keep its turbines competitive. That depended in part on keeping maintenance costs as low as possible. So far it was doing well. Maintenance costs on its Frame 7 were from five to 14 times lower than its competitors' machines of similar power. But GE was coming under increasing pressure from rivals. It searched for ways to make its workers even more productive. Work-Out supplied an answer.

To implement Work-Out at Power Generation five vice presidents began working in the spring of 1991 with "Empowered Process Ownership" teams, the equivalent of the High Involvement teams in Louisville. Such teams had been operating in other GE facilities for two years. But Schenectady had a difficult union environment, so it took longer to organize them there. Management wanted to make sure the unions were aboard.

Though Jack Welch had asked GE Work-Out organizers to steer clear of the numbers, the people at Power Generation happily noted that as of the fall of 1991 roughly a quarter of its 10,000 employees had been through Work-Out sessions. Several hundred Empowered Process Ownership teams with cycle time and quality as their key concerns were in place.

One of the great success stories of Work-Out at Schenectady involved customer Work-Outs. David Genever-Watling, senior vice president for industrial and power systems, recalled how nervous some at GE were about discussing work problems with customers. Yet Genever-Watling was convinced that much good could come out of such discussions. Numerous sessions were held. Sometimes the customers were brutally honest. They told GE management that the company excelled at selling a product but not at servicing it. "We can't figure out what to do when things go wrong," they said. One person had to be called to get a generator serviced; a second, to get a steam turbine serviced; a third, to get a gas turbine serviced. Thanks to Work-Out, a new system was devised: Seventy customer service managers were placed around the country, each of whom was assigned to a specific customer. Now a customer had only one address no matter what broke down.

Suppliers were included in some of the Power Generation business teams to help design a completely new gas turbine. In this way GE was able to come up with the turbine in eight months. The old system would have taken four years! The trick was that GE used components currently made by its suppliers—instead of specifying new components. Thanks to ideas generated in Work-Out sessions, the business now sources 90 percent of its materials from a mere 170 suppliers, unusual for a company of General Electric's size. And it had reduced the cycle time on ordering components from these vendors from 36 days to only 2 days.

Quality had improved as well. In the old days managers had to confirm many thousands of workstation instructions in order to achieve acceptable standards of quality on the turbines. To attain speed and added quality GE turned quality control over to High Involvement employee teams on the floor. "Not only is this going to drive the process more quickly," commented Rodger Bricknell. "There's no way these people are going to make life miserable for themselves by creating a paper bureaucracy. They're going to create a sensible work environment that combines quality with the speed and simplicity that we need to survive in the 90s."

Work-Out unleashed a set of practices in Power Generation that would have been taboo in the old GE. One such practice was calling in outside consultants. To reduce production cycle time GE sought out the consulting firm of Booz, Allen, which worked with engineering personnel. "The idea of bringing Booz, Allen in," said Bricknell, "is something that would have been unthinkable in the old culture. We thought then that we were the kings of the hill. The idea that anybody had anything to offer GE was unthinkable. We had to be the best of the best at everything, and the idea of taking a fresh look was just not in the old culture".[18]

Welch's stress on candor and openness had gotten through to these people. In the fall of 1991 GE arranged for members of some High Involvement teams to meet with the author. Before the session Jim Carter, general manager of manufacturing, confessed, "I don't have any idea who's going to be in that room," as he pointed to the room in which the members were gathering. "That's part of the environment change. Two years ago I would have known everyone in the room. I would have talked to everyone in the room. I would have known what they were going to say."[19]

Four High Involvement teams sat around a large conference table. A few people appeared eager to return to the factory floor. First the teams discussed the difficult times during downsizing.

"It was almost as if we were the patient going through an operation," said James O. Pollock, a manager in the finished machine area, "and Jack Welch was the skilled surgeon. Certainly there was a lot of pain and a lack of understanding for what we were going through." Pollock had been in the wire mill for two years, in the foundry for the next eight years. These two businesses comprised seven buildings that had been leveled. The buildings had been replaced by flat parking lots.

Most of the bitterness created by downsizing was gone. "Now," said Pollock, "we're at the recovery stage where it still hurts a little bit. You still remember the operation, but you can see things getting better. We trimmed out inefficiency, fat; we took out layers of management and bureaucracy. Things really are simpler, faster, more effective.

"I feel a lot more involved in running a business today. In the past everybody had their little niche and everybody stayed in that niche. The emphasis today is to find a way to expand above and beyond those niches, to help the other guy, to solve problems. Together as a team we're a whole lot smarter and more effective than as individuals. It really is starting to feel good. There's an excitement about coming to work to see where we can contribute, to find out what things we can improve."[20]

When problems arose on the factory floor, members of the High Involvement teams tried to deal with them at once, without referring to management. Wally Croote, one of the team members, recalled: "We might not even talk to our manager about a problem. Once it gets up to his level, it's a pretty dandy good one. We now try to get together and figure things out before they get to a certain level. On the floor we try to weed out problems. If we have one, we all get together, if it's only for five minutes. We shoot the shit a little bit. The thing is: Don't slow this process down.

"Now I may raise a problem at our Monday morning meetings or go talk to the manager in his office. A few years ago I wouldn't even want to be there. Once you start thinking about these guys just bullshittin' back and forth with you, you actually see that they have families and you start to let loose a little bit." Five years ago Croote would not have talked to a manager more than once or twice every few years. Now he may talk to one three times a day. "I feel comfortable going in to see a manager. If a problem isn't ironed out at a Monday morning meeting, it continues up the chain of command. Normally about 85 percent of our problems have been dealt with and ironed out at this Monday morning meeting."[21]

Fran Ahl, the spray painter and union man who had been less than enthusiastic about Work-Out at the start, was by now a zealous convert. He liked the idea that employees could "control their own destiny without someone hanging over their backs and constantly hounding them. They know what they have to do when they come to work in the morning. No one has to tell them what to do. They go to their punch presses and assembly areas and winding areas. They don't need to be told."[22]

If Work-Out was so beneficial, why had it taken so long to implement? The answer came from Wally Croote: "A few years before it started to get tough and the businesses were closing, we all thought we had the world by the ass. Nothing was going to change. We were going to live here in this big 10,000-person community, and nothing would ever change. GE will always be here, and that's it.

"Then along came Jack Welch, and he seemed to line us all up on a fence like crows. He had a bag of rocks, and he took us off one at a time. And I was one of the crows, and I was angry.

"OK. It was getting close to the time that a rock would be sent in my direction. But we all woke up and saw that he was trying to do something with a business that was virtually going under because of competition. It took a little time for all of us to figure that we're going to have to try to help this man out. Now we feel really good about what the man's done. If he hadn't done something, if he hadn't torn those foundries down, torn the motors building down and all these buildings I worked at, most likely our competition would have done it for us. So what's he done? He's saved my job. I'm back up on the fence now. And no stones are being thrown. Matter of fact, we're putting more crows up there and I feel damn good about it."[23]

Ed Synfelt, a Louisville manager, thought that if a High Involvement plan had been in effect in earlier years, many jobs might have been saved. "The energy that was put into the mistrustful relations between employers and employees could have been diverted to more productive uses. Our customers today prefer to work with people who are involved in 'high involvement,' because they know they'll probably get more of a quality product."[24]

While the town meetings and the High Involvement teams looked inward to improve productivity, the Best Practices effort—a major innovation of the Work-Out program—looked outward. Its purpose was to uncover how certain companies became more productive. Best Practices teams went to each of these companies and "lived" in them for a week or two. It was not a one-way street. GE reciprocated by explaining the measures it had employed to step up productivity. GE quickly realized that highly productive companies usually achieved their results, not because they had specific "secrets," but because they had a coordinated, internally coherent view of how to become more productive. In-depth studies of two dozen companies proceeded quietly. A report on each company was then written, organized around a number of themes. Senior GE executives then were shown these reports.

In December 1989 the Best Practices effort moved into high gear. That month three-day workshops took place to pass on to GE employees what the Best Practices teams had learned from their visits to the targeted companies. Each of the workshops was attended by 10 employees from 10 GE businesses. The first theme was "Process over Product." Why had certain companies devised such efficient business processes? What could be learned from those processes?

Another theme was "Partnering with Suppliers." How did a company get on well with its suppliers? This topic had become of growing importance to GE as it turned increasingly to outsiders for its raw materials. With customers making new, tougher demands and competition sharper, GE hoped that good relations with its suppliers might induce them to reduce the cost of their raw materials. Thanks to Best Practices, GE had started to invite suppliers to its Work-Out sessions in Louisville.

The most exciting discovery from Best Practices research had to do with reducing the time it took to deliver a product to the customer. Some GE businesses were better suited than others to pursue this goal. Plastics and Major Appliances were especially well suited to what General Electric called "Quick Response."

The Quick Response effort began when Serge Huot, a French Canadian and the manufacturing manager of Camco, the GE appliance subsidiary in Canada, was working on a Best Practices study. As part of that study, he discovered that a New Zealand firm had achieved some remarkable reductions in cycle time. He and a few senior people flew down under to see for themselves. Huot and his team remained in New Zealand for a week. Upon his return Huot introduced Quick Response into Camco. Gary Rogers, then head of Major Appliances, visited Huot and was dazzled by the Quick Response effort. Within a short time Rogers had introduced the concept into the entire Major Appliances business. The excitement trickled up to corporate as well. Welch decided to push Quick Response throughout GE (except for businesses in which it had no application, such as

Financial Services). Jim Baughman was ecstatic about what Huot had done: "A guy in Canada gets religion, gets the spirit, finds out a company that makes sense to him, that's credible to him. He gets on a plane. He absorbs, he brings it back on his own authority, he doesn't have to ask anybody. That's boundaryless, that's speed, simplicity, and self-confidence."[25] (Huot later became head of manufacturing for GE's Medical Systems business in France.)

One of the first major trials of Quick Response occurred in Louisville. Although GE had the best product delivery system in the appliance industry, it wasted a great deal of money by virtue of its inability to forecast inventory accurately. Sometimes the situation grew so severe that GE had to rent public warehousing to store its products for a couple of months during the high-demand summer period. Cutting product cycle time dramatically could lower inventory, saving huge amounts of money.

At the time Quick Response began, it had been taking an average of 18 weeks for GE appliances to be produced and delivered to the distribution centers. Once a customer ordered an appliance from a store it took 48 hours for a distribution center to deliver the product to the store. The problem, then, was how to cut the time it took between an order, scheduling the plant to manufacture appliances, and their delivery to the distribution centers. Of the 18 weeks, fully 6 were spent in forecasting the number of appliances to manufacture. Another 10 weeks were required to make the appliances and 2 weeks to get the appliances from the factory to the distribution centers.

The forecasting not only took far too long. It was also wildly inaccurate—and no one quite knew why. Broken down to specific model numbers, the forecasts had an average error rate of 20 percent at best, 50 percent at worst. The forecasts were all but useless. Because of these poor forecasts it became necessary to build up protective inventories.

To reduce those inventories and save money Gary Rogers aimed at instituting Quick Response in Louisville as of June 1990. He encountered skeptics who considered it hopeless to try to do this in an operation on the scale of Appliance Park. These GE cynics had not been impressed by the attempts of other companies to improve production cycle times. The breakthrough came with the news that Quick Response had worked wonders at Camco. Although that appliance facility was only $\frac{1}{10}$ the size of the Louisville facility, its experience seemed relevant. Dubious employees from Louisville visited Camco to learn more. "The biggest problem you'll have," they were told, "is mind-set. Convincing your people that it's doable."

Despite such cautionary notes the cynics came back convinced it could work.

In the summer of 1990 Rogers asked for assistance from staffers at Corporate Business Development, Corporate Audit, and Corporate Management Development. These people spent nearly a year training Louisville personnel in process mapping, a technique used to identify and then streamline the steps involved in business operation processes. Process mapping teams were set up in factories. The teams learned that for Quick Response to work, it would have to take into account, not just manufacturing and distribution processes, but everything from design to service. Very quickly efficiencies were introduced. Suppliers were asked to deliver raw materials more speedily. GE personnel increased the amount of spare parts on hand. Assembly lines were changed over more rapidly so that the factory could move from the production of one model to another more expeditiously. The six-week forecasts were cut to monthly ones which were updated each week.

By the fall of 1991 all nine of Louisville's manufacturing plants had made significant progress toward implementing Quick Response. The electric range facility had gone from a 10-week cycle to a three-day cycle. That was the best. Dishwashers had the cycle down to 6 days; home laundry, to 15; refrigerators, to 12. By the end of 1991 the 18-week cycle had been cut to 5 weeks. The savings in money was enormous: In September 1991 warehousing and other costs were $280 million lower than they had been the previous September.

At the plant in which electric ranges were made, 1,000 employees were turning out 2,300 ranges a day in a million-square-foot facility. The range facility had been chosen as the pilot for Quick Response because it had few product lines, its products required few spare parts, and it was the least automated of the nine Louisville plants.

With deadlines so drastically compressed, any problem that arose became a crisis that had to be resolved immediately. An example was a problem with the broil unit that had to be dealt with by a manager named Tom Tiller, who, though 30 years old, looked like a college student. Tiller finished a master's at the Harvard School of Business in June 1991 and then became head of the range facility, having worked for GE off and on for 10 years. His business school experience, while stimulating, had not trained him for one of the most crucial elements of the business world: meeting deadlines. "The weakness of the business school approach is you turn to page 17 of the case and here are the facts. The problem in real life is there's no page 17 of the case, and so you have to make some assumptions."[26]

Working for Jack Welch, Tiller knew that one of those assumptions was that speed counted. He quickly assembled a team, including suppliers, to solve the broil unit problem, which the team did without a loss of much production time.

Tiller remembered that crisis as "perhaps the longest week of my work life. Our team of about 40 people formed a war room to update everyone on test methods, results, and next steps, and essentially worked 24 hours a day. It took us about a week to solve the problem. We discovered the cause to be a combination of a blown voltage regulator in the building power supply and some process control problems with our wire supplier. A number of things happened at the same time to form this quality problem, all of which were of a low probability."[27]

If Quick Response had added pressure to Tom Tiller's job, it had been no less challenging for Roger Creal, a 28-year veteran at GE who was also an executive officer of the local union. Quick Response changed his work style. "Your reaction time is quite condensed. When something goes wrong, you have to make some pretty quick fixes and they have got to be the right ones."

Creal credited Jack Welch with realizing early on that the key to success in business was to understand that "the competition is not with the union or the employees; it's with the other manufacturers of appliances in the world." He was pleased that this had meant the arrival of a different kind of manager in Louisville. More caring toward the employee. Eager to employ the minds of the workers. "They set out to tap that resource, not just because it was good for business, but because morally, ethically, it was right."[28]

Quick Response enjoyed positive reviews on Wall Street. Analysts liked hearing that GE would be able to increase productivity in its Major Appliances business by 30 percent in just two years. That could lead to a 30 percent cut in the cost of producing Major Appliances products, meaning higher profits and the chance to capture a larger segment of the appliance market through increased advertising, improved customer service, and better customer financing terms. With others in the industry struggling just to keep a positive cash flow, GE stood to gain a great deal in its assault on domestic and global appliance markets. Once the Quick Response program penetrated all of GE the company's gains would be dizzying. The company's $4 billion inventory levels could be cut by 40 percent, enabling GE to reduce its costs by $3.5 billion annually over the next few years. Nicholas Heymann, vice president of County NatWest Securities, said that it was "revolutionary" for a company as large as GE to push a program like Quick Response throughout its businesses. No other company, he noted, was able to replace its appliances in a week, yet GE hoped to be averaging that response rate by the end of 1992.[29]

Jack Welch liked what was happening in Louisville. At a Crotonville session in the fall of 1991 someone in the audience asked him if he was troubled by the possibility that Work-Out might go too far. It was not clear what "too far" meant, but Welch said, "What a nice problem that will be." He talked about Louisville. "I am so damn proud of that team. What they [Louisville] did right was to define Work-Out as an umbrella of Quick Response, lower inventories, and faster availability. You have to get Work-Out under a high enough umbrella because there are cynics everywhere. The cynics can't argue with Quick Response. Who can be for slower [response], worse quality?"[30]

CHAPTER FOURTEEN

◊

"What Means Profit?"

The company just kept making more and more money. By the end of the 80s General Electric was stronger than ever. It had had 40 consecutive quarterly earnings increases, ending the decade with a 16.6 percent growth in earnings. GE began the 80s ranked 11th in market value, at $12 billion; it ended the 80s ranked 2nd in market value, at $58 billion—with the greatest market value increase of any American company during the decade. Thanks to Work-Out and other efforts, GE's productivity had by the end of the decade risen to an average 5–6 percent a year, up from 1–2 percent in 1980.

GE's businesses were leaders in their fields: Aircraft Engines, Electric Motors, Engineering Plastics, Industrial and Power Systems, and Medical Systems were first in the United States and first in the world; Broadcasting (NBC) was first in the United States; Circuit Breakers was first in the United States and tied for first with several other firms in the world; Locomotives was first in the United States and tied for first with General Motors in the world; Defense Electronics was second in the United States and second in the world, behind Hughes Electronics in both; Factory Automation was second in the United States and third in the world; Lighting was first in the United States and second in the world; Major Appliances was first in the United States and second in the world, behind Whirlpool.

GE turned in a stellar financial performance in 1989. Its sales were up 7 percent, to $58.4 billion; its earnings were up 11 percent, to $3.9 billion. A large portion of those earnings came from Power Systems ($1.057 billion). Other large earners were Aircraft Engines

◊

($1.050 billion), GE Financial Services ($927 million), and Aerospace ($646 million). The company ranked fifth on the Fortune 500 list of American industrial corporations, behind General Motors, Ford, Exxon, and IBM. It was the third most profitable industrial corporation.

As 1989 began, General Electric derived no joy from its purchase of Kidder, Peabody. It was time for a change of leadership. The Kidder purchase, the *New York Times* wrote in January, "has turned out worse than anyone's lowest expectations."[1] To salvage Kidder, Welch replaced Silas Cathcart as its CEO with Michael Carpenter, Welch's 41-year-old strategic planning genius, executive vice president of GE Capital.

The main purpose of selecting Carpenter was to signal Kidder that GE was going to run things. "I am the chief executive of Kidder but an employee of GE," asserted Carpenter. His mandate was to keep the 124-year-old firm from slipping even further.

No one thought that Carpenter, however bright and imaginative, would have an easy time of it. He tried to sound optimistic. "This firm, relatively speaking, is not troubled. It's not GE's best acquisition, but it's not bad. We want to make Kidder as successful as possible, and we will use all the resources at GE to get that done."[2]

According to the 1991 Annual Report, Kidder's operating profits of $119 million for 1991 reflected an improvement over the losses of about $50 million for both 1989 and 1990. By the end of 1991 revenue had increased 38 percent; return on equity had exceeded 20 percent. The firm had gained a significant market share in targeted businesses as well as gaining in the industry rankings.

Welch appeared to be slowing down, buying less. Not entirely true. It was simply that his acquisitions—$10 billion worth of purchases between early 1989 and October 1991—garnered little publicity. One reason for the lack of interest: $1 billion worth of those acquisitions consisted of container leasing companies under the wing of GE Financial Services. Such deals are not as sexy as a network or a brokerage house, noted Joyce Hergenhan, vice president for public relations.[3]

With the stock market at an all-time high, buying American companies made little sense. Globalization, especially entering into joint ventures overseas, looked increasingly attractive. Infected by the bug, Welch sought to turn General Electric into a truly international force.

In 1989 GE announced that it was investing $580 million in a joint venture with Britain's General Electric Company—unrelated to the American firm—to manufacture appliances and medical equipment. Linking up with a British firm required little adjustment for GE.

However, doing business in Eastern Europe would mean a large adjustment. Communist regimes were falling, and the regimes that succeeded them hoped for Western investment. Jack Welch was at first hesitant, worried about the negative effects of collapsing economies and continued government meddling in management. He was eager, though, to globalize his businesses, including Lighting. GE was the world's second-largest producer (behind Philips) in lighting, with 1989 sales of $2.3 billion, but it was sixth in Europe, with only 3 percent of the European light bulb market. So when Welch heard about the Hungarian lighting firm of Tungsram, he looked it over thoroughly.

He liked what he saw. Founded in 1896 and the third-oldest lighting firm in the world (behind GE, founded in 1878, and Philips, founded in 1891), Tungsram was a strong exporter, obtaining 70 percent of its $300 million in revenues from the West. It commanded a respectable 7 percent of the West European market. Mercedes Benz and BMW used Tungsram headlamps on some models. The $20 million profit the Hungarian firm turned in for 1989 showed that it had a solid foundation. The firm's name was a cross between the German and Hungarian words for tungsten. For GE, the strategic fit was clear: Tungsram would give GE Lighting a European manufacturing base and European distribution channels and, hopefully, would play a crucial role in developing global leadership for GE Lighting.

What a tempting combination: getting a better market share in Western Europe and paying East European wages! One week after the Berlin Wall came down, in November 1989, GE announced that it planned to spend $150 million to purchase Tungsram. The deal was big news. At the time it was the largest single investment by a Western company in Eastern Europe.

Though Tungsram needed considerable fine-tuning, GE thought it had great potential. Lagging far behind in quality, Tungsram had an assembly line that broke one of every four bulbs. Lagging equally far behind in technology, Tungsram employed bookkeepers who did their accounting with pencils. Some of Tungsram's limitations could be rectified without much fuss. Some could not: A staff of 150 Tungsram employees stuffed 17,000 pay envelopes with cash each month—because checking accounts hardly existed in Hungary!

GE sensed that Tungsram had potential. After having mass-produced the classic tungsten filament light bulb since 1906, Tungsram derived more than 50 percent of its sales from this low-tech, inexpensive product. By the 80s, costlier, high-tech, energy-efficient products had become more popular—compact fluorescent bulbs for homes and offices; high-pressure sodium lamps for street lighting; miniature spotlights for shop windows displaying jewelry and antiques. GE decided to invest $15 million a year, three times Tungsram's yearly investment for the 80s, to earn profits from such segments of the business.

Now the hard part began.

Move over Karl Marx. Here comes Jack Welch.

A major American corporation hoped to take a factory that the Communists had been running with little derring-do for decades and to make it profitable.

To run the new Tungsram Welch selected a 28-year GE veteran named George Varga who had been running a $500 million-a-year plastics plant for GE in the Netherlands. The impeccable credentials of the 55-year-old Varga included the fact that he had been a Hungarian refugee!

Varga, then 19, was a law student and a nationally known soccer hero when Soviet tanks rolled into his country to crush the 1956 revolt. Fleeing to the West, he crawled under barbed wire into Austria. Ironically, searchlights made by Tungsram swept the border as he made his escape. He reached the United States "with only the clothes on my back" and soon won a scholarship to Western Maryland College, where he became an All-American soccer star. He obtained a master's degree in economics from Stanford. By 1970, on the strength of a general amnesty given to all of those who fled, Varga began regular visits to his family in Hungary. To his disappointment the country had not shifted much from its rigid, backward ways. Nonetheless, he hoped to succeed at Tungsram.

Varga knew that General Electric intended to shake the place up. Half of Tungsram's senior managers were dismissed to make way for American GE managers who literally had to begin with the fundamentals of American capitalism. David Gadra, one of these, began to grasp how colossal the task was while lecturing to Tungsram employees on the value of keeping close track of inventory and receivables in order to measure their effect on profit.

"What means profit?" The question came from a bewildered Hungarian engineer.

Though bewildered himself, Gadra went to the blackboard and began putting graphs and flowcharts up by way of reply.

"Why profits?" someone else asked.

Gadra knew then that he—and GE in general—had their work cut out for them.

How could managers, used to being told what to do, be expected to take on responsibility? How could employees be expected to care about achieving 100 percent quality in the products they produced when they and the rest of the country had become accustomed to standing in line to buy whatever was available? Tungsram managers were able to describe what had gone wrong the day before. When it came to solutions for the problem, they fell silent. GE had to teach the Tungsram staff that *profit* was not a dirty word, that quality mattered, that criticism was permissible. A weekly Tungsram newsletter dropped Lenin's sayings and instead offered one from Vince Lombardi, the American football coach: "We want to win, not just exist."

Tungsram's seven plants were top-heavy with workers, 18,000 in all, roughly the same number that GE employed in the rest of its Lighting business (which had sales seven times as large as those of the Hungarian firm). Such a firm might ordinarily have been a classic target for downsizing. But downsizing to save on salaries would not have helped: Tungsram paid its workers only $3,000 a year, 1/10 the amount paid to comparable workers in the United States and Western Europe.

Still, productivity could be improved. One production line turned out 3 million outdoor spotlights a year for yards and driveways. In the process it broke another half million. The result: a large financial loss due to the waste of glass, tungsten wire, and other raw materials. A visitor to a Tungsram plant frequently found the floor covered with glass shards and tall trash cans overflowing with discarded bulbs. Reducing breakage and breakdowns could save half a million dollars a year, GE officials estimated.

Karl Marx's ideas had not been kind to Tungsram. It had too much bureaucracy, too many management layers, too many reporting requirements, too much data and too little analysis, and almost no office automation. What could one expect from a company that was, as Frank Doyle, senior vice president for external and industrial relations, put it in a wonderful understatement, "constrained by the accumulated inheritance of four decades of regional problems."[4]

In its first years under GE Tungsram was transformed radically. Though the desired savings were not realized, the bloated work force was cut 30 percent. GE committed itself to investing $50 million during the first three years and reinvesting Tungsram's profits for at least the same period. As a result of restructuring costs and investment Tungsram posted an $18 million local loss in 1990. But its sales rose to $400 million, up by nearly a third since 1989, the year before GE took over.

In November 1990, to bolster its lighting effort in Europe even more, General Electric spent $138 million to purchase the British-based lighting operations of THORN EMI. As with the Tungsram brand name, the THORN brand name was retained. The purchase of Tungsram and THORN helped move GE from sixth to third in the European lighting market. Tungsram lost money in 1990, but in 1991 it earned $10 million. GE Lighting's revenues, which in 1990 amounted to more than $2 billion, approached $3 billion in 1991. GE would not release the earnings figures for Lighting for these two years.

In late 1989 Welch was still searching for fresh ways to bolster GE's stock price. Though the stock had been only $15.31 at the end of 1980, it had reached $55 in 1989; its ascent had been shaky. Even after a decade of unrivaled success GE was still regarded tentatively and cautiously on Wall Street. Welch used the few public speeches he gave to foster the impression that the company was focused and unified in its purpose. Forging whole new patterns of behavior in the workplace through Work-Out and Best Practices, he sensed that these schemes, while important, would take years of running in. He looked for short-term measures in the hope of jump-starting the stock.

He had a number of options. One was to make another major acquisition. Even if such a sale were in the cards, the reaction from Wall Street, hopefully positive, would not necessarily be immediate. A onetime dividend increase was another option, but that did not seem the best means of increasing long-term share value. The best choice appeared to be a stock buyback scheme. "We feel," Welch wrote in a pamphlet explaining the plan, "the best investment is not another large company's stock; it's our own."

The time appeared right. The company was in great shape: Annual productivity increases had risen from 1–2 percent to 5–6 percent. Operating margins were 30 percent higher than they had been at the start of the decade. Working capital turnover, one more measure of efficiency, had risen 30 percent during the decade, freeing up $2.6 billion in cash. This led Welch to assert that GE had "now reached the point in its strategic development where we believe it can grow earnings substantially, increase dividends in line with those earnings, maintain a high degree of internal investment, make complementary acquisitions—and purchase a significant amount of company stock."

In November 1989 he settled on a controversial, but effective, scheme that called for General Electric to repurchase $10 billion worth of its stock over the next five years. This was the largest stock repurchase program ever undertaken by an American firm. On the surface the gambit appeared shrewd, for stock buybacks invariably increase the stock price since they reduce the number of shares in circulation.

The price of General Electric's stock shot up! Six months later, by May 1990, it had reached $68 a share, a 23 percent increase at a time when the Standard & Poor's 500 index ascended only 3 percent.

The move brought scorn on Welch and GE, however. Critics argued that, rather than buying back their own stock, CEOs like Jack Welch should be investing in new products and processes. To abandon that game, they argued, was to permit countries in Europe and Asia to surpass the United States, as they had done in consumer electronics, semiconductors, and machine tools.

Welch tried to put a good face on the step. Repurchasing the stock, he insisted, was a better way for GE to generate value for shareholders than taking a "wild swing" on an acquisition or investing in new technology. Amid fears that GE would now have less available cash to spend on research and development, Welch assured everyone that the company would spend as much on its research and development efforts as it always had.

Yet it all seemed so out of character. Welch had always prided himself on spending huge amounts of money on R&D and plant improvements. He had insisted that such investments would generate the new products, the greater efficiencies, and the added earnings that would create added value for share owners. The repurchase of GE's stock was viewed as a cop-out, as an acknowledgment that no other way existed to increase its value. Worst of all, it appeared to reflect the company's lack of confidence in its ability to be a major global competitor.

The balance sheet looked bright again in 1990. Revenues had reached $58.414 billion. Earnings had climbed to $4.303 billion. For all his worry and concern, Jack Welch could take pride in the surveys that recognized General Electric as the number one company in America.

It was first in the Forbes Super 50—based on revenue, net income, assets, and market value. Trailing GE were Exxon, IBM, Philip Morris, and AT&T. GE had been second in 1989.

It was first in the Corporate Finance Performance 1,000—a new survey based on shareholder value created.

It was sixth on the Fortune 500 list—based on revenues. The top five were General Motors, Exxon, Ford, IBM, and Mobil. GE had been fifth in 1989.

It was fourth in a *Wall Street Journal* survey of the world's 100 largest public firms—based on market value.

By the spring of 1990 Wall Street analysts sounded increasingly upbeat about GE. County NatWest's Nicholas Heymann called GE "one of the world's largest growth companies." In a newsletter dated April 20, 1990, he wrote: "We believe that during the past 10 years, GE has successfully accomplished what virtually all companies' 1980s restructuring programs were intended to do: remake the business into dominant global competitors capable of sustaining above-average growth in their remaining businesses. . . . No other large diversified

U.S. industrial corporation has achieved such sizable progress on a sustainable basis this decade." Heymann predicted that over the next 6 to 12 months GE's stock would rise from 65½, where it had been on April 20, to $74–79 per share. The stock closed at $57.38 at the end of 1990, but by December 31, 1991, it had risen to $76.50.

The environmental issue threatened General Electric with continuing headaches. Though the company had been spending $300 million a year to deal with complaints from environmental authorities, it could not escape the protests of various groups that continued to view GE as a giant irritant. The protests caused the company little financial damage. The campaigns of the protest groups, however, kept General Electric in the public eye as an alleged environmental polluter.

Through the late 80s one group, the Boston-based Infact, tried to drive GE out of the nuclear weapons business. In 1986 the group began a boycott of GE because GE produced nuclear missile systems. In June 1991 Nancy Cole, Infact's director, announced that the boycott had cost GE $30 million in medical equipment sales. GE spokesmen retorted that the boycott had not even dented the sales of its Medical Systems business.[5]

As part of the Infact struggle, the sisters of St. Francis, 1,100 strong, took on GE's estimated $3 billion Medical Systems business, ordering their college, high school, and 12 hospitals to avoid GE products. The sisters complained that GE was making parts for Trident submarines and nuclear-armed missiles, creating safety, health, and environmental hazards. Their effort deprived GE of $2 million in orders for such items as CT-scanners. With $58 billion in sales in 1990, General Electric found the $2 million loss a drop in the bucket. Its spokesmen argued that the company's nuclear efforts were aimed not only at making a profit but also at building a strong national defense.[6]

Infact focused fresh attention on its cause by making a documentary film called "Deadly Deception: General Electric, Nuclear Weapons and Our Environment." On March 30, 1992, the film, produced by Debra Chasnoff, won an Academy Award for the best documentary short subject. Producer Chasnoff accepted the award, noting that: "Infact supporters all over the world helped us tell the real story about the company that falsely claims it brings good things to life." Grabbing the Oscar in her left hand and raising it above her head, she smiled triumphantly and shouted: "Thank you very much and boycott GE!"

This verbal attack against General Electric was made before a worldwide audience of hundreds of millions of people. What effect would this sudden burst of massive publicity have on General Electric?

The people at GE waited tensely over the next few days to see how the nation would react. Would consumers respond to the appeal from the Oscars ceremony and decide in large numbers to heed the plea to boycott GE's products?

To the relief of the people at General Electric, Chasnoff's statement to "boycott GE" did not set off a fresh onslaught against the company. Only three people phoned GE, all of whom were supportive. GE spokespersons sought to convince everyone that the Oscar triumph did not mean the message of the film was correct. "Deadly Deception," they pointed out, had won for its artistic merit; and winning did not validate its substance.

That may have been technically true; but undoubtedly the Oscar triumph encouraged the view that the message of the film deserved to be taken seriously.

In a prepared statement, GE assailed Infact for mistakenly pursuing a goal of unilateral disarmament. "GE wants peace every bit as much as anyone does, but we along with the overwhelming majority of the American people believe peace can be assured only by an adequately strong national defense, not by weakness or unilateral disarmament."

GE sought to argue, as it had on previous occasions, that Infact had had no significant effect on the company's revenues. And indeed that appeared to be true. However, Infact had clearly scored points in its campaign against GE by managing to turn the capturing of the Oscar into a dramatic eruption of publicity to encourage people to "boycott GE."

The protests kept General Electric in the news and presented it with an ongoing predicament. According to government data, GE was not among the worst polluters in general. Nor was it among the top 10 water polluters. It did rank 9th among the 10 worst air polluters.[7]

Some environmental experts predicted that the environmental issue could become GE's biggest financial burden in the 90s. One GE consultant said that environmental efforts could cost the company billions of dollars, eating heavily into its profits.[8] Noting that such efforts were already costing GE a couple of hundred million dollars a year, Jack Welch nonetheless thought the consultant's gloomy forecast an exaggeration.

When he addressed the issue in the spring of 1990, Welch pledged to give priority to environmental concerns. "In the environment our advanced technology—from plastic recycling to power generation combustion to emission control systems to jet engine noise control to bioremediation—gives us the opportunity for world leadership in meeting this important challenge. Every product we make—every process we use—will be subject to an intense environmental review to ensure that we exercise the best available technology. We intend to have environmental concern as culturally embedded in every GE employee as are the need for integrity and the quest for excellence."[9]

One of the most controversial aspects of the environmental issue, that of PCBs, had been plaguing General Electric during the 80s and continued to plague it in the early 90s.

The company stood accused of having polluted a 40-mile stretch of the Hudson River between Fort Edward and Troy, in upper New York State, by dumping about 500,000 pounds of PCBs into the river as waste products from its manufacturing plants at Fort Edward and Hudson Falls between 1946 and 1975.[10]

PCBs—polychlorinated biphenyls—are complex chemicals that were formerly used as insulators in heavy electrical equipment but were barred as toxic in 1976. Since then, due to PCB contamination, New York State has banned commercial fishing for striped bass in the Hudson and has advised people not to eat fish caught in the river. In 1976 GE and the New York State Department of Environmental Conservation agreed to spend $7 million to assess potential solutions to the contamination of the Hudson.[11]

The state determined that dredging PCB-laden sediments from the bottom of the Hudson and creating new landfills were the best means of resolving the problem. But legal suits of local residents who objected to toxic landfills delayed implementation of that plan.

Meanwhile, GE came up with an alternative to dredging: biological destruction of the PCB molecules. Such biological approches have been getting wider attention as scientists have tried to find easier and cheaper ways to clean up oil spills and hazardous waste sites. GE hoped to show that its scientists could eliminate the need to dredge by helping nature to cope with PCB toxicity. GE objected to dredging in part because of its far greater cost (nearly $300 million) and in part because GE believed that dredging would lead to new environmental hazards.

Though company officials considered the accusations against GE unfair, GE was making an effort to show good faith—and at the same time to avoid a higher bill in cleanup costs. By the spring of 1990 the company had invested $20 million and committed $30 million more to a research and development program aimed at speeding up the natural process that had been removing PCBs from sediment in the contaminated part of the Hudson. On August 9, 1991, GE scientists pounded half a dozen 6-foot-wide pipes into the bed of the upper Hudson.

The experiment lasted 10 weeks. A key objective was to show that PCB biodegradation could occur under field conditions. The scientists concluded that it was possible to accelerate PCB biodegradation in the Hudson River sediments by adding nutrients and supplemental oxygen. More research is needed to establish the rate and extent of the PCB biodegradation and to understand the role of nutrients in the process. But for now, scientists seemed satisfied that a way existed to significantly reduce the amount and availability of PCBs in these sediments. These findings were turned over to the Environmental Protection Agency in early 1992.

For all its efforts to eradicate unethical behavior within the company, General Electric was caught in another web of scandal during the early 90s. This case spread all the way to the Middle East and involved the Israeli Air Force.

The case broke in Israel before GE learned about it. Only in December 1990, when Israeli investigators showed up at the GE Aircraft Engines plant at Evendale, near Cincinnati, did the company learn that it was under investigation.

The Israeli investigators said that a General Rami Dotan of the Israeli Air Force had admitted setting up phony corporations and diverting funds from them to his own pocket. Dotan had headed the IAF propulsion engines and aircraft divisions before being promoted to head the IAF Equipment Branch. The Israeli probers said Dotan had confessed that his coconspirator was Herb Steindler, GE's international sales manager. [12]

The case had embarrassing ramifications for Israel, which received $1.8 billion from the American government each year to finance the purchase of weapons from American contractors.

Upon learning of Dotan's confession, GE officials traveled to Washington and informed both the Justice and Defense departments of the Israeli probers' information. GE launched its own investigation. In March 1991 it fired Steindler based on Dotan's testimony.

That same month, in Israel, Dotan pleaded guilty to fraud and bribery charges, closing the Israeli side of the case. Dotan's confession and plea bargain sent him to prison for 13 years. [13]

As a result of the Dotan disclosures, in August 1991 the Justice Department accused GE of defrauding the Pentagon of more than $30 million on the sale of jet engines and support services to the Israeli Air Force. [14]

Details of this GE scandal emerged in a lawsuit that was made public in August 1991, though it had been filed the previous November by GE employee Chester L. Walsh under the Federal False Claims Act, known also as "the whistle-blowing statute." [15] That act requires the Justice Department to investigate claims made by whistle-blowers and to decide whether the claims should be pursued by the government. Walsh was the GE Aircraft Engines manager in Israel from 1984 to 1988.

According to Walsh's suit, between 1985 and 1988 General Electric conspired with Israel's Rami Dotan to submit fraudulent claims for Israeli Air Force work for which the American government would pay. These claims were for engine-testing equipment, software, and support services that GE never provided. This was allegedly part of an arrangement between Israel and General Electric to overcharge the Pentagon for F–16 fighter engines. Named in the suit as a key participant in the transactions was Herbert Steindler. [16]

In October 1991 GE officials were fuming over the Walsh suit, enraged that instead of blowing the whistle on Steindler and Dotan at once, Walsh had taken four years to turn them in, meanwhile taping conversations between the participants. Now he stood to gain $3–4 million if he won the suit. A GE official complained: "It went on for four years longer than it should have. If Walsh had reported it four years earlier, it would have been stopped four years earlier."

Yet, the official said, every year he had signed the GE policy statement requiring him to speak up immediately upon learning of ethical
violations.

Walsh, who had been suspended with pay, could collect 30 percent of the amount the government received from General Electric.
As of the spring of 1992 GE was still considering whether to bring suit
against Walsh. GE's reluctance appeared, at least in part, to be due to
a concern that legal action would be construed as designed to discour-
age whistle-blowers. The company's main interest was to make sure
that Walsh did not gain financially.[17]

Jack Welch was sick at heart about the Dotan scandal. "We had a
rotten apple. We also have the dark side of customer service. The guy
who was in with him [Welch meant Steindler] could always call back
and say: 'The general will kill us if we don't do this.' Everything was
under the guise of 'You've got to do this for the customer.' "[18]

By March 1992 General Electric had taken various forms of dis-
ciplinary action ranging from dismissal to demotion against some 20
employees in GE Aircraft Engines for not having been more vigilant
in uncovering the Dotan-Steindler scam. Officials at GE would not
comment on this development other than to say that any such actions
were a matter between the company and its employees.

On June 1, 1992, the Defense Department suspended GE's Aircraft Engines business from receiving new government contracts. Five
days later the suspension was lifted after GE promised to set up a
panel to monitor all foreign arms sales.

By most measurements Jack Welch should have felt that he was
sitting on top of the world. Yet Welch seemed pressured, noting with
great emotion that his businesses were "under siege." True, the American recession had taken its toll on the entire business community.
Times were indeed tough. To Welch they had never been tougher.
"There's nobody out there getting business easily." Between price pressures and global competition, "you've got to be more on your toes every second. If you're out of step for a minute . . . " He did not finish
the sentence. He did not want to. He could not bring himself to en-
tertain the thought that GE collectively might come up short.

Aircraft Engines, the most profitable of GE's businesses, had
$1.263 billion profits on $7.558 billion of revenues in 1990. Yet in
1991 its situation became increasingly precarious. One of the two

main producers of military aircraft engines (the other being Pratt & Whitney), GE faced difficulties because of the shrinking defense budget and reduced spare parts orders for commercial engines.

GE built $3 billion worth of engines for the military in 1990, nearly half of its revenues, but it expected to build only $2.5 billion worth in 1992. Though GE had a $20 billion backlog in orders for commercial jet engines, that was not expected to offset the predicted drop in military spending.

In April 1991 GE lost a bid to build the ATF, the U.S. Air Force's Advanced Tactical Fighter—the fighter jet meant to replace the F–15. Pratt & Whitney won the estimated $60 billion contract to make engines for 650 of the radar-evading planes. Of the $1 billion it cost GE to develop the engine for the ATF, $800 million came from the air force. As a result of losing its bid, GE laid off 1,500 employees in an attempt to save $450 million.

GE rebounded in August by winning a $1.4 billion contract to supply engines for Boeing 777 wide-body jets for British Airways.

The sharpest competition in the aircraft engine field was over contracts to build engines for the latest generation of wide-body jets: the McDonnell Douglas MD–11, the Boeing 777, and Airbus Industrie's A330 and A340. The engines for those jets would account for an estimated half of the $170 billion in engines and spare parts bought in the West over the next 15 years. The wide-body market was crucial to a commercial engine maker, for without gaining a significant share of that market, it would be unable to afford the research and development it needed to stay in business.

The new GE90 engine, which cost GE $1.1 billion to develop, was built for wide-body planes. The engine represented a new generation of commercial jet engines that provided more fuel savings, noise reduction, emission reduction, and power than any jet engine had ever produced. Engines for the wide-body planes required up to 100,000 pounds of thrust, 10 times as much as the thrust that had propelled the first Boeing 707s 25 years earlier.

GE defense businesses faced great pressure. "Everyone is spending the peace dividend before they have it," said Welch. He predicted a "downsizing in defense that makes what happens now just peanuts." He suspected that the defense budget might be sliced in half in the next five to six years. From just under $300 billion to under $150 billion. "I think it could be devastating," he said. In his view the only way of coping was to become more cost effective.

Second in profits to Aircraft Engines in 1990 was Financial Services. Welch could not say enough nice words about this business. "They have the capital, the power. They can grow as big as their dreams can take them." Competition remained fierce, but Financial Services could get "as big as their eyes and brains can take them." In 1990 this business generated a whopping $1.1 billion profit, an 18 percent hike over its profit in the previous year. Because it had such a diversified array of businesses, GEFS was less vulnerable to changes in the economy than other financial service firms.

Third in profits in 1990 was Materials (Plastics), with profits of $1.017 billion. Fourth was Power Generation. Its profits in 1990 were $739 million on sales of $5.8 billion. NBC, Welch acknowledged, was "at a trough," with earnings of only $477 million in 1990 on sales of $3.2 billion. Though advertising was down, Welch believed that "the network is still the only game in town for mass advertising."

Major Appliances had a productive year in 1990, with earnings of $467 million on $5.7 billion in sales. Welch doubted that GE would get "booming growth" from either Major Appliances or Lighting in the near future, but he was confident that Lighting would grow globally.

Motors did not do well and was suffering, Welch said, from "a series of management missteps. If you want to rate our management performance, I would rate Motors at the bottom of our scale."[19]

That finishing school of executives, General Electric, was again supplying American corporations with its veterans. In June 1991 Larry Bossidy, GE vice chairman, became the chief executive officer of $12 billion Allied Signal. Bossidy's departure from General Electric might have been considered a blow to Jack Welch and to the company. It was not. This finishing school had enough bench talent to survive the departure of even someone as senior as Bossidy.

Still, Welch had to reshape the office of the Chief Executive Officer, which, with Bossidy's departure, was left with only Vice Chairman Ed Hood and himself as members. The system of direct reports had to be changed. Until Bossidy left, the businesses had been distributed among the three members of the CEO's office. Welch decided that he and Hood would monitor the businesses collectively. Obviously the final say was the chairman's. After the new system had been in place for three months, Ed Hood thought it was working out fine. "We've worked together long enough so that we pretty much know how the other thinks." In practice Hood still took the lead in the Aerospace and Aircraft Engines businesses because he knew them so well. Welch took charge of GE Financial Services because he had been involved with that business since the late 70s. The two shared the rest of the businesses. "We sort of put ourselves in a blender," Welch said.

Hood noted that the new system had one advantage over its predecessor. When the businesses had reported to only one of the three men—Welch, Bossidy, or Hood—"there was an element of turf that crept in that was pretty natural." If a dispute arose between two businesses, each man felt proprietary about his business. Hood said: "It doesn't work that way anymore. It's much easier to ask yourself the question: What is the right thing to do for the enterprise? Not what's the right thing to do for NBC or Aerospace."[20]

As the 90s began, Jack Welch steered clear of another "quantum leap," a Kidder or an RCA. It was clear by 1991 that Welch's goal had become the internal expansion of the 13 GE businesses. Rumors persisted that he wanted to sell off NBC, but the price appeared too high for potential buyers.

If Welch was planning another RCA-type quantum leap, he kept his cards close to his chest. Still, Wall Street advisers kept pushing ideas on him. One landed on his desk in the summer of 1991.

It called for General Electric to merge with Time Warner, the American entertainment and information giant. Trying to raise $2.8 billion to cut down its debt, Time Warner announced a plan that would give shareholders securities called "rights" to buy 34.5 million new shares of Time Warner for anywhere from $63 to $105 a share, depending on how many shareholders took part. The proposal came to Welch from an investment banker friend who thought that if the Securities and Exchange Commission forced Time Warner to cancel its rights offering, the Time Warner stock, then at 66, would plunge. "If it goes to 60 bucks, why not offer 85 or 90?" was the gist of the proposal laid before Welch.

The investment banker thought that GE would be better off acquiring Time Warner than selling NBC. From time to time he suggested that companies move on the basis of sudden events such as a cancellation of the rights offering. GE came to mind "because there's nobody that can move faster on sudden events than this company. Nobody. And that's one of their real strengths."

Welch answered the proposal politely, never referring to it specifically but making his rejection clear. "Thanks for your note. We'll pass on this one. Have a great summer. Best, Jack." The note was written on stationery that simply said "John F. Welch, 3135 Easton Turnpike, Fairfield, Ct." It was dated July 2, 1991.

The SEC did not order the plan scrapped; but when it and shareholders complained that the sliding price scale made it impossible for purchasers to know how much they were paying until the offer was completed, Time Warner did scrap it. In mid-July it replaced the original offering with an offering of rights to buy Time Warner shares for $80 a share.

CHAPTER FIFTEEN

"Winning in the 90s"

In the late 80s and early 90s Jack Welch gave continued thought to the kind of company General Electric should become in the future. In articulating that dream, he was in effect offering a prescription for the way all large American corporations should behave. In a speech given in September 1989, he outlined the qualities that would be required for business success in the coming decade.

"The 80s have forced business to change. The complacent and timid had a date with hostile takeover people. Ten million manufacturing jobs were eliminated and shifted to the service sector. Seventeen million new jobs were created, and unemployment dropped to its lowest point in 15 years. American firms began to globalize. The results of the 80s show that things worked. Productivity growth in American manufacturing at the end of the 80s is more than twice what it was at the start of the decade. America is now growing faster than West Germany and getting closer to Japanese growth levels. The weak dollar and strong productivity have helped America's trade position in the 80s. American real net exports of goods and services improved 40 percent since 1986.

"The biggest mistake we could make right now is to think that simply doing more of what worked in the 80s will be enough to win the 90s. It won't. Productivity still lags behind Japan despite major gains in the 80s. And the competitive arena is much tougher and complex. Whereas at the start of the 80s Japan was the one powerful competitor, today it is Europe and Korea and Taiwan. Korea and Taiwan, once sourcing areas for labor-intensive electronic products, are now major manufacturing powerhouses in electronics, autos, steel, and many other industries. Others in the Far East are following in their paths.

"Simply going after more of the hardware solutions that worked in the 80s will just not be enough to win in the 90s.

"The point is—the competitive world of the 90s will make the 80s look like a walk in the park.

"How does America win the 90s?

"To win we have to find the key to dramatic, sustained productivity growth. . . . Why is it that people don't question the limits of productivity growth in Japan—or other Asian countries? They accept it because they understand that the source of that growth is cultural—not cutting, combining, or all the things it's come to be associated with in this country.

"Cultural. That's what productivity has to become here. The Japanese have the software, the culture which ties productivity to the human spirit—which has practically no limits.

"That's where we have to turn in the 90s—to the software of our companies—to the culture that drives them."

Changing the culture fundamentally meant, Welch said, going beyond incentive plans and a hundred other suggestions from the how-to books; beyond the hero of the week who single-handedly saves or transforms a company. "We have to move from the incremental to the radical, toward a fundamental revolution in our approach to productivity and to work itself—a revolution that must touch every single person in the organization every business day."

Welch summed up his prescription in three words: *speed, simplicity,* and *self-confidence.*

Speed occurred when people made decisions in minutes, face-to-face, without producing months of staff work or forests of paper.

Simplicity had many definitions: "To an engineer it's clean, functional designs with fewer parts. For manufacturing it means judging a process not by how sophisticated it is, but how understandable it is to those who must make it work. In marketing it means clear messages and clean proposals to consumers and industrial customers. And, most importantly, on an individual, interpersonal level it takes the form of plainspeaking, directness—honesty." Simplicity was also indispensable to a leader's most important function: projecting a vision. "The leader's unending responsibility must be to remove every detour, every barrier to ensure that vision is first clear, and then real. The leader must create an atmosphere in the organization where people feel not only free to, but obliged to, demand clarity and purpose from their leaders."

Self-confidence: "It takes enormous self-confidence to be simple—particularly in large organizations. Self-confidence does not grow in someone who is just another appendage on the bureaucracy, whose authority rests on little more than a title. Bureaucracy is terrified by speed and hates simplicity. It fosters defensiveness, intrigue, sometimes meanness. Those who are trapped in it are afraid to share, can't be passionate, and—in the 90s—won't win."

A company cannot distribute self-confidence. But it can provide opportunities to dream, risk, and win and hence to earn self-confidence.

"Speed. Simplicity. Self-confidence. We can grow a work ethic that plays to our strengths, one that unleashes and liberates the awesome productive energy that we know resides in our work force. If we can let people see that what they do counts, means something; if you and I and the business leadership of the country can have the self-confidence to let people go—to create an environment where each man and woman who works in our companies can see a clear connection between what he or she does every day, all day, and winning and losing in the real world—we can become productive beyond our wildest dreams—certainly beyond the abilities of our international competitors, most of whom are hobbled by cultures that make it virtually impossible for them to liberate and empower their people.

"It is we who have the ultimate advantage, one that few of us, if pressed, would ever wish to trade. It is the fact that our system, while providing no guarantees, also has the fewest barriers to the stuff that creates real productivity—stuff like innovation, boldness, and risk-taking.

"Our natural strong suit is the energy and creativity of an irreverent, aggressive, impatient, and curious people. It is ours to win with—if we can shift gears from decades of controlling things—to a decade of liberating—turning people loose to dream, dare, and win."[1]

Six months later, in March 1990, Welch spoke about making General Electric "boundaryless" in order to deal with the 90s:

"The pace of change will be felt in several areas. Globalization is now no longer an objective but an imperative, as markets open and geographic barriers become increasingly blurred and even irrelevant. Corporate alliances, whether joint ventures or acquisitions, will increasingly be driven by competitive pressures and strategies rather than financial structuring. . . .

"Simply doing more of what worked in the 80s—the restructuring, the delayering, the mechanical, top-down measures that we took—will be too incremental. More than that, it will be too slow. The winners of the 90s will be those who can develop a culture that allows them to move faster, communicate more clearly, and involve everyone in a focused effort to serve ever more demanding customers.

"To move toward that winning culture we've got to create what we call a 'boundaryless' company. We no longer have the time to climb over barriers between functions like engineering and marketing, or between people—hourly, salaried, management, and the like. Geographic barriers must evaporate. Our people must be as comfortable in Delhi and Seoul as they are in Louisville or Schenectady. The lines between the company and its vendors and customers must be blurred into a smooth, fluid process with no other objective than satisfying the customer and winning in the marketplace.

"If we are to get the reflexes and speed we need, we've got to simplify and delegate more—simply trust more. The 80s had no shortage of individual business heroes. In the 90s the heroes, the winners, will be entire companies that have developed cultures that instead of fearing the pace of change, relish it."[2]

In a speech given on April 24, Welch asked how a company gets faster, what stands between a company and the speed it needs.

"In designing a high-performance airplane, engineers work incessantly at eliminating or flattening any protruding surfaces that produce a drag. The result is a clean design that moves quickly and smoothly through the air. In a company the drag comes from boundaries—the walls that grow between functions such as finance and marketing and manufacturing; boundaries between suppliers and the company; between the company and customers. Each of these boundaries is a speed bump that slows the enterprise. Each piece of turf within these boundary walls is defended by the watchdogs of bureaucracy. The process of getting through function after function can be so time-consuming and complex that it can force the organization to focus on itself, on its own inner workings, and distract it from its real mission: serving customers."

How do you get rid of these boundaries? The vertical ones—layer after layer of management, Welch said, were relatively easy targets, and GE had reduced or compressed them substantially in the 80s. "The horizontal ones, primarily between functions, are much more difficult. The barriers between them grow, basically, because of insecurity." The answer was to build self-confidence. That, Welch said, was being done through Work-Out when people were "wrestling with the boundaries, the absurdities that grow in large organizations. We're all familiar with those absurdities: too many approvals, duplication, pomposity, waste."[3]

Believing that the defense industries of the 90s would experience difficulties analogous to those that the rust belt businesses experienced in the 80s, in a speech given on the following day, Welch said that "accepting this reality was the first step in dealing with it—and rightsizing is the second. Only those who move quickly to resize themselves will survive and prosper in the 90s."

Welch saw change occurring around the world that GE could exploit. He thought that Eastern Europe was an area of significant business potential. On the Pacific Rim Japan, Taiwan, Korea, Singapore, Malaysia, Thailand, and Indonesia had rapidly growing economies. The Soviet Union was shifting from defense spending to other priorities. And great promise was being shown by two other countries—Mexico and India. Mexico might become prosperous, as Spain did in the 80s. It might become part of a North American trading bloc with the United States and Canada. India, with 840 million people, 120 million of them in the middle class, had the potential of becoming a major economic player in the next century.

Education, Welch declared, was a great challenge for the 90s. "If we ask our employees at every level of the work force to win in a world seething with change, we must provide them with the tools to do so."

Accordingly, General Electric was spending over $500 million a year on education and training—a figure that would grow to over a billion dollars in the mid-90s.[4]

In December 1991 comments by Welch bearing the title "What I Want U.S. Business to Do in '92" appeared in *Fortune* magazine. The magazine had also asked other leaders in commerce, politics, religion, and academic life for like comments.

"The job all of us have in business is to flatten the building and break down the walls. If we do that, we will be getting more people coming up with more ideas for the action items that a business needs to work with.

"Not every idea is a capital I idea. A breakthrough in biotech—that's the wrong view of an idea. An idea is an error-free billing system. An idea is taking a process that requires six days and getting it done in one. Everyone can contribute—every single person. The people who process the work in general have better ideas than those in the office, far better ideas. The key is to give them respect, dignity. When you spend three days in a room with people mapping a process, the ideas just about bubble up inside. Just give them respect—everybody in the organization—and the improvement is enormous. . . .

"Neatness and orderliness are not what we are after. We are after getting information to people who can act on it. . . . All we have to do is open up, give people a chance, get them in the process, and I am convinced we can make quantum leaps. But we can't rest. Because while many American companies are improving dramatically against themselves, globally we still have a hell of a long way to go to win this game."[5]

To Welch 1991 was a watershed year for General Electric, an important test of the effect his rhetoric and his accent on soft values had had on the company's balance sheet. Welch sensed that he was trying the patience of both GE shareholders and Wall Street analysts by touting the virtues of speed, simplicity, and self-confidence, of boundarylessness, and of Work-Out. He knew that cynics would contend that while his hardware changes of the early 80s had brought growth and profit to GE, the company had been aided in great measure by the nation's decade-long prosperity. The early 90s, however, had witnessed yet another American recession along with a decline in the world economy. The Welch revolution faced its most serious challenge.

Happily for Welch and GE, the 1991 balance sheet showed that the company had turned in a reasonable performance despite the nasty business environment. GE's revenues grew 3 percent, to $60.236 billion. Its earnings also grew 3 percent, to $4.435 billion.

According to the March 16, 1992, edition of *Business Week*, among American companies, GE was fifth in sales (behind General Motors, Exxon, Ford, and IBM, in that order); and second in earnings (behind Exxon). In the Fortune 500 for 1991, published in the magazine's April 20, 1992, edition, GE was ranked fifth in sales, up from number 6 in 1990 (behind General Motors, Exxon, Ford, and IBM, in that order). In profits it ranked third, up from number 5 the year before (behind Exxon and Philip Morris). Its assets of $168.2 billion placed it third for 1991 behind General Motors with $184.3 billion; and Ford with $174.4 billion. GE's earnings per share grew 5 percent, to $5.10. GE's adoption of a new accounting rule reduced its earnings by $1.8 billion but did not use up the company's cash. That accounting rule required large companies to set aside large sums for 10 to 20 years' worth of retiree health benefits no later than 1993. What particularly pleased Welch was that GE's total cost productivity increased 4 percent, which was more than double the rate of increase during the 1981–82 recession. GE's stock produced a 38 percent return for share owners in 1991.

In the 1991 annual report Welch led off his report on the GE businesses by crediting GE Financial Services with "another terrific year." In 1991 GE Financial Services brought in an earnings increase of 17 percent. Of its 22 businesses, 17 were profitable, 11 of them with impressive double-digit growth. Welch also noted that Power Generation, Lighting, Medical Systems, and Information Services had produced double-digit sales increases and that GE's exports had risen 21 percent, to $8.6 billion.

He noted the "misses" as well. NBC, suffering from a decline in ratings and a soft advertising market, turned in a "significant decline" in earnings. Motors and Plastics had a difficult year.

For Welch, the annual report was not merely a chance to wrap up the numbers of the previous year. It was a platform from which he could inveigh against all of those at GE who still had not joined the Welch revolution. He wrote only briefly of how the company had done in 1991: His principal emphasis was on getting employees to pay closer attention to his message.

Increasing productivity remained Welch's chief concern. He observed that if GE's productivity growth in 1990 and 1991 had been at the lower level of 1980 and 1981, GE's 1991 earnings would have been $3 billion rather than $4.435 billion. He sensed that despite his late 80s efforts to remove management layers and other features of bureaucracy, much more work of this kind needed to be done. "Unfortunately," he wrote in the 1991 annual report, "it is still possible to find documents around GE businesses that look like something out of the National Archives, with 5, 10, or even more signatures necessary before action can be taken. In some businesses you might still encounter many layers of management in a small area—boiler operators reporting to the supervisor of boilers, who reports to the utility manager, who reports to the manager of plant services, who reports to the plant manager, and so on."

Clearly, Welch wanted more delayering. It was an old message. The analogies were new. "Layers insulate," he wrote. "They slow things down. They garble. Leaders in highly layered organizations are like people who wear several sweaters outside on a freezing winter day. They remain warm and comfortable but are blissfully ignorant of the realities of their environment. They couldn't be further from what's going on."

Welch stressed the need for greater speed within GE. He congratulated the Quick Response effort in Louisville, noting that Louisville, having cut product delivery cycle time from 18 weeks to 5 weeks, was now striving to build appliances virtually to order—through a three-day cycle. He then rhapsodized about the virtues of speed: "There is something about speed that transcends its obvious business benefits of greater cash flow, greater profitability, higher share due to greater customer responsiveness, and more capacity from cycle-time reductions.

"Speed exhilarates and energizes. Whether it be fast cars, fast boats, downhill skiing, or a business process, speed injects fun and excitement into an otherwise routine activity. This is particularly true in business, where speed tends to propel ideas and drive processes right through functional barriers, sweeping bureaucrats and their impediments aside in the rush to get to the marketplace. Speed helps force a company 'outside of itself' and prevents the inward focus that institutions tend to develop as they get bigger."

Welch then turned to the company programs that were designed to encourage speed and other means of achieving greater productivity. As for Best Practices, the GE chairman stated that nowhere did GE learn as much as at Sam Walton's Wal-Mart, which Welch described as "something very special." He added: "Many of our management teams spent time there observing the speed, the bias for action, the utter customer fixation that drives Wal-Mart; and despite our progress we came back feeling a bit plodding and ponderous, a little envious, but ultimately, fiercely determined that we're going to do whatever it takes to get that fast."

Work-Out took time to develop, Welch wrote, but the results had continued to justify GE's investment in the program. "Suddenly things began to pop, here and there, with big ideas, process breakthroughs; and today they roar almost everywhere, with both radical transformations in the way we do business and with tangible business results." Welch said that thanks to Work-Out and the team efforts that had evolved from it, "GE has become faster and more energized than any of us ever thought possible."

Welch then described the four types of GE managers and assessed which would succeed at GE, which would fail. The first type delivered on commitments—financial or otherwise—and shared GE's values. "His or her future is an easy call. Onward and upward." The second type did not meet commitments (read "bring in a healthy balance sheet") and did not share GE's values. "Not as pleasant a call," wrote Welch, "but equally easy." The third type missed commitments but shared the values. "He or she," wrote Welch, "usually gets a second chance, preferably in a different environment."

The fourth type delivered on commitments but did not subscribe to GE's values. This type was the most difficult to deal with. "This is," wrote Welch, "the individual who typically forces performance out of people rather than inspires it: the autocrat, the big shot, the tyrant. Too often all of us have looked the other way—tolerated these 'Type 4' managers because 'they always deliver'—at least in the short term.

"And perhaps this type was more acceptable in easier times, but in an environment where we must have every good idea from every man and woman in the organization, we cannot afford management styles that suppress and intimidate. Whether we can convince and help these managers to change—recognizing how difficult that can be—or part company with them if they cannot will be the ultimate test of our commitment to the transformation of this company and will determine the future of the mutual trust and respect we are building."

GE's most profitable business in 1991 was Aircraft Engines, with $1.414 billion in profits on sales of $7.899 billion—this despite the recession and despite the Gulf War, which adversely affected Aircraft Engines' commercial customers, the world's airlines. Still, in 1991 GE and CFM International engines were chosen for 57 percent of the new commercial aircraft (CFM International is a joint company of GE and SNECMA of France). One of Aircraft Engines' major orders for 1991 came from British Airways, which chose the GE90 engine for its new Boeing 777 twin-engine aircraft. British Airways ordered 15 of the 777s, with options to order 20 more.

Second most profitable for GE in 1991 was GE Financial Services, with $1.275 billion in profits. GE Capital was the business most responsible for Financial Services' rosy balance sheet, bringing in $105 million more in earnings in 1991 than in 1990. Employers Reinsurance Corporation had stable earnings. Kidder, Peabody had one of the most profitable years in its history.

Power Generation was GE's third most profitable business, with $932 million in profits on sales of $6.185 billion. It captured the leading share in major world markets in 1991. Its advanced gas turbine design had won 77 percent of advanced heavy-duty gas turbine opportunities since it came on the market. In 1991 GE introduced the 9F, the world's most powerful gas turbine, which was rated at 226 megawatts and designed for 50-hertz markets in Europe and Asia.

NBC's balance sheet was not sparkling. Its profits, $477 million in 1990, dropped to only $209 million in 1991. GE acknowledged that despite NBC's cost control efforts the network had been unable to turn in a better financial record because it had had to deal with too many negatives: lower prime-time ratings, higher programming costs, the costs of covering the Gulf War, and the worst network advertising market in 20 years. NBC did win the 1990–91 network contest, but by the narrowest margin in six years. "Cheers" was again the top series; NBC had 5 of the top 10 shows.

However harsh the American economy in 1992, General Electric managed to ward off its worst effects. On April 13, 1992, GE announced its earnings for the first quarter of 1992: revenues of $13.5 billion, a 2 percent increase over 1991's first quarter; and earnings of $1.058 billion, a 6 percent increase over the previous year's first quarter. "The strength of GE's performance," said Jack Welch in the communiqué issued by GE at the time, "was a direct result of continued growth in Power Systems, Medical Systems, and GE Financial Services. . . . While the global economy remains fragile, the upturn in U.S. short-cycle order trends, combined with faster cycle times, continued productivity, and improving cash generation capabilities, gives us confidence that 1992 will be another good year at GE."

Hence, the titan called General Electric continued to register impressive financial achievements.

The spring of 1992, however, brought other, sobering news. Once again, the company was embroiled in scandal, this time involving its diamond business. In late April it was reported that the Justice Department was conducting a criminal investigation into allegations that GE had conspired with a South African diamond cartel to fix prices in the global market for industrial diamonds.[6] Those allegations had been brought to the Justice Department several months earlier by a former GE official, Edward J. Russell, a vice president and general manager of GE's Superabrasives business, based in Worthington, Ohio. That business manufactures industrial diamonds. Along with companies linked to DeBeers Consolidated Mines Ltd., of South Africa, it controls 90 percent of the $600 million-a-year market, according to a lawsuit filed by Russell on April 21, 1992, in Federal Court in Cincinnati.[7]

While the $600 million-a-year industrial diamond market might not seem so important to General Electric, the company has generated solid earnings from its diamond-making operations—$166 million over the past three years on sales of about $840 million.

In his suit, Russell outlined the alleged price-fixing scheme and what he said were other improprieties by current and former senior GE officers. He charged that high-level GE executives approved a sham $80 million stock transaction in late 1989 in order to bolster the profit of GE Plastics and that they covered up evidence of a kickback scheme and serious expense-account cheating. Russell alleged that one GE manager spent $20,000 of GE's funds to visit prostitutes in Bangkok.

Russell charged as well that his boss Glen Hiner, who headed GE Plastics until December 1991, told Russell that Jack Welch was aware of a secret meeting that Hiner scheduled with DeBeers in London in September 1991, "and was interested in seeing what developed." GE's vice president for public relations, Joyce Hergenhan, called that statement "absolutely outrageous."[8] Hiner, interviewed by *The Wall Street Journal*, would not say whether he had met with DeBeers, but strongly denied the charges: "The allegations about price-fixing are absolutely untrue. Our conduct was always aboveboard."[9]

In an April 21, 1992, statement GE said that Russell had been removed from his job in the fall of 1991 due to "performance shortcomings. . . . He's had many conversations with GE people attempting to improve the conditions of his termination package. During these conversations, he never mentioned the alleged antitrust issues. . . . We can say that Mr. Russell's removal was based solely on his level of performance as a manager." In another statement the next day GE asserted that "Based on our current information, we have no reason to believe that an antitrust violation occurred."

Welch, in an interview with *The Wall Street Journal* on April 23, 1992, called allegations that GE had conspired to fix prices of industrial diamonds "pure nonsense." He denied that there had been any "antitrust" violations in GE's dealings with other manufacturers of industrial diamonds. He also said it was "nonsense" that certain GE officials secretly met in London with representatives of DeBeers Consolidated Mines, as Russell alleged. "We're talking with other companies all the time as part of normal business," Welch said in the interview. "It's crazy to say that we're price-fixing." He called the entire suit "crazy" and said the company would contest all its charges.[10]

In a letter to GE officers dated April 29, 1992, and signed "Jack," Welch wrote that GE would investigate the charges fully. He added; "Ed Russell was removed from his job as head of Superabrasives for one simple reason—he was not performing effectively as a GE leader. Any charges by Mr. Russell that I personally was aware of any antitrust or securities law violations are outrageous. . . . Furthermore, I have no knowledge that any Company employees engaged in any of these alleged acts."

On May 4, 1992, a civil antitrust lawsuit was filed against GE and a subsidiary of South Africa's giant DeBeers Consolidated Mines Ltd., alleging that they are fixing the prices of industrial diamonds at artificially high levels. The class action suit, filed in Manhattan, was brought by Kidder Concrete Cutting Co., a unit of the New Hamp-

shire–based Kidder Building & Wrecking Inc. A GE spokesman, reacting to the indictment, said "there was no reason to believe that any
antitrust violation occurred."

What of the future? What kind of company did Jack Welch want
GE to become in the 90s? He sounded as if he had no special strategy in mind except to push the businesses to do as well as they
could. "I want GE to be the mix of businesses that its ideas take it to
be, not some preconceived grand plot to be 25 percent of this, 35 percent here. [The businesses'] organic growth will take us where it will
take it."

In that sense GE had to guess which way the country's tastes
would move?

"They will move," Welch agreed. "In Southeast Asia [there will
be] as many opportunities as your eye can see. I think we know
enough now not to put a lot of money into defense. Materials
will always be a good business in some form or another. Power
Generation will have its cycles, but the world's going to need to power
up. Commercial airlines will in fact go through this awful moment
and someday in the next decade will lead very healthy lives. They'll
consolidate, they'll rationalize. Lighting for as long as I breathe
will be an important product in the world's infrastructure. You can
take money out of certain businesses and not worry about it. Defense
now is a place you don't want to put money into, so we'll allocate
money away from there. We'll put it in medical and in new gas
turbines."

Welch was sanguine about the future. In the fall of 1991 the GE
businesses had turned in projections on productivity to him. "Our
productivity numbers are staggering. They're scary. Many businesses
are over 7 [percent] in their plan for next year. If we ever get volume,
it'll come out of our ears, I hope."

In April 1991 Welch had said, "We are in the midst of the biggest
change in work culture in the history of this company, perhaps in
the history of any large company."[11] How far along was he in creating
that change?

"Work-Out and employee empowerment and trust between manager and worker have got a long way to go. [They] will probably have

a long way to go when I leave here. There's a lot of water that has to pass under this bridge, and we've got to get a lot of people to believe. You can see different degrees."

What about the hardware? "I certainly think I can take on more businesses if the right value comes, the right opportunity comes."[12]

Would one man continue to run 13 major businesses indefinitely? One former senior GE official and a close friend of Jack Welch's addressed this question. Larry Bossidy said: "I don't know whether that can last. I don't know that you can be a hands-on company and have one man run 13 businesses even if you're as capable and broad-based and as informed as Jack Welch is. I don't know what will happen there, but if it needs to get changed, it will get changed. I think it's unique—to be that size and be that ambitious and be as free of bureaucracy as it is."[13]

Did Welch believe that over the next 10 or 15 years GE would remain in its current configuration of 13 major businesses?

The question, he believed, was beside the point if only because one of those businesses, GE Capital, was actually an aggregate of 21 individual businesses, some of them larger than three of the 13 GE businesses. Though back in the early 80s he had been the one who redefined GE's hundreds of business units into 15 businesses, a decade later Jack Welch admitted, "We're really a much more complicated thing than the definition [of 13 businesses]." Welch said that he would not want to lock the company into a configuration of a certain number of businesses. "The system we have can handle a large number of businesses."

Were there businesses that Jack Welch would have liked to be involved in?

Indeed there were. Two in particular, which he regretted not having done something about earlier. These were businesses that he had "talked about too long but done nothing because I couldn't afford them." One was the food business. He had held back "because I was afraid in the early days. I didn't have enough self-confidence to buy in the food business. I liked the food business for the same reason that I liked the network business. Cash flow and no foreign competition. I didn't have the guts to make the move. I talked about it a lot. At Crotonville. Around here in Fairfield. I didn't quite have the guts to do it. I wasn't sure enough of myself in the early 80s about the way to go with big acquisitions."

The other business was pharmaceuticals. "I've talked about [that business] for seven years, and I've always been a dollar short. The PEs [price-earnings ratios] have always been so high I'd never get my money back. Never. Not three years or four years. I wouldn't get it back."[14]

What was Welch's long-range goal? To be number one in sales? Number one in market value? In 1991 *Forbes* magazine had rated General Electric the number one company in America. I asked Welch how he felt about this.

"Well," he replied without the slightest bit of emotion, "it was better than not being the number one company. OK?"

Welch insisted that he put little stock in the business media's rankings of the major companies.

Was not the number one ranking a kind of pinnacle? The height of Jack Welch's career?

Welch remained unfazed. "Let's face it. A company gains more and more respect by a whole series of things: our Work-Out program; our consistency of earnings; I'm proud of the fact that we are well thought of today. You can't pick up a paper that doesn't say the words '*well managed*'. We like to be thought of as well managed. We like to be thought of as a good company."[15]

Jack Welch's story is incomplete. Barring the unforeseen, he will be the chairman and CEO of General Electric for nearly another decade. We catch him therefore in the midst of his efforts—one revolution behind him, a second just starting. Who knows how many more revolutions he will want to start? Some have decided that as Welch moved from the first revolution (in hardware) to the second (in software), he had in fact abandoned his earlier "tough" views on management. That he had gone through a conversion. This was a misunderstanding of Jack Welch. It was not that Welch had changed his mind about the virtues of tough management (i.e., the need to get rid of bureaucracy and excessive rank-and-file jobs). It was, rather, that he had reached a saturation point in downsizing and was now placing his emphasis on the "software," on getting more productivity out of GE's employees.

Just how well has Welch positioned General Electric for the future? An impossible question to answer. But given his record over the past decade, there seems every reason to believe that the company is on a stable path of ascent. Some charge that Welch has missed the boat by not involving GE in some of the high-flying businesses of the 90s, especially telecommunications. Some charge that the RCA merger has not turned out too well, that NBC is becoming ever less profitable, and that Kidder, Peabody's balance sheets have yet to prove golden.

Such accusations miss an important point. The General Electric that Jack Welch wrought is built on the premise that mistakes will be made in certain acquisitions; and that GE's businesses will go through cyclical ups and downs. Welch would agree that neither NBC nor Kidder—today—are superstars of American business. But NBC once was. And perhaps Kidder will be. As long as GE is strong enough—that is, as long as other GE businesses are doing well—the Welch system will work and the bottom line will remain strong.

Of course, Welch would like to be involved in industries that are thriving today. He mentioned food and pharmaceuticals. Others mention telecommunications and computers. But the decision to develop businesses in these industries at an early enough stage for it to pay off is complicated. Large amounts of resources are required. Foresight and perseverance help too. Asking Welch and GE to bat 1.000 is asking too much. Errors of judgments were made before. They will undoubtedly be made again. The key question is: How has GE been doing overall? On that there can be no debate.

In October 1991 Welch was nearly 56 years old. He still had nine more years to serve as CEO. Had he, like his predecessor, already begun thinking of his successor? "From now on, it's the most important decision I'll make. It occupies a considerable amount of thought almost every day. As I watch different people do different things, I'm always looking for the right person. Thinking about the right person. We have a lot of very good people here. Times change. People change. Some grow. Some swell. The difference between growing and swelling is a big difference."

Welch must step down by age 65. Would he remain that long? Other CEOs had stepped down before the mandatory age. Welch was ambiguous: "I like to think I'm smart enough to get out at the right time. The question is sometime between 60 and 65. What's the right time? A lot of people determine that."[16]

What about a senior position in government? Lee Iacocca, in *Talking Straight*, chose Welch as secretary of defense in his imaginary cabinet. Other choices: Don Rumsfeld as secretary of state, Felix Rohatyn or Paul Volcker as secretary of the Treasury, Peter Uberroth as secretary of commerce.[17] Yet Jack Welch's closest friends and business associates doubted that he longed for a cabinet post. They doubted that he would respond favorably even if the right job were proffered. Even Reg Jones, Mr. Outside, turned down cabinet positions to remain at GE. Why should Jack Welch, Mr. Inside, be any different?

Everyone's best guess was that Welch would have no trouble saying no—even to the president. Washington held out little appeal for him. Welch loved power, loved exercising it, loved seeing results. All of that was antithetical to the way Washington operated. He had no great love for politicians, believing that most of them were ineffectual. He had no strong taste for politics, sensing that it was too difficult to get the truly important things done. Do not expect to find Jack Welch inside the Beltway.

What would happen if he got a call from the president? A cabinet position, perhaps even secretary of defense?

"Oh, don't even talk about it," Welch shot back. "I'm comfortable doing this. I'm a lot better off in business. I know this game. I think everyone has to know what he's good at and what he might not be good at. It's not part of my long-term plan."

Of course it wasn't. Jack Welch was a businessman, not a politician. He was too blunt, too practical, too daring to want to reshape Washington as he had reshaped GE. So it seemed likely that he would stick it out at GE. He had every reason to. He had built the new GE, taken it through the worst of times, and molded this American institution into a rough, tough enterprise that stood near the top of the heap. In doing so, Jack Welch had earned a reputation as the best CEO in America.

Notes

Chapter One

1. John Winthrop Hammond, *Men and Volts: The Story of General Electric* (Philadelphia: J. B. Lippincott, 1941), p. 22.
2. Ibid., p. 47.
3. Ibid., p. 90.
4. Hall of History, *The General Electric Story, 1876–1986: A Photo History*, vol. 4 (Schenectady, N.Y.: A Hall of History, October 1989), p. 76.
5. Ibid., p. 43.
6. Ibid., p. 37.
7. Hammond, *Men and Volts*, p. 199.
8. Richard Pascale, *Managing on the Edge: How Successful Companies Use Conflict to Stay Ahead* (Harmondsworth, Middlesex, England: Penguin Books, 1991), p. 192.

Chapter Two

1. Reginald Jones, interview with author, October 7, 1991.
2. Ibid.
3. "America's Most Influential Jones," *New York Times Sunday Magazine*, September 16, 1979.
4. Reginald Jones, interview with author, October 7, 1991.
5. Ibid.
6. "America's Most Influential Jones."
7. Reginald Jones, interview with author, October 7, 1991.

Chapter Three

1. "The Mind of Jack Welch," *Fortune*, March 27, 1989, pp. 39–50.
2. Jack Welch, interview with author, July 8, 1991.
3. Jack Welch, interview with author, October 22, 1991.

4. Ibid.

5. "The Mind of Jack Welch," pp. 39–50.

6. Michael Gartner, interview with author, October 8, 1991.

7. Jack Welch, interview with author, October 22, 1991.

8. "The Dynamo," *Business Week*, June 30, 1986, pp. 40–45.

9. Jack Welch, interview with author, July 8, 1991.

10. Jack Welch, interview with author, October 22, 1991.

11. Ibid.

12. Ibid.

13. "Jack Welch: The Man Who Brought GE to Life," *Fortune*, January 5, 1987, pp. 76–77.

14. From "Daniel W. Fox, 1923–1989," *Bulletin of the National Academy of Engineering*, February 1989, pp. 103–06.

15. Jack Welch, interview with author, July 8, 1991.

16. Eva M. Smith, "How GEP [General Electric Plastics] Became an International Business," *GE Plastics*, May 1986, pp. 1–23.

17. Jack Welch, interview with author, July 8, 1991.

18. Robert Wright, interview with author, October 23, 1991.

19. Ibid.

20. Ibid.

21. Ibid.

22. Jack Welch, interview with author, July 8, 1991.

23. Ibid.

Chapter Four

1. Reginald Jones, interview with author, June 24, 1991.

2. Ibid.

3. Richard F. Vancil, *Passing the Baton: Managing the Process of CEO Succession* (Boston: Harvard Business School Press, 1987), p. 38.

4. Edward Hood, interview with author, October 15, 1991.

5. Reginald Jones, interview with author, June 24, 1991.

6. Jack Welch, interview with author, July 8, 1991.

7. Edward Hood, interview with author, October 15, 1991.

8. Paul Van Orden, interview with author, July 2, 1991.

9. Ibid.

10. "The Dynamo," *Business Week*, June 30, 1986, pp. 40–5.

11. "The Toughest Bosses in America," *Fortune*, August 6, 1984, pp. 18–23.

12. Jones's description of these meetings is reported in Vancil, *Passing the Baton*, p. 189.

13. Material on the first Welch-Jones "airplane interview" came from interviews with Jack Welch, July 8, 1991, and Reginald Jones, October 7, 1991.

14. Robert Wright, interview with author, October 23, 1991.

15. Vancil, *Passing the Baton*, p. 188.

16. Reginald Jones, interview with author, June 24, 1991.

17. Reginald Jones, interview with author, October 7, 1991.

18. Jack Welch, interview with author, July 8, 1991.

19. Reginald Jones, interview with author, October 7, 1991.

20. Gertrude Michelson, interview with author, June 18, 1991.

21. Interview with Jack Welch, *Monogram*, January–February 1981, pp. 2–9.

22. "G.E. Names Welch, 45, Chairman," *New York Times*, December 20, 1980.

23. Ibid.

24. Reginald Jones, interview with author, June 24, 1991.

25. J. P. Donlon, editor of *Chief Executive*, reported Walter Wriston's comment to the author.

26. Walter Wriston, interview with author, June 26, 1991.

27. Edward Hood, interview with author, October 15, 1991.

28. Jack Welch, interview with author, October 22, 1991.

Chapter Five

1. Reginald Jones, interview with author, October 7, 1991.

2. "General Electric: The Financial Wizards Switch Back to Technology," *Business Week*, March 16, 1981, pp. 110–15.

3. Paul Van Orden, interview with author, July 2, 1991.

4. Jim Baughman, interview with author, June 20, 1991.

5. Gertrude Michelson, interview with author, June 18, 1991.

6. Welch made these comments to students at the Harvard Business School on April 27, 1981.

7. Richard Burke, interview with author, October 21, 1991.

8. Jim Baughman, interview with author, June 20, 1991.

9. Paul Van Orden, interview with author, July 2, 1991.
10. "Our Changing Cultures," *Monogram*, Bill Lane, Fall 1987, pp. 2–7.
11. Jack Welch, interview with author, July 8, 1991.
12. *Monogram*, September-October 1981.
13. "Trying to Bring GE to Life," *Fortune*, January 25, 1982, pp. 52–7.
14. To be consistent in presenting the stock price between 1980 and the present, I have adopted GE's practice, started after the 2-for-1 stock split in April 1987, of referring to the stock price prior to the stock split as if the stock had already been split.
15. Jack Welch, interview with author, October 22, 1991.
16. Walter Wriston, interview with author, June 26, 1991.
17. Jack Welch, interview with author, July 8, 1991.

Chapter Six

1. Michael Carpenter, interview with author, October 23, 1991.
2. Jim Baughman, interview with author, June 20, 1991.
3. Dennis Dammerman, interview with author, June 24, 1991.
4. Paul Van Orden, interview with author, July 2, 1991.
5. "Letters to *Fortune*," *Fortune*, May 8, 1989, p. 164.
6. Jim Baughman, interview with author, June 20, 1991.
7. "General Electric—Going with the Winners," *Forbes*, March 26, 1984, pp. 97–106.
8. Jack Welch, interview with author, July 8, 1991.
9. David Genever-Watling, interview with author, October 11, 1991.
10. Jack Welch, interview with author, July 8, 1991.
11. Ibid.

Chapter Seven

1. Fran Ahl, interview with author, October 21, 1991.
2. Jim Carter, interview with author, October 12, 1991.
3. Bill Bywater, interview with author, October 16, 1991.
4. Roger Creal, interview with author, October 21, 1991.
5. Jack Welch, interview with author, July 8, 1991.
6. Walter Wriston, interview with author, June 26, 1991.
7. "From the Bottom Line to Share of the Market," *The Wall Street Journal*, July 12, 1982.

8. "How GE Bobbled the Factory of the Future," *Fortune*, November 11, 1985, pp. 52–63.

9. Frank Doyle, interview with author, October 4, 1991.

10. "What Welch Has Wrought at GE," *Fortune*, July 7, 1986, pp. 43–7.

11. Rodger H. Bricknell, interview with author, October 11, 1991.

12. Reginald Jones, interview with author, June 24, 1991.

13. Paul Van Orden, interview with author, July 2, 1991.

14. Jim Baughman, interview with author, June 20, 1991.

15. Joyce Hergenhan, interview with author, June 17, 1991.

16. "Federal Jury Charges $800,000 Fraud by G.E.," *New York Times*, March 27, 1985.

17. Quoted in letter from Jack Welch to all GE employees, March 29, 1985.

18. "Federal Jury Charges $800,000 Fraud by G.E."

19. Ibid.

20. "Three Indicted in Fraud Case Involving GE," *The Wall Street Journal*, July 17, 1985.

21. Quoted in letter from Jack Welch to all GE employees, March 29, 1985.

22. Quoted in letter from Jack Welch to all GE employees, April 19, 1985.

23. Joyce Hergenhan, interview with author, October 22, 1991.

24. "Three Indicted in Fraud Case Involving GE."

25. "Scandal Rocks General Electric," *Time*, May 27, 1985, p. 60.

26. Quoted in letter from Jack Welch to all GE employees, September 16, 1985.

27. "Jury Acquits Two in General Electric Contract Fraud," *The Wall Street Journal*, December 4, 1985.

28. Jack Welch, interview with author, October 22, 1991.

29. Walter Wriston, interview with author, June 26, 1991.

30. This information was supplied by the office of GE's vice president for public relations.

31. In a speech to the Commercial Club, Cincinnati, Ohio, October 17, 1985.

32. Dennis Dammerman, interview with author, June 24, 1991.

33. Nicholas Heymann, interview with author, July 11, 1991.

34. Jack Welch, interview with author, October 22, 1991.

Chapter Eight

1. Michael Carpenter, interview with author, October 23, 1991.

2. Jack Welch, interview with author, October 22, 1991.

3. Robert Wright, interview with author, October 23, 1991.
4. Michael Carpenter, interview with author, October 23, 1991.
5. Walter Wriston, interview with author, June 26, 1991.
6. "Jack Welch: GE's Live Wire," *Newsweek*, December 23, 1985, p. 48.
7. Jack Bergen, interview with author, July 3, 1991.
8. "Jack Welch: GE's Live Wire," p. 48.
9. "Could the GE–RCA Merge Mean New Role for Carson?" *The Wall Street Journal*, December 16, 1985.
10. "John Welch," *Business Week*, April 18, 1986, p. 241.
11. "A Reunion of Technological Titans," *Time*, December 23, 1985, pp. 48–9.
12. Ibid.
13. "Jack Welch: GE's Live Wire," p. 48.
14. "Tinker, NBC's Chairman, 'Delighted' with Merger," *New York Times*, December 13, 1985.
15. Jack Welch, interview with author, October 22, 1991.
16. Ibid.
17. "G.E. Names Lineup for Financial Unit," *New York Times*, September 3, 1986.

Chapter Nine

1. "NBC Official Foresees Reassessment," *New York Times*, October 2, 1986.
2. Ken Auletta, *Three Blind Mice* (New York: Random House, 1991), p. 238.
3. Robert Wright, interview with author, October 23, 1991.
4. The source asked not to be identified.
5. Dennis Dammerman, interview with author, June 24, 1991.
6. Robert Wright, interview with author, October 23, 1991.
7. Ibid.
8. "Column One: The Press—Belt Tightening," *New York Times*, November 7, 1986.
9. "GE's Hard Driver at NBC," *Fortune*, March 16, 1987, pp. 98–104.
10. Robert Wright, interview with author, October 23, 1991.
11. "The Dishwasher League," *New York Times*, December 18, 1986.
12. Ibid.

13. "NBC Head Proposes Staff Political Contributions," *New York Times*, December 9, 1986.

14. Jack Welch, interview with author, October 22, 1991.

15. Robert Wright, interview with author, October 23, 1991.

16. Ibid.

17. Auletta, *Three Blind Mice*, p. 393.

18. Michael Gartner, interview with author, October 8, 1991.

19. Ibid.

20. "NBC Is No Longer a Feather in GE's Cap," *Business Week*, June 3, 1991, pp. 88–92.

21. Robert Wright, interview with author, October 23, 1991.

22. Jack Welch, interview with author, October 22, 1991.

23. "G.E. Tells NBC Chiefs to Change or Go Home," *New York Times*, June 12, 1987.

24. Ibid.

25. Ibid.

26. Michael Gartner, interview with author, October 8, 1991.

27. Ibid.

28. "The Endangered NBC Peacock," *Washington Post*, March 29, 1991.

29. "NBC Retains First Place in Very Close Ratings Race," *The Wall Street Journal*, April 15, 1991.

30. Larry Bossidy, interview with author, October 16, 1991.

31. Jack Welch, interview with author, October 22, 1991.

32. Robert Wright, interview with author, October 23, 1991.

Chapter Ten

1. From "Daniel W. Fox, 1923–1989," *Bulletin of the National Academy of Engineering*, February 1989, pp. 103–06.

2. Jack Welch, interview with author, October 22, 1991.

3. Jim Baughman, interview with author, June 20, 1991.

4. Walter Wriston, interview with author, June 26, 1991.

5. Paul Van Orden, interview with author, July 2, 1991.

6. Alvin Toffler, *Power Shift* (New York: Bantam Books, 1990), p. 26.

7. "GE Chairman Welch, Though Much Praised, Starts to Draw Critics," *The Wall Street Journal*, August 4, 1988.

8. Ibid.

9. Jim Baughman, interview with author, June 20, 1991.

10. Michael Gartner, interview with author, October 8, 1991.

11. "General Electric—Going with the Winners," *Forbes*, March 26, 1984, pp. 97–106.

12. Frank Doyle, interview with author, October 4, 1991.

13. Interview with Jack Welch, *Monogram*, Fall 1984, pp. 8–15.

14. Jack Welch, interview with author, October 22, 1991.

15. Joyce Hergenhan, interview with author, February 13, 1992.

16. Nancy Dodd McCann, interview with author, February 17, 1992.

17. Noel Tichy and Ram Charan, "Speed, Simplicity, Self-Confidence," *Harvard Business Review*, September–October 1989, pp. 112–20.

18. Paul Van Orden, interview with author, July 2, 1991.

19. Jack Welch, interview with author, October 22, 1991.

20. Leonard Schlesinger, interview with author, July 3, 1991.

21. Ralph Nader and William Taylor, *The Big Boys: Power and Position in American Business* (New York: Pantheon Books), p. xv.

22. Joyce Hergenhan, interview with author, June 17, 1991.

23. Larry Bossidy, interview with author, October 16, 1991.

24. Jack Welch, interview with author, October 22, 1991.

25. From a speech Welch gave on July 15, 1991, after accepting the National Management Association's Manager of the Year award.

26. Interview with Jack Welch, *Monogram*, Fall 1989, pp. 2–5.

27. Interview with Jack Welch, *Monogram*, Fall 1984, pp. 8–15.

28. Speech to the annual meeting of GE shareholders in Waukesha, Wisconsin, on April 27, 1988.

29. Ibid.

30. Jack Welch, interview with author, July 8, 1991.

31. Speech to the annual meeting of GE shareholders in Waukesha, Wisconsin, on April 27, 1988.

32. Paul Van Orden, interview with author, July 2, 1991.

33. "GE's Management Mission," *Washington Post*, May 22, 1988.

34. Speech to the annual meeting of GE shareholders in Waukesha, Wisconsin, on April 27, 1988.

35. Frank Doyle, interview with author, October 4, 1991.

36. "GE's Management Mission."

37. Jack Welch, interview with author, October 22, 1991.

Chapter Eleven

1. Reginald Jones, interview with author, June 24, 1991.
2. Jim Baughman, interview with author, June 20, 1991.
3. "CEO of the Year: Welch on Welch," *Financial World*, April 3, 1990, pp. 62–7.
4. Jim Baughman, interview with author, June 20, 1991.

Chapter Twelve

1. "Having It All, Then Throwing It All Away," *Time*, May 25, 1987, pp. 22–3.
2. Jack Welch, interview with author, October 22, 1991.
3. "GE Chairman Welch, Though Much Praised, Starts to Draw Critics," *The Wall Street Journal*, August 4, 1988.
4. Interview with Jack Welch, *Monogram*, Fall 1987, pp. 2–7.
5. "GE Chairman Welch."
6. Noel Tichy and Ram Charan, "Speed, Simplicity, Self-Confidence," *Harvard Business Review*, September–October 1989, pp. 112–20.
7. "At G.E. Plant, Familiar Fears," *New York Times*, July 28, 1987.
8. J. P. Donlon, interview with author, June 21, 1991.
9. Jack Welch, interview with author, July 8, 1991.
10. "GE Chairman Welch."
11. Interview with Jack Welch, *Monogram*, Fall 1987, pp. 2–7.
12. Bob Lewis, interview with author, October 18, 1991.
13. Jim Corman, interview with author, October 11, 1991.
14. Jim Allen, interview with author, October 21, 1991.
15. Richard Burke, interview with author, October 21, 1991.
16. Jack Welch, interview with author, October 22, 1991.

Chapter Thirteen

1. "Letters to Fortune," *Fortune*, May 8, 1989, p. 164.
2. Jim Carter, interview with author, October 12, 1991.
3. Wally Croote, interview with author, October 12, 1991.
4. Jack Welch, interview with author, October 22, 1991.
5. Jim Baughman, interview with author, June 20, 1991.
6. Fran Ahl, interview with author, October 11, 1991.
7. Mary Byrum, interview with author, October 21, 1991.

8. Rodger Bricknell, interview with author, October 11, 1991.

9. Jack Welch, interview with author, October 22, 1991.

10. Jack Welch, interview with author, July 8, 1991.

11. Welch spoke to GE employees at Crotonville on October 14, 1991.

12. "Seeking a Better Idea," *Washington Post*, October 7, 1990.

13. Jack Welch, interview with author, October 22, 1991.

14. Bob Colman, interview with author, October 21, 1991.

15. Gary Rogers, interview with author, October 21, 1991. Rogers became senior vice president in charge of GE Plastics as of January 1, 1992.

16. Richard Burke, interview with author, October 21, 1991.

17. Carl Liebert, interview with author, October 21, 1991.

18. Rodger Bricknell, interview with author, October 12, 1991.

19. Jim Carter, interview with author, October 12, 1991.

20. James Pollock, interview with author, October 21, 1991.

21. Wally Croote, interview with author, October 21, 1991.

22. Fran Ahl, interview with author, October 21, 1991.

23. Wally Croote, interview with author, October 21, 1991.

24. Ed Synfelt, interview with author, October 21, 1991.

25. Jim Baughman, interview with author, June 20, 1991.

26. Tom Tiller, interview with author, October 21, 1991.

27. Ibid.

28. Roger Creal, interview with author, October 21, 1991.

29. Nicholas Heymann, interview with author, July 11, 1991.

30. During an appearance at Crotonville on October 14, 1991.

Chapter Fourteen

1. "Remaking Kidder in G.E.'s Image," *New York Times*, January 29, 1989.

2. Ibid.

3. Joyce Hergenhan, interview with author, October 22, 1991.

4. In remarks to the National Foreign Trade Conference on Opportunities for American Business in Hungary on June 18, 1991, in New York City.

5. "Going After G.E.," *New York Times*, June 16, 1991.

6. "The Gnat Trying to Sting an Elephant Called GE," *Business Week*, June 24, 1991, p. 44.

7. "The Nation's Polluters—Who Emits, What, and Where," *New York Times*, October 15, 1991. The *Times* gave as its source Environmental Protection Agency data.

8. The source asked not to be identified.
9. In a speech to the annual meeting of GE share owners in Erie, Pennsylvania, on April 25, 1990.
10. "G.E. to Test Alternative Method of PCB Disposal," *New York Times*, October 29, 1989.
11. "New York Expands Plan to Rid Hudson of PCB's," *New York Times*, December 21, 1989.
12. Joyce Hergenhan, vice president for public relations at GE, explained what the Israeli investigators had told GE Aircraft Engines officials in December 1990.
13. "U.S. Accuses G.E. of Fraud in Israeli Deal," *New York Times*, August 15, 1991.
14. Ibid.
15. Ibid.
16. Ibid.
17. GE's attitude toward the Walsh whistle-blower issue was recounted to the author by General Electric officials who asked not to be identified.
18. Jack Welch, interview with author, October 22, 1991.
19. Ibid.
20. Edward Hood, interview with author, October 15, 1991.

Chapter Fifteen

1. From a speech given in San Francisco, California, on September 6, 1989, to the Bay Area Council, a group of San Francisco businessmen.
2. "Today's Leaders Look to Tomorrow," *Fortune*, March 26, 1990, pp. 30–31.
3. Speech given to GE share owners in Decatur, Alabama, April 24, 1991.
4. Speech given to the annual meeting of GE share owners in Erie, Pennsylvania, on April 25, 1990.
5. "What I Want U.S. Business to Do in '92," *Fortune*, December 30, 1991, pp. 44–61.
6. "Allegations of Price-fixing Effort by GE Are Being Investigated in U.S." *The Wall Street Journal*, April 23, 1992.
7. Ibid.
8. Ibid.
9. Ibid.
10. Ibid.
11. Speech to GE share owners in Decatur, Alabama, April 24, 1991.
12. Jack Welch, interview with author, October 22, 1991.

13. Larry Bossidy, interview with author, October 16, 1991.
14. Jack Welch, interview with author, October 22, 1991.
15. Ibid.
16. Ibid.
17. Lee Iacocca with Sonny Kleinfield, *Talking Straight* (Toronto, N.Y.: Bantam Books, 1988), p. 287.

Index